## What others are saying about this book:

"Finding an old buddy may be an easier chore since the release of this book."
*The American Legion Magazine*

"A book that can help former service men and women find friends they have served with or locate specific people to substantiate a claim."
*Disabled American Veterans Magazine*

"The title of this specialized little niche-filler describes it perfectly.  This book lists just about every conceivable private, federal, and state agency that one might contact."
*American Reference Books Annual*

"The author has brought together a whole group of options available to those searching for military personnel."
*The Genealogical Helper*

"I have accomplished more with this book in two months than I did in three years on my own.  I have found all of my World War II unit."
Howard Ashcraft, Virginia

"It will be valuable to users of public, some academic, and especially military libraries."
*Booklist, American Library Association*

"This book is the standard in twentieth century military research."
*Association Of Professional Genealogists' Quarterly*

Other favorable reviews and articles have been published by VFW, Purple Heart, AMVETS, US Air Force Afterburner, Soldier of Fortune, International Combat Arms, The Retired Officer, Off Duty magazines, as well as the Philadelphia Inquirer and Stars and Stripes  newspapers.  This book is listed in Directories In Print.

### *Armed Forces Locator Directory*
**The book that has helped thousands locate thousands.**

# How To Locate Anyone Who Is Or Has Been In The Military

## Armed Forces Locator Directory

### Lt. Col. Richard S. Johnson

**1995 Edition, completely revised**

**MIE Publishing**     **San Antonio, Texas**

# How To Locate Anyone Who Is Or Has Been In The Military

## Armed Forces Locator Directory

### by Lt. Col. Richard S. Johnson

Published by:

 MIE Publishing
PO Box 340081
San Antonio, Texas  78234

MIE Publishing                              (800) 937-2133
PO Box 5143
Burlington, North Carolina  27216

Library of Congress Cataloging in Publication Data
Johnson, Richard S., 1933-
How to locate anyone who is or has been in the military.

"A new version, revised ..."
Includes index.
1. United States—Armed Forces—Directories.
2. Veterans—United States—Societies, etc.—
Directories. I. Title.
UA23.J58 1988   355'.0225'73   89-60697
ISBN 1-877639-16-8

# Table of Contents

# About The Author

Lt. Col. Richard (Dick) S. Johnson served 28 years in the US Army. He was an enlisted man for three years, an Armor officer for ten years and a member of the Adjutant General Corps for 15 years. He served in various positions involved with personnel records and management, military postal operations and automated data processing. The latter involved the collection of military personnel records on computers and the operation of two Army locators. He served tours in Germany, Italy, Korea and Vietnam and was stationed at numerous bases in the United States. He retired from the Army in December 1979. During his military career, he received several Army decorations for outstanding and meritorious service to include the Bronze Star Medal, four awards of the Meritorious Service Medal and the Army Commendation Medal.

For the last several years, he has done extensive research on methods of locating current and former members of the military. In 1988, he authored and published the first edition of *How to Locate Anyone Who is or Has Been in the Military*. 65,000 copies of this unique book are in print and it is now in its sixth edition. He is also the author of "Searching", a column that appears in *Reunions* magazine and *Stars and Stripes* newspaper.

Dick has appeared on numerous TV and radio shows, has been the subject of several newspaper articles and is a frequent speaker on the subject of locating missing people.

He acts as a consultant and accepts individual cases to locate missing people. Dick has located hundreds of people for "Reunion", the television program, numerous military reunion organizations, attorneys, private investigators, heir searchers, people seeking missing relatives and birth parents and many other individuals. He has assisted the 11th Armored Cavalry's Veterans of Vietnam and Cambodia in locating over 15,000 of their former members. He is the foremost authority in the nation on locating people with a military connection.

# Foreword

*William Childs Westmoreland*
*General, United States Army, Retired*
*Charleston, South Carolina*

Lt. Col. Richard Johnson has provided a useful and welcomed service to all men and women who have been privileged to wear the military uniform of our Nation.

It is my opinion that virtually every veteran of our military services, in peace or war, does at some time want to contact a buddy with whom he or she served. Until now, that has been usually difficult. But now, thanks to Colonel Johnson, it can be expeditiously accomplished.

William C. Westmoreland

# Dedication

*This book is dedicated to the 27 million living veterans who have served their country with distinction.*

# Acknowledgement

It is impossible to cite all the authorities I have consulted in the preparation of this book. To do so would require more space than is available. The list would include department heads in the Department of Defense, the Department of Veterans Affairs and other federal and state agencies.

I wish to acknowledge the contributions made by Charles Pellegrini of the National Personnel Records Center; Dorothy Kennedy formerly of the National Personnel Records Center for unique information on service numbers and records; Alice Hunter of the VA Records Processing Center; Julie Delpho, Technical Editor; Gil Gilstrap for information concerning thousands of reunion organizations; Darwin Dahl and Debbie Knox for endless research and assistance; and my wife Mickey for sound advice.

Special acknowledgement is made to the artist of the cover illustration of "The Ghost Troop" by:

Norman Hines                    (916) 373-0466
555 Douglas #100
West Sacramento, CA  95605

# Preface

The purpose of this book is to provide the reader with information on how to locate present or former members of the military. This includes members of the Air Force, Army, Coast Guard, Marine Corps, Navy, the reserve and National Guard, retired members and former members. Whatever the reason for your search, this book provides the best methods to locate and contact present and former military members. There are many alternative methods that can be used, so it is recommended that you read the entire book before beginning your search.

A portion of this book concerns military reunions and veterans organizations. These may be another method to locate a missing veteran. A great deal of information is provided concerning military records and service numbers, which are important sources for obtaining units of assignment, date of birth, and service numbers. This information can be used to provide a current address.

This book is the only one available that contains this much detailed information for this specialized subject. It reflects many years of research and experience that can save you time and expense. Of far greater importance, if you use the information this book contains, you will find the person you are looking for.

This book contains hundreds of telephone and FAX numbers, area codes and addresses. Every attempt has been made to ensure that all addresses and telephone numbers are correct. In the event you encounter a number that is incorrect, call the area information operator, (area code) 555-1212. For toll free numbers, call (800) 555-1212. If you encounter a military telephone number that is incorrect, call the appropriate base information operator listed in Chapter Two (Base and Post locator service) for the correct number. The Pentagon information operator, (703) 545-6700, can provide numbers for both the Washington, DC area and numbers for military installations world-wide.

The pronoun "he" is generic as is "serviceman". They refer to both men and women without intending a slight or demeaning attitude toward women service members and veterans.

# Chapter One

## Service And
## Social Security Numbers

*This chapter provides important information concerning the military service number and the Social Security number. Both of these numbers can be used to obtain the former and current locations of the person you are seeking.*

### Service Numbers

Service numbers were first issued on February 28, 1918, for enlisted men in the Army. Army officer service numbers were not issued until 1921. Prior to this, the name of the individual was the only means of identification.

Regular Army service numbers ranged from the numbers 1 through 19,999,999 (8 numerical digits not included in any letter prefix or suffix, see Chart Four) until July 1, 1969 when the Social Security number became the identifying number. The Air Force shared these numbers after its establishment on September 25, 1947, until July 1, 1969, when it also began using Social Security numbers.

During the period 1918 through 1939 Army enlisted service numbers were assigned at random without regard to any geographical area.

Beginning in 1940 each entrance and examining station in the US was allocated certain sets of service numbers for enlisted Army personnel. At times not all numbers were used because of an overestimate of needs in that area.

The US was divided into six Service areas which were later changed to Army areas. A set of numbers was allocated to each entrance station identified with that Army area. For example First Army 11,000,000 through 12,999,999 and 31,000,000 through 32,999,999 and 51,000,000 through 51,999,999; Second Army 13,000,000 through 15,999,999 and 52,000,000 through 52,999,999 also 33 and 35 million numbers; Third Army 14 million through 34 million and 53 million; Fourth Army 18 million through 38 million and 54 million; Fifth Army 16 million through 17 million and 36 million through 37 million and 55 million; Sixth Army 19 million through 39 million and 56 million.

Numbers in the 10 millions and 50 millions were assigned to members who entered the service outside the Continental US. Numbers in the 20,000,000 through 20,999,999 were assigned to members of the National Guard on active duty (1940-1946). Numbers 21 million through 29 million were assigned to members of the National Guard (1946-1969) (see Chart Three).

Numbers in the 30 million series were assigned to those men who were inducted (drafted) during World War II (1940-1946). 42 through 46 million were assigned to members inducted between 1943-1946. Numbers in the 50 million series were assigned to those who were inducted in the Korean and Vietnam wars (1948-1966).

Also, some 57 million numbers were issued during the Vietnam war. Numbers in the 60 million series were assigned to Army and Air Force enlisted men from 1966-1969. Numbers in the 90 million series (approximately 20,000) were assigned to members of the Philippine Army during World War II. 40 and 41 million numbers, 47 through 49 million and 70 through 89 million numbers were not allocated.

Army officers service numbers never exceeded seven numerical digits plus letter prefix for non-regular officers and six numerical digits plus letter prefix for regular officers (1919 through 1969). See Chart Four for explanation of prefixes and suffixes to service numbers.

The Navy, Marine Corps and Coast Guard began using service numbers in 1918 for enlisted members. These consisted of different sets of numbers ranging from one digit numbers to seven digit numbers and had no significance as to where they were issued. Blocks of numbers were assigned to recruiting offices throughout the world and to some headquarters activities. Navy officer service numbers were called file numbers.

# To Use Charts One, Two And Three

1. To determine where and when a Regular (10 through 19 million series) Army or Air Force service number was assigned:
   a. Determine in what state the service number was issued. See Chart One.
   b. Determine on what date the service number was issued. See Chart Two.
   Example: 12,250,000 was issued in Delaware or New Jersey (Chart One) and was issued between 1946 and 1948.

2. To determine where and when a draftee service number (31 - 37 million and 50 - 57 million) was issued:
   a. Determine in what state the service number was issued. See Chart Two.
   b. 31 - 37 million service numbers were assigned between 1940 and 1946.
   c. 51 and 57 million service numbers were assigned between 1948 and 1969.
   Example: A service number 38,945,340 was issued in Texas, Louisiana, Oklahoma or New Mexico between 1940 and 1946. Service numbers beginning with 50 were assigned in Alaska, Hawaii, Panama, and Puerto Rico between 1948-1969.

3. To determine where and when a National Guard service number was assigned:
   a. Determine to which state the service number was assigned. See Chart Three.
   b. Service numbers were utilized from 1946-1969.
   Example: 25,914,500 was assigned to Texas between 1946 and 1969.

## Chart One

### Service Number Prefixes

These examples apply to the first two numbers of the eight digit service numbers (e.g., 14,000,000). These service numbers were assigned by the following entrance stations to Air Force and Army enlisted male personnel.

| (1) | (2) | (3) | (4) | (1) | (2) | (3) | (4) |
|-----|-----|-----|-----|-----|-----|-----|-----|
| AL | 14 | 34 | 53 | NV | 19 | 39 | 56 |
| AK | 19 | 39 | 502 | NH | 11 | 31 | 51 |
| AZ | 19 | 39 | 56 | NJ | 12 | 32 | 51 |
| AR | 18 | 38 | 54 | NM | 18 | 38 | 54 |
| CA | 19 | 39 | 56 | NY | 12 | 32 | 51 |
| CO | 17 | 37 | 55 | NC | 14 | 34 | 53 |
| CT | 11 | 31 | 51 | ND | 17 | 37 | 55 |
| DE | 12 | 32 | 51 | OH | 15 | 35 | 52 |
| FL | 14 | 34 | 53 | OK | 18 | 38 | 54 |
| ID | 19 | 39 | 56 | OR | 19 | 39 | 56 |
| GA | 14 | 34 | 53 | PA | 13 | 33 | 52 |
| IL | 16 | 36 | 55 | RI | 11 | 31 | 51 |
| IN | 15 | 35 | 52 | SC | 14 | 34 | 53 |
| IA | 17 | 37 | 55 | SD | 17 | 37 | 55 |
| KS | 17 | 37 | 55 | TN | 14 | 34 | 53 |
| KY | 15 | 35 | 52 | TX | 18 | 38 | 54 |
| LA | 18 | 38 | 54 | UT | 19 | 39 | 56 |
| ME | 11 | 31 | 51 | VT | 11 | 31 | 51 |
| MD | 13 | 33 | 52 | VA | 13 | 33 | 52 |
| MA | 11 | 31 | 51 | WV | 15 | 35 | 52 |
| MI | 16 | 36 | 55 | WA | 19 | 39 | 56 |
| MN | 17 | 37 | 55 | WI | 16 | 36 | 55 |
| MS | 14 | 34 | 53 | WY | 17 | 37 | 55 |
| MO | 17 | 37 | 55 | HI | 101 | 301 | 50 |
| MT | 19 | 39 | 56 | Panama | 102 | 302 | 501 |
| NE | 17 | 37 | 55 | PR | 104 | 304 | 501 |

(1) Name of state and territory;  (2) Regular and reserve Air Force and Army; (3) Draftees 1940-1946;  (4) Draftees 1948-1969

## Chart Two
## Regular Army And Air Force
## Service Numbers

Service numbers 10,000,000 through 19,999,999 were issued to Regular Air Force and Regular Army enlisted men for periods indicated below. These numbers were also assigned to enlisted male reservists.

| 10,000,000-10,999,999 | 1940-1969 | | |
|---|---|---|---|
| 11,000,000-11,142,500 | 1940-1945 | 12,000,000-12,242,000 | 1940-1945 |
| 11,142,501-11,188,000 | 1946-1948 | 12,242,001-12,321,000 | 1946-1948 |
| 11,166,001-11,238,500 | 1949-1951 | 12,321,001-12,393,500 | 1949-1951 |
| 11,238,501-11,283,000 | 1952-1954 | 12,393,501-12,469,000 | 1952-1954 |
| 11,283,001-11,344,500 | 1955-1957 | 12,469,001-12,553,375 | 1955-1957 |
| 11,344,501-11,384,000 | 1958-1960 | 12,553,376-12,614,900 | 1958-1960 |
| 11,384,001-11,999,999 | 1961-1969 | 12,614,901-12,999,999 | 1961-1969 |
| 13,000,000-13,197,500 | 1940-1945 | 14,000,000-14,204,500 | 1940-1945 |
| 13,197,501-13,299,700 | 1946-1948 | 14,204,501-14,300,770 | 1946-1948 |
| 13,299,701-13,408,700 | 1949-1951 | 14,300,771-14,454,000 | 1949-1951 |
| 13,408,701-13,511,500 | 1952-1954 | 14,454,001-14,547,500 | 1952-1954 |
| 13,511,501-13,621,140 | 1955-1957 | 14,547,501-14,661,000 | 1955-1957 |
| 13,621,141-13,705,500 | 1958-1960 | 14,661,001-14,745,000 | 1958-1960 |
| 13,705,501-13,999,999 | 1961-1969 | 14,745,001-14,999,999 | 1961-1969 |
| 15,000,000-15,201,000 | 1940-1945 | 16,000,000-16,201,500 | 1940-1945 |
| 15,201,001-15,280,500 | 1946-1948 | 16,201,501-16,307000 | 1946-1948 |
| 15,280,501-15,465,760 | 1949-1951 | 16,307,001-16,398,890 | 1949-1951 |
| 15,465,761-15,530,600 | 1952-1954 | 16,398,891-16,481,925 | 1952-1954 |
| 15,530,601-15,593,615 | 1955-1957 | 16,481,926-16,600,497 | 1955-1957 |
| 15,593,616-15,639,615 | 1958-1960 | 16,600,498-16,683,100 | 1958-1960 |
| 15,639,616-15,999,999 | 1961-1969 | 16,683,101-16,999,999 | 1961-1969 |
| 17,000,000-17,183,500 | 1940-1945 | 18,000,000-18,247,100 | 1940-1945 |
| 17,183,501-17,254,500 | 1946-1948 | 18,247,101-18,360,800 | 1946 |
| 17,254,501-17,338,840 | 1949-1951 | 18,360,801-18,546,000 | 1947-1957 |
| 17,338,841-17,410,300 | 1952-1954 | 18,546,001-18,607,725 | 1958-1960 |
| 17,410,301-17,512,785 | 1955-1957 | 18,607,726-18,999,999 | 1961-1969 |
| 17,512,786-17,592,940 | 1958-1960 | | |
| 17,592,941-17,999,999 | 1961-1969 | | |
| 19,000,000-19,235,500 | 1940-1945 | Numbers 10,000,000 to 10,999,999 | |
| 19,235,501-19,324,485 | 1946-1948 | were used for initial enlistments | |
| 19,324,486-19,420,000 | 1949-1951 | occurring outside the continental limits | |
| 19,420,001-19,520,770 | 1952-1954 | (AK, HI, PR, Panama). | |
| 19,520,771-19,590,665 | 1955-1957 | | |
| 19,590,666-19,597,661 | 1958 | | |
| 19,597,662-19,999,999 | 1959-1969 | | |

## Chart Three
## National Guard Service Numbers

Service numbers 21,000,000 through 29,999,999 were issued to National Guard enlisted men in these designated states from 1946 to 1969.

### First Army

| State | Beginning | Ending |
|-------|-----------|--------|
| CT | 21,000,000 | 21,139,999 |
| ME | 21,190,000 | 21,259,999 |
| MA | 21,260,000 | 21,619,999 |
| NH | 21,620,000 | 21,689,999 |
| NJ | 21,690,000 | 21,899,999 |
| NY | 21,900,000 | 22,699,999 |
| NJ | 22,700,000 | 22,789,999 |
| RI | 22,790,000 | 22,859,999 |

### Second Army

| State | Beginning | Ending |
|-------|-----------|--------|
| DE | 21,140,000 | 21,189,999 |
| VT | 22,860,000 | 22,909,999 |
| DC | 22,910,000 | 22,959,999 |
| IN | 22,960,000 | 23,169,999 |
| KY | 23,170,000 | 23,269,999 |
| MD | 23,270,000 | 23,379,999 |
| OH | 23,380,000 | 23,729,999 |
| PA | 23,730,000 | 24,259,999 |
| VA | 24,260,000 | 24,409,999 |
| WV | 24,410,000 | 24,479,999 |

### Third Army

| State | Beginning | Ending |
|-------|-----------|--------|
| AL | 24,480,000 | 24,619,999 |
| FL | 24,620,000 | 24,729,999 |
| GA | 24,730,000 | 24,879,999 |
| MS | 24,880,000 | 24,959,999 |
| NC | 24,960,000 | 25,109,999 |
| SC | 25,110,000 | 25,249,999 |
| TN | 25,250,000 | 25,409,999 |

### Fourth Army

| State | Beginning | Ending |
|-------|-----------|--------|
| AR | 25,410,000 | 25,499,999 |
| LA | 25,500,000 | 25,629,999 |
| NM | 25,630,000 | 25,679,999 |
| OK | 25,680,000 | 25,839,999 |
| TX | 25,840,000 | 26,239,999 |

### Fifth Army

| State | Beginning | Ending |
|-------|-----------|--------|
| CO | 26,240,000 | 26,329,999 |
| IL | 26,330,000 | 26,799,999 |
| IA | 26,780,000 | 26,919,999 |
| KS | 26,920,000 | 27,009,999 |
| MI | 27,010,000 | 27,339,999 |
| MN | 27,340,000 | 27,499,999 |
| MO | 27,500,000 | 27,659,999 |
| NE | 27,660,000 | 27,729,999 |
| ND | 27,730,000 | 27,789,999 |
| SD | 27,790,000 | 27,849,999 |
| WI | 27,850,000 | 28,019,999 |
| WY | 28,020,000 | 28,039,999 |

### Sixth Army

| State | Beginning | Ending |
|-------|-----------|--------|
| AZ | 28,040,000 | 28,089,999 |
| CA | 28,090,000 | 28,639,999 |
| ID | 28,640,000 | 28,709,999 |
| MT | 28,710,000 | 28,759,999 |
| NV | 28,760,000 | 28,769,999 |
| OR | 28,770,000 | 28,909,999 |
| UT | 28,910,000 | 28,969,999 |
| WA | 28,970,000 | 29,029,999 |
| HI | 29,030,000 | 29,119,999 |
| PR | 29,120,000 | 29,239,999 |
| AK | 29,240,000 | 29,249,999 |
| Unused | 29,250,000 | 29,999,999 |

Service numbers 20,000,000 to 20,999,999 were assigned to National Guard enlisted men between 1940 and 1946.

## Chart Four

### Service Number Prefixes And Suffixes

The majority of prefixes and suffixes were letters used with Air Force and Army service numbers. None are known to have been used with Coast Guard service numbers. The Marine Corps used "O" to denote officer and "W" to denote enlisted women. The Navy also used "W" to denote enlisted women. From December 1965 Navy enlisted personnel received six digit numbers with a "B" prefix (B100000 thru B999999). Following the "B" series was the "D" series (D100000 thru D999999). EM and EW are used to show enlisted men and enlisted women.

| Letter | Use | Service | Designation |
| --- | --- | --- | --- |
| A | prefix | Army | Enlisted women (WAC) without specification of component |
| A | suffix | Air Force | Used until 1965 for Regular AF male officers |
| AA | prefix | Air Force | Women enlisted personnel (WAF) |
| AD | prefix | Air Force | Aviation cadets |
| AF | prefix | Air Force | Male enlisted personnel other than aviation cadets |
| AO | prefix | Air Force | Reserve officers from about 1947-1965 |
| AR | prefix | Air Force | Used until about 1965 for enlisted reserve of the AF and USAF dietitians |
| AW | prefix | Air Force | Used from about 1947-1965 for male reserve of the AF and USAF warrant officers |
| E | suffix | Air Force | Used until 1965 for Regular AF male warrant officers |
| ER | prefix | Army | Members of Army Reserve, including those enlisted personnel of Army National Guard transferred from AUS, RA, or NGUS |

| Letter | Use | Service | Designation |
|---|---|---|---|
| F | prefix | Army | Used with field clerks numbers in 800,000 series in WW I |
| FG | prefix | Air Force | Air National Guard officers and warrant officers (male and female) |
| FR | prefix | Air Force | Regular AF officers and warrant officers (male and female) |
| FR | prefix | Army | Certain Army enlisted reservists from date unknown through October 3, 1962 |
| FT | prefix | Air Force | Officers and warrant officers without component (male and female) |
| FV | prefix | Air Force | Reserve officers and warrant officers |
| H | prefix | Air Force | Used until 1965 for Regular AF female warrant officers |
| K | suffix | Air Force | Used until about 1965 for AF academy cadets |
| K | prefix | Army | Female officers except Regular Army with SNs 100,001 or higher, Army Nurse Corps, Army Medical Specialists Corps, and Women's Army Corps |
| KF | prefix | Army | Regular Army women officers with service numbers 100,001 and higher |
| L | prefix | Army | Women's Army Corps (officers) |
| MJ | prefix | Army | Occupational Therapy officers |
| MM | prefix | Army | Physical Therapy officers |
| MN | prefix | Army | Male officers of Army Nurse Corps |
| MR | prefix | Army | Dietitians |
| N | prefix | Army | Female nurses (officers) |
| NG | prefix | Army | Army National Guard enlisted personnel |
| O | prefix | Army | Male officers except Regular Army with SNs 100,001 and higher after October 28, 1963; and Army Nurse Corps and Army Medical Specialists Corps |
| O | prefix | Marines | Marine Corps officers |

| Letter | Use | Service | Designation |
|--------|-----|---------|-------------|
| OF | prefix | Army | Regular Army male officers with SNs 100,001 and higher after October 28, 1963 |
| R | prefix | Army | Officer dietitians |
| R | prefix | Army | Used on Army WW I EM numbers 1 thru 5,999,999 if man re-enlisted |
| RA | prefix | Army | Regular Army enlisted personnel (used since approximately October 1945) |
| RM | prefix | Army | Regular Army EM holding appointments as warrant officer in the active Army reserve |
| RO | prefix | Army | Regular Army enlisted holding commissions in the active Army reserve |
| RP | prefix | Army | Retired EM recalled to active duty now on retired status (used only for those transferred to retired Army reserve) |
| RV | prefix | Army | Women's Army Corps warrant officers holding commissions in active reserves |
| RW | prefix | Army | Warrant officers holding commissions in active reserves |
| T | prefix | Army | Flight officers appointed from enlisted ranks number range from T10,000 thru T223,600 (1942 to date unknown) |
| UR | prefix | Army | Inductees holding commissions or warrants in active Army reserve |
| US | prefix | Army | Enlisted men without specification of component |
| V | prefix | Army | Women's Army Corps officers |
| W | prefix | Army | Warrant officers |
| W | prefix | Marines | Women enlisted personnel |
| W | suffix | Air Force | Used until 1965 for Regular AF women commissioned officers |

| Letter | Use | Service | Designation |
|--------|-----|---------|-------------|
| W | suffix | Navy | Women enlisted personal |
| WA | prefix | Army | Regular Army enlisted women (WAC) |
| WL | prefix | Army | Regular Army enlisted women holding commissions in the active Army reserve |
| WM | prefix | Army | Regular Army enlisted women holding warrants in the Army active reserve |
| WR | prefix | Army | Enlisted women reservists (WAC) |

## Social Security Numbers

The Social Security number (SSN) is the most important item other than the name of the individual you are trying to locate. Every member of the military, active, reserve, National Guard or retired is identified and listed by his SSN. The same is true for veterans though they can also be listed by their VA claim number or their former service number by the Department of Veterans Affairs. Service numbers were discontinued and were replaced by Social Security numbers on the following dates:

| | |
|---|---|
| Army and Air Force | July 1, 1969 |
| Navy and Marine Corps | July 1, 1972 |
| Coast Guard | Oct. 1, 1974 |

Records in the National Personnel Records Center are identified by SSN except for records received before the SSN replaced the service number, in which case the service numbers are used.

There are several ways you may find a SSN. It is contained on military orders, discharges (DD 214), officers, commissions, and in the Register of Officers published by each military service from 1970 to 1976. Many bank statements contain it as well as some driver licenses. If you have canceled checks from the individual they may list the SSN. Personal letters from military members usually have their SSN included with the return address. All VA claim numbers issued after June 1974 included the veteran's SSN preceded by the letter "C" (example C123456789). You can look at old investments such as money market funds, mutual funds and stock certificates for a SSN. Most department stores ask for a person's SSN when charge accounts are opened. You might get it from schools or places of civilian employment. SSN can also be obtained from voter registration information in most states. In many states, DD forms 214 (discharge) are recorded in county courthouses. Many of these discharges contain SSN. It will speed your search to know the SSN of the person you are seeking. If you do not know it, the government will not tell you what it is. The Privacy Act of 1974 prohibits the military and federal agencies from giving out this information.

You may need the SSN to have your letters forwarded by the military, Social Security Administration, or the Department of Veterans Affairs. You may also be asked for the SSN when you call an installation locator (see Base/Post Locators in Chapter Two), especially if there is more than one person with the same name. Many times individuals are listed by their SSN because it is easier and quicker to find a number on computer records than trying to find the person by name.

But if you do not have the person's SSN, do not let this stop your search. You may still locate or contact a present or former military member without their SSN if you have one of the following:

- name and date of birth
- name and VA claim or file number
- name and former service number
- name and former unit or ship assignment (with approximate date assigned)
- name and a former address
- name only in some cases

# Social Security Number Allocations

The Social Security Administration (SSA) was formed in 1933. Between 1933 and 1972 SSN were assigned at field offices in each state. The area number identified the state in which the field office was located. Since 1973, SSN have been issued by the SSA central office.

The Social Security number consists of nine (9) digits. The first three (3) digits are the area number. The middle two (2) digits are the group number. The last four (4) digits are the serial number. (Do not confuse this with the military service numbers.)

EXAMPLE:  123-45-6789

123    45    6789
Area  Group  Serial
No.    No.    No.

# Area Number

The area number assigned by the central office identifies the state indicated in the application.

The chart below shows the first 3 digits (area number) of the Social Security numbers allocated to each state and US possession.

| | |
|---|---|
| 004-007.....................Maine | 440-448...............Oklahoma |
| 008-009.................Vermont | 449-467, 627-645...... Texas |
| 010-034........Massachusetts | 468-477...............Minnesota |
| 035-039.......... Rhode Island | 478-485.........................Iowa |
| 040-049............. Connecticut | 486-500................... Missouri |
| 050-134................ New York | 501-502.......... North Dakota |
| 135-158.............New Jersey | 503-504......... South Dakota |
| 159-211.......... Pennsylvania | 505-508................. Nebraska |
| 212-220..................Maryland | 509-515................... Kansas |
| 221-222................ Delaware | 516-517................. Montana |
| 223-231, 691-699* ... Virginia | 518-519...................... Idaho |
| 232-236.......... West Virginia | 520...................... Wyoming |
| 232, 237-246, 681-690* ....... | 521-524, 650-653* .Colorado |
| .................... North Carolina | 525, 585, 648-649*.............. |
| 247-251, 654-658*S Carolina | ........................ New Mexico |
| 252-260, 667-675* ...Georgia | 526-527, 600-601..... Arizona |
| 261-267, 589-595...... Florida | 528-529, 646-647* ........Utah |
| 268-302.......................Ohio | 530, 680*................. Nevada |
| 303-317.....................Indiana | 531- 539........... Washington |
| 318-361..................... Illinois | 540-544............... Oregon |
| 362-386.................. Michigan | 545-573, 602-626* California |
| 387-399................ Wisconsin | 574............................ Alaska |
| 400-407..................Kentucky | 575-576, 750-751* .....Hawaii |
| 408-415, 756-763* | 577-579. District of Columbia |
| ...........................Tennessee | 580.................... Virgin Islands |
| 416-424.................. Alabama | 580-584, 596-599Puerto Rico |
| 425-428, 587, 588*, 752-755* | 586............................ Guam |
| .......................... Mississippi | 586...........American Samoa |
| 429-432, 676-679* Arkansas | 586.......... Philippine Islands |
| 433-439, 659-665* Louisiana | 700-728**..... Railroad Board |

* New areas (prefixes) allocated but not yet issued.

** 700-728 RRB (Railroad Board). Issuance of these numbers to railroad employees was discontinued July 1, 1963.

NOTE: The same area number, when shown more than once, means that certain numbers have been transferred from one state to another, or that an area number has been divided for use among certain geographic locations.

Area numbers range from 001 through 587, 589 through 649, and 700 through 728. Social Security numbers containing area numbers other than these are invalid.

Prior to converting from service numbers to Social Security numbers as a means of identification, the military assigned dummy Social Security numbers to individuals who did not have them. These dummy area numbers range from 900 through 999 and appear on some military orders and unit rosters in the late 1960s and early 1970s. These dummy numbers were later replaced with valid Social Security numbers.

# Group Number

The first three (3) digits denote the area (or state) of the SSN. Within each area, group numbers (middle two (2) digits) are allocated. These numbers range from 01 to 99 but are not assigned in consecutive order. For administrative reasons, group numbers issued first consist of the odd numbers from 01 through 09 and then even numbers from 10 through 98, within each area number allocated to a state. After all even numbers in group 98 of a particular area have been issued, the even numbers 02 through 08 are used, followed by odd numbers 11 through 99 as shown:

| ODD | EVEN | EVEN | ODD |
|---|---|---|---|
| 01, 03, 05, 07, 09 | 10 to 98 | 02, 04, 06, 08 | 11 to 99 |

The chart below shows the highest group number allocated for each area number as of September 1, 1994.

| | | | | | |
|---|---|---|---|---|---|
| 001-003 | 86 | 387-393 | 13 | 525-529 | 99 |
| 004-006 | 94 | 394-399 | 11 | 530 | 81 |
| 007 | 92 | 400-404 | 47 | 531-535 | 31 |
| 008-019 | 78 | 405-407 | 45 | 536-539 | 29 |
| 020-034 | 76 | 408-415 | 75 | 540-544 | 43 |
| 035-039 | 62 | 416-417 | 43 | 545-573 | 99 |
| 040-047 | 92 | 418-424 | 41 | 574 | 15 |
| 048-049 | 90 | 425-428 | 77 | 575 | 69 |
| 050-124 | 82 | 429-430 | 87 | 576 | 67 |
| 125-134 | 80 | 431-432 | 85 | 577-579 | 25 |
| 135-146 | 96 | 433-436 | 89 | 580 | 29 |
| 147-158 | 94 | 437-439 | 87 | 581-585 | 99 |
| 159-206 | 74 | 440-442 | 06 | 586 | 19 |
| 207-211 | 72 | 443-448 | 04 | 587 | 75 |
| 212-220 | 41 | 449-467 | 99 | 588 | 00 |
| 221-222 | 84 | 468 | 29 | 589-595 | 43 |
| 223-226 | 71 | 469-477 | 27 | 596-597 | 44 |
| 227-231 | 69 | 478 | 29 | 598-599 | 42 |
| 232-236 | 41 | 479-482 | 23 | 600-601 | 41 |
| 237-239 | 79 | 483-485 | 21 | 602-603 | 76 |
| 240-246 | 77 | 486-500 | 08 | 604-626 | 74 |
| 247-248 | 95 | 501 | 21 | 627-639 | 42 |
| 249-251 | 93 | 502 | 19 | 640-645 | 40 |
| 252 | 91 | 503 | 25 | 646-647 | 20 |
| 253-260 | 89 | 504 | 23 | 648-649 | 03 |
| 261-267 | 99 | 505-507 | 33 | 650-699 | 00 |
| 268-298 | 96 | 508 | 31 | 700-723 | 18 |
| 299-302 | 94 | 509-511 | 11 | 724 | 28 |
| 303-309 | 15 | 512-515 | 08 | 725-726 | 18 |
| 310-317 | 13 | 516-517 | 27 | 727 | 10 |
| 318-336 | 90 | 518-519 | 45 | 728 | 14 |
| 337-361 | 88 | 520 | 33 | 750-763 | 00 |
| 362-375 | 17 | 521-523 | 93 | | |
| 376-386 | 15 | 524 | 91 | | |

# Serial Number

Within each group, the serial numbers (last four (4) digits of the Social Security number) run consecutively from 0001 through 9999.

# Chapter Two

# How To Locate
# Active Duty Military

*This chapter describes the ways to locate members of the armed forces who are on active duty. The Armed Forces World-Wide Locators, Base and Post locators and Army, Air Force and Fleet Post Offices (APO and FPO) provide means to locate active duty members.*

## Armed Forces
## World-Wide Locators

The Armed Forces World-Wide Locators will either forward a letter or provide you with the current military unit of assignment. The latter may be limited to unit of assignments in the United States. The latter may be limited to unit of assignments in the United States.

If you want to have a letter forwarded, place the letter in a sealed, stamped envelope. Put your name and return address in the upper left hand corner. In the center of the envelope put the rank, full name of the service member, followed by the Social Security number or date of birth (if known). On a separate sheet of paper put everything you know that may help the military locator such as:

- name
- rank
- social security number
- military service e.g., active air force
- date of birth (estimated if actual is unknown)
- sex
- officer or enlisted (if you are not sure of the rank)
- date entered service
- last assignment (if known)

In another envelope, preferably legal size, enclose the letter you want forwarded along with the fact sheet and a check for the search fee (the current search fee for all armed forces is $3.50, make check payable to Treasurer of the US). If you are active, reserve, National Guard, retired military or a family member, state this on the fact sheet. Show your rank and SSN or relationship, and you will not need to send the search fee. On the outer envelope, include your name and return address. Address it to the appropriate locator below.

If the military locator can identify the individual, it will forward your letter. It is up to the individual to reply to your letter. The military cannot require a reply in this process. If the military locator cannot identify the person you are seeking, it will return your letter and tell you why. Common problems include: the locator cannot identify the individual without a SSN or the name is not unique; the individual has been separated from the service; the SSN is incorrect; or the individual is deceased.

To determine what unit and military installation a person is assigned, write a letter to the appropriate address below and include as much information as possible that will assist in identifying the person (include the same information as shown above).

If you already know the installation, you can call directly to that installation's assistance operator or the installation locator (see instructions under "Base and Post Locator Service" located in this chapter). You can also mail a letter to the individual in care of the installation locator (see list of base and post locators for proper mailing address).

# To Locate Active Duty
# Air Force Personnel

The Air Force locator will forward only one letter per each request and will not provide overseas unit of assignment of active members. Requests for more than one address per letter will be returned without action. Include self-addressed stamped envelope with request for unit assignment. If the individual is separated from the Air Force, they will tell you.

USAF World-Wide Locator
AFMPC-RMIQL                    Recording (210) 652-5774
55 C Street West, Room 50              (210) 652-5775
Randolph AFB, TX 78150-4752

# To Locate Active Duty Army Personnel

This locator furnishes military addresses for individuals currently serving on active duty in the Army and for the Department of the Army civilians. All requests must contain the individuals full name, Social Security number or date of birth. No information will be given without one of the above identifying numbers. The hours of operation are 7:30 a.m. to 4:00 p.m. EST, Monday through Friday. Written requests should be mailed to the above address with a check or money order in the amount of $3.50 for each name submitted. Check or money order should be made payable to "Finance Officer". (Do not send cash.) Approximate time for processing written requests is seven to ten working days.

The locator system holds separation data for two years after a soldier is separated. The only separation information available is date and place of separation.

To forward a letter to an active duty member, put your return address on envelope to be forwarded and in the body of the letter of request.

World-Wide Locator               (317) 542-4211
US Army Enlisted Records
   and Evaluation Center
Ft. Benjamin Harrison, IN  46249-5301

For bona fide emergencies, call Total Army Personnel Command Locator at (703) 325-8852. It is open 24 hours a day.

# To Locate Active Duty
# Coast Guard Personnel

The Coast Guard will provide ship or station of assignment and unit telephone number of active duty personnel when requested by telephone. A $5.20 search fee is charged to provide a written verification of unit assignment. If you know the ship the member is assigned, see Fleet Post Office listing in this chapter for correct mailing address.

Military Personnel Command          (202) 267-1340
Locator Service(MPC-S-3)       FAX (202) 267-4985
2100 Second Street, SW
Washington, DC  20593-0001
($5.20 search fee)

## To Locate Active Duty
## Marine Corps Personnel

U.S.  Marine Corps-CMC          (703) 640-3942
(MMSB-10)
2008 Elliot Road, Room 201
Quantico, VA  22134-5030
(no search fee)

## To Locate Active Duty Navy Personnel

This locator will forward letters only for a fee of $3.50.

Bureau of Naval Personnel          (703) 614-3155
P-324D                            (703) 614-5011
2 Navy Annex                  FAX (703) 614-1261
Washington, DC  20370-3240

If you know the name of the ship the member is assigned, see Fleet Post Office listing in this chapter for correct mailing address.

## To Locate National Oceanic And Atmospheric Administration Personnel

Commissioned Personnel Center          (301) 713-3444
1315 E West Hwy
SSCM3  Room 12100
Silverspring, MD  20910-3233

## To Locate US Public Health Service Personnel

US Public Health Service               (301) 443-3087
Department of Health and Human Services
PHS/CPOD
5600 Fishers Lane
Parklawn Bldg Room 4-35
Rockville, MD  20857

## Base and Post Locator Service

The armed forces provide locator service at most of their installations.  The Freedom of Information Act provides that the services may release a military member's unit or ship assignment.  They may provide their duty telephone number, but will not give out their SSN or home address, except when the individual has authorized the release of this information.  You may need to provide SSN or rank if there is more than one person with the same name.  You can call the locator if you know the installation where the person is assigned.  Locators normally operate during normal duty hours, usually 7:00 or 7:30 AM to 4:00 or 4:30 PM Monday through Friday.  Locator service is normally provided by a separate office at larger bases. Sometimes it is provided by the telephone information operator, the personnel office or by the Staff Duty Officer (SDO) after normal working hours and holidays. When you call, give the name and rank of the person you are looking for and ask for their duty assignment, work telephone number, home address and telephone number. Some Individuals may have authorized release of their home addresses and telephone numbers.

Many enlisted people live in barracks, dormitories, or quarters on the base as do many single non-commissioned officers (NCO) and officers. They can be contacted through the Charge of Quarters of their unit after normal duty hours. Some married NCO and officers live on base in quarters and they usually have telephone numbers that are available through the local telephone company. Call the local civilian information operator to find out if they have a listed telephone number. Many military members live in the civilian communities close to the military installation they are assigned.

To obtain the telephone number of an installation locator not listed in the following pages, you can call the installation information operator to get the number. If you know the unit of the person you are trying to reach, the operator can give you that telephone number. You may also write to the locator to obtain the number. Locators keep forwarding addresses for all personnel who are separated from the service or have been transferred for six months after departure. Mail for personnel who were assigned to decommissioned ships or closed installations will be forwarded for sixty days after closing or decommissioning.

# Armed Forces Installations
# In The United States

The following pages list the major military installations in the Unites States and its territories. It also lists the closest city, the ZIP code, the telephone number for the base or post information operator and the telephone number for the base or post locator.

This information may be utilized to locate current military members assigned to a particular installation by either calling or writing the base or post locator. Telephone numbers of units, offices and individuals who live in base quarters may be obtained through the base and post information operator.

These abbreviations are used in the list of major installations:

AAF - Army Air Field
AF - Air Force
AFB - Air Force Base
AFRB - Air Force Reserve
    Base
AFS - Air Force Station
AMC - Army Medical Center
ANG - Air National Guard
CG - Coast Guard
CGAS - Coast Guard Air
    Station
Cp - Cape
Ctr - Center

Ft - Fort
HQ - Headquarters
MC - Marine Corps
MCAS - Marine Corps Air
    Station
NAB - Naval Amphibious Base
NAS - Naval Air Station
NS - Naval Station
NSA - Naval Support Activity
NSB - Naval Submarine Base
Pt - Point
Stn - Station
Trng - Training

| City | Installation | ZIP Code | Information Number | Locator Number |
|------|-------------|----------|-------------------|----------------|
| **ALABAMA** | | | | |
| Anniston | Anniston Army Depot | 36201 | 205-235-7501 | 235-7501 |
| Anniston | Fort McClellan | 36205 | 205-848-4611 | 848-3795 |
| Dothan | Hall ANG Station | 36301 | 334-792-6793 | 792-6793 |
| Gadsden | Martin ANG Station | 35901 | 205-442-9700 | 442-9700 |
| Huntsville | Redstone Arsenal | 35898 | 205-876-2151 | 876-3331 |
| Mobile | Coast Guard Aviation Training Center | 36608 | 334-694-6110 | 694-6127 |
| Mobile | Coast Guard Base | 36615 | 334-690-3109 | 690-3109 |
| Montgomery | Dannelly Field ANG | 36125 | 334-284-7100 | 284-7411 |
| Montgomery | Gunter Annex | 36114 | 334-416-1110 | 953-5027 |
| Montgomery | Maxwell AFB | 36112 | 334-416-1110 | 953-5027 |
| Ozark | Fort Rucker | 36362 | 334-255-1030 | 255-3156 |
| **ALASKA** | | | | |
| Adak | Naval Station | 98791 | 907-592-4201 | 592-4395 |
| Anchorage | Elmendorf AFB | 99506 | 907-552-1110 | 552-4860 |
| Anchorage | Fort Richardson | 99505 | 907-873-1121 | 873-3255 |
| Anchorage | Kulis ANG Base | 99502 | 907-249-1176 | 249-1176 |
| Attu | Coast Guard Station | 96512 | 907-392-3000 | 392-3000 |
| Clear | Air Force Station | 99704 | 907-585-6113 | 585-6209 |
| Delta Junct'n | Fort Greely | 96508 | 907-873-1121 | 873-3255 |
| Fairbanks | Eielson AFB | 99702 | 907-377-1110 | 377-1841 |
| Fairbanks | Fort Wainwright | 99703 | 907-353-7500 | 353-6586 |
| Ketchikan | Coast Guard Base | 99901 | 907-228-0220 | 228-0213 |
| King Salmon | King Salmon Airport | 99613 | 907-552-1110 | 552-4860 |
| Kodiak | Kodiak CGAS | 99619 | 907-487-5163 | 487-5163 |
| Kodiak | CG Support Center | 99619 | 907-487-5525 | 487-5525 |
| Shemya | Air Force Base | 96512 | 907-392-3000 | 392-3000 |
| Sitka | CG Air Station | 99835 | 907-966-5555 | 966-5555 |
| **ARIZONA** | | | | |
| Gila Bend | AF Auxiliary Field | 85337 | 520-683-6200 | 683-6200 |
| Glendale | Luke AFB | 85309 | 520-856-7411 | 856-6405 |
| Phoenix | Phoenix ANG | 85034 | 520-231-8000 | 231-8000 |
| Sierra Vista | Fort Huachuca | 85613 | 520-538-7111 | 538-7111 |

| City | Installation | ZIP Code | Information Number | Locator Number |
|------|-------------|----------|-------------------|----------------|
| **ARIZONA (cont.)** | | | | |
| Tucson | Davis-Monthan AFB | 85707 | 520-750-3900 | 750-3347 |
| Yuma | Army Proving Ground | 85365 | 520-328-2151 | 328-2151 |
| Yuma | MC Air Station | 85369 | 520-341-2011 | 341-2011 |
| **ARKANSAS** | | | | |
| Fort Smith | Fort Chaffee | 72905 | 501-484-2141 | 484-2933 |
| Jacksonville | Little Rock AFB | 72099 | 501-988-3131 | 988-6461 |
| Pine Bluff | Pine Bluff Arsenal | 71602 | 501-540-3000 | 540-3000 |
| **CALIFORNIA** | | | | |
| Alameda | CG Support Center | 94501 | 510-437-3151 | 437-3151 |
| Atwater | Castle AFB | 95342 | 209-726-2011 | 726-4848 |
| Barstow | Fort Irwin | 92310 | 619-386-4111 | 380-3369 |
| Barstow | MC Logistical Base | 92311 | 619-577-6211 | 577-6675 |
| Bridgeport | MC Warfare Trng Ctr | 93517 | 619-932-7761 | 932-7761 |
| China Lake | Naval Weapons Ctr | 93555 | 619-939-2303 | 939-9011 |
| Concord | Naval Weapons Stn | 94520 | 510-246-2000 | 246-5040 |
| Coronado | NAB Coronado | 92155 | 619-437-2011 | 437-2011 |
| Coronado | NAS North Island | 92135 | 619-524-1011 | 545-0496 |
| Costa Mesa | ANG Station | 92627 | 714-979-1343 | 979-1343 |
| El Centro | Naval Air Facility | 92243 | 619-339-2555 | 339-2699 |
| El Toro | MC Air Station | 92709 | 714-726-2100 | 726-3736 |
| Fairfield | Travis AFB | 94535 | 707-424-5000 | 424-2798 |
| Fresno | Fresno ANG Base | 93727 | 209-454-5100 | 454-5100 |
| Hayward | Hayward ANG Stn | 94545 | 510-783-1661 | 783-1661 |
| Herlong | Sierra Army Depot | 96113 | 916-827-4000 | 827-4328 |
| Jolon | Fort Hunter Liggett | 93928 | 408-385-2350 | 385-2350 |
| Lancaster | Edwards AFB | 93523 | 805-277-1110 | 277-2777 |
| Lathrop | Sharpe Army Depot | 95331 | 209-982-2000 | 982-2000 |
| Lemoore | Naval Air Station | 93246 | 209-998-0100 | 998-3789 |
| Lompoc | Vandenberg AFB | 93437 | 805-734-8232 | 734-8232 |
| Long Beach | Naval Station | 90822 | 562-547-6721 | 547-6004 |
| Los Angeles | Air Force Base | 90245 | 562-363-1100 | 363-1876 |
| Los Angeles | CG Air Station | 90045 | 562-215-2204 | 215-2204 |
| Mare Island | Naval Station | 94592 | 707-646-1111 | 646-4196 |

| City | Installation | ZIP Code | Information Number | Locator Number |
|---|---|---|---|---|
| **CALIFORNIA (cont.)** | | | | |
| Marysville | Beale AFB | 95903 | 916-634-3000 | 634-2960 |
| McKinleyville | CGAS Humboldt Bay | 95521 | 707-839-6115 | 839-6115 |
| Moffett Field | Naval Air Station | 94035 | 415-603-9527 | 603-4088 |
| Monterey | Coast Guard Group | 93940 | 408-647-7300 | 647-7300 |
| Monterey | Presidio of Monterey | 93944 | 408-647-2211 | 647-5119 |
| Oakland | Naval Hospital | 94627 | 510-633-5000 | 633-5000 |
| Oakland | Naval Supply Center | 94625 | 510-302-2000 | 302-2000 |
| Oakland | Oakland Army Base | 94626 | 510-466-9111 | 466-9111 |
| Oceanside | Camp Pendleton | 92055 | 619-725-4111 | 725-5171 |
| Petaluma | CG Training Center | 94952 | 707-765-7212 | 765-7211 |
| Point Mugu | Naval Air Station | 93042 | 805-989-1110 | 989-8031 |
| Point Mugu | Pacific Missile Test Center | 93042 | 805-989-1110 | 989-8031 |
| Point Reyes | Coast Guard Station | 95456 | 707-765-7212 | 765-7211 |
| Prt Hueneme | ANG Station | 93041 | 805-986-8000 | 986-8000 |
| Prt Hueneme | Naval Construction Battalion Center | 93043 | 805-982-4711 | 982-4711 |
| Riverside | March AFB | 92518 | 909-655-1110 | 655-3192 |
| Sacramento | Army Depot | 95813 | 916-388-2211 | 388-2211 |
| Sacramento | CG Air Station | 95652 | 916-643-2081 | 643-2081 |
| Sacramento | McClellan AFB | 95652 | 916-643-2111 | 643-2111 |
| San Diego | CG Air Station | 92101 | 619-557-5870 | 557-5510 |
| San Diego | MC Recruit Depot | 92140 | 619-524-1011 | 524-1719 |
| San Diego | NAS Miramar | 92145 | 619-537-1011 | 537-6018 |
| San Diego | Naval Station | 92136 | 619-556-1011 | 556-1011 |
| San Diego | Naval Hospital | 92134 | 619-532-6400 | 532-6400 |
| San Diego | Naval Sub Base | 92106 | 619-553-8663 | 553-8663 |
| San Diego | Naval Trng Center | 92133 | 619-524-1011 | 524-1011 |
| San Francis. | CG Air Station | 94128 | 415-876-2920 | 876-2920 |
| San Francis. | NSA Treasure Island | 94130 | 415-395-1000 | 395-3419 |
| San Francis. | Presidio | 94129 | 415-561-2211 | 561-3204 |
| San Francis. | Letterman AMC | 94129 | 415-561-2231 | 561-2231 |
| San Obispo | Cp San Luis Obispo | 93403 | 805-549-3800 | 549-3800 |
| San Miguel | Camp Roberts | 93451 | 805-238-3100 | 238-3100 |
| San Pedro | CG Support Center | 90731 | 562-514-6402 | 514-6402 |

| City | Installation | ZIP Code | Information Number | Locator Number |
|------|--------------|----------|--------------------|----------------|
| **CALIFORNIA (cont.)** | | | | |
| Santa Ana | MCAS El Toro | 92709 | 714-726-2100 | 726-2100 |
| Seal Beach | Naval Weapons Stn | 90740 | 562-594-7011 | 594-7011 |
| Stockton | Naval Comm Stn | 95203 | 209-944-0284 | 944-0284 |
| Sunnyvale | Onizuka AFB | 94088 | 408-752-3000 | 752-4539 |
| Tracy | Defense Depot | 95296 | 209-832-9000 | 832-9000 |
| Vallejo | NS Mare Island | 94592 | 707-646-1111 | 646-2115 |
| **COLORADO** | | | | |
| Aurora | Buckley ANG Base | 80011 | 970-340-9011 | 340-9011 |
| Aurora | Fitzsimons AMC | 80045 | 970-361-8241 | 361-8202 |
| CO Springs | Air Force Academy | 80840 | 719-472-3110 | 472-4262 |
| CO Springs | Falcon AFB | 80912 | 719-550-4113 | 556-4020 |
| CO Springs | Fort Carson | 80913 | 719-526-5811 | 526-3341 |
| CO Springs | Peterson AFB | 80914 | 719-550-4112 | 556-4020 |
| Denver | Air Force Reserve Personnel Center | 80280 | 970-676-6307 | 676-6307 |
| Pueblo | Army Depot | 81001 | 719-549-4111 | 549-4111 |
| Commerce | Rocky Mountain Arsenal | 80022 | 970-288-0711 | 361-8202 |
| **CONNECTICUT** | | | | |
| East Granby | Bradley ANG Base | 06026 | 203-623-8291 | 623-8291 |
| Groton | NSB New London | 06349 | 203-449-3011 | 449-3087 |
| New Haven | Long Island Snd CG | 06512 | 203-468-4450 | 468-4450 |
| New London | Coast Guard Academy | 06320 | 203-444-8444 | 444-8444 |
| Orange | ANG Communications Station | 06477 | 203-795-4786 | 795-4786 |
| **DELAWARE** | | | | |
| Dover | Dover AFB | 19902 | 302-677-2113 | 677-3000 |
| **DISTRICT OF COLUMBIA** | | | | |
| Washington | DC ANG | 20331 | 301-981-1110 | 981-1110 |
| Washington | Andrews AFB | 20331 | 301-981-1110 | 981-1110 |
| Washington | Naval Air Facility | 20390 | 301-981-5848 | 981-5848 |

| City | Installation | ZIP Code | Information Number | Locator Number |
|------|-------------|----------|-------------------|----------------|
| **DISTRICT OF COLUMBIA (cont.)** | | | | |
| Washington | Bolling AFB | 20332 | 703-545-6700 | 767-5393* |
| Washington | Coast Guard HQ | 20593 | 202-267-2229 | 267-1340 |
| Washington | Fort McNair | 20319 | 703-545-6700 | 475-2005* |
| Washington | Marine Barracks | 20390 | 703-545-6700 | 694-3793* |
| Washington | Marine Corps HQ | 20380 | 703-614-2479 | 614-2344 |
| Washington | NG Bureau | 20310 | 703-697-4841 | 697-4841 |
| Washington | Navy Yard | 20374 | 703-545-6700 | 433-3273* |
| Washington | Pentagon | 20310 | 703-545-6700 | 545-6700 |
| Washington | Walter Reed AMC | 20307 | 202-576-3501 | 576-3767 |
| *Area code (202) | | | | |

**FLORIDA**

| City | Installation | ZIP Code | Information Number | Locator Number |
|------|-------------|----------|-------------------|----------------|
| Avon Park | Air Force Range | 33825 | 813-452-4114 | 452-4114 |
| Cp Canaveral | Air Force Station | 32925 | 407-853-1110 | 494-4542 |
| Clearwater | CG Air Station | 34622 | 813-535-1437 | 535-1437 |
| Cocoa Bch | Patrick AFB | 32925 | 407-494-1110 | 494-4542 |
| Crestview | Duke Field AFS | 32542 | 904-882-1110 | 882-1110 |
| Cuedjoe Kys | Cuedjoe Keys AFS | 33044 | 305-292-3121 | 292-3121 |
| Ft Walton Bc | Eglin AFB | 32542 | 904-882-1110 | 882-1110 |
| Ft Walton Bc | Hurlburt Field | 32544 | 904-882-1110 | 884-6333 |
| Homestead | Homestead AFRB | 33039 | 954-257-8011 | 257-7621 |
| Jacksonville | Naval Air Station | 32212 | 904-772-2338 | 772-2340 |
| Jacksonville | NAS Cecil Field | 32215 | 004-770-0020 | 778-5240 |
| Key West | Coast Guard Group | 33040 | 954-292-8500 | 292-8700 |
| Key West | Naval Air Station | 33040 | 954-293-2434 | 293-2256 |
| Mayport | Coast Guard Base | 32267 | 904-247-7301 | 247-7301 |
| Mayport | Naval Station | 32228 | 904-270-5401 | 270-5401 |
| Miami | Seventh CG District | 33139 | 954-536-5632 | 536-5632 |
| Miami | Coast Guard Base | 33139 | 954-535-4300 | 535-4300 |
| Milton | NAS Whiting Field | 32570 | 904-623-7437 | 623-7437 |
| Opa Locka | CG Air Station | 33054 | 305-953-2100 | 953-2100 |
| Orlando | Naval Training Center | 32813 | 407-646-4111 | 646-4501 |
| Panama City | Naval Coastal System Center | 32407 | 904-234-4011 | 234-4011 |
| Panama City | Tyndall AFB | 32403 | 904-283-1113 | 283-1113 |

| City | Installation | ZIP Code | Information Number | Locator Number |
|------|--------------|----------|-------------------|----------------|
| **FLORIDA (cont.)** | | | | |
| Pensacola | Naval Air Technical Training Center | 32508 | 904-452-0111 | 452-4693 |
| Pensacola | Corry Naval Station | 32511 | 904-452-0111 | 452-6226 |
| Pensacola | Naval Hospital | 32512 | 904-452-0111 | 452-6831 |
| Pensacola | Shufley Field | 32509 | 904-452-0111 | 452-4519 |
| St Petersburg | Coast Guard Station | 33701 | 813-893-3434 | 893-3434 |
| Starke | Camp Blanding | 32091 | 904-533-3100 | 533-3100 |
| Tampa | MacDill AFB | 33608 | 813-828-1110 | 828-2444 |
| **GEORGIA** | | | | |
| Albany | MC Logistic Base | 31704 | 912-439-5000 | 439-5103 |
| Athens | Naval Supply Corps School | 30606 | 706-354-1500 | 354-1500 |
| Atlanta | Fort McPherson | 30330 | 404-752-3113 | 752-3113 |
| Augusta | Fort Gordon | 30905 | 706-791-0110 | 791-4675 |
| Columbus | Fort Benning | 31905 | 706-545-2011 | 545-5217 |
| Dahlonega | Camp Merrill | 30533 | 706-864-3367 | 864-3367 |
| Forest Park | Fort Gillem | 30050 | 404-363-5000 | 363-5000 |
| Hinesville | Fort Stewart | 31314 | 912-767-1110 | 767-2862 |
| Kings Bay | Naval Submarine Bse | 31547 | 912-673-2000 | 673-2160 |
| Marietta | NAS Atlanta | 30060 | 404-421-5503 | 421-5503 |
| Marietta | Dobbins AFB | 30069 | 404-421-5000 | 421-5000 |
| Savannah | Hunter Army Airfield | 31409 | 912-352-6521 | 767-2862 |
| Savannah | CG Air Station | 31409 | 912-352-6237 | 352-6237 |
| Valdosta | Moody AFB | 31699 | 912-333-4211 | 333-3585 |
| Wmr Robins | Robins AFB | 31098 | 912-926-1110 | 926-6027 |
| **HAWAII** | | | | |
| Barbers Pt | Naval Air Station | 96862 | 808-471-7110 | 684-1005 |
| Ewa Beach | Barbers Point CGAS | 96862 | 808-682-2614 | 682-2614 |
| Hilo | Pohakuloa Trng Area | 96720 | 808-471-7110 | 536-2294 |
| Honolulu | MC Camp HM Smith | 96861 | 808-471-7110 | 477-0411 |
| Honolulu | Fort Shafter | 96858 | 808-471-7110 | 655-2299 |
| Honolulu | Tripler AMC | 96859 | 808-471-7110 | 655-2299 |
| Honolulu | Hickam AFB | 96853 | 808-471-7110 | 449-0165 |

| City | Installation | ZIP Code | Information Number | Locator Number |
|------|-------------|----------|-------------------|----------------|
| **HAWAII (cont.)** | | | | |
| Honolulu | Sand Island CG Base | 96819 | 808-541-2481 | 541-2481 |
| Kaneohe Bay | MC Air Station | 96863 | 808-471-7110 | 257-2008 |
| Kekaha | Barking Sands Pacific Missile Range/USN | 96752 | 808-471-7110 | 471-6737 |
| Pearl Harbor | Naval Base | 96860 | 808-471-7110 | 614-3155 |
| Wahiawa | Naval Ammo Area | 96786 | 808-471-7110 | 614-3155 |
| Wahiawa | Schofield Barracks | 96857 | 808-471-7110 | 655-2299 |
| Wahiawa | Wheeler AAF | 96854 | 808-471-7110 | 655-2299 |
| Wahiawa | Kunia Field Station | 96819 | 808-471-7110 | 655-2299 |
| Wahiawa | Helemano Military Reservation | 96857 | 808-471-7110 | 655-2299 |
| Waianae | Lualualei Naval Magazine | 96792 | 808-471-7110 | 614-3155 |
| Waianae | Army Recreation Ctr | 96792 | 808-471-7110 | 655-2299 |
| Waimanalo | Bellows AFS | 96853 | 808-471-7110 | 449-0165 |
| **IDAHO** | | | | |
| Boise | Gowen ANG Base | 83707 | 208-389-5011 | 389-5011 |
| Mt'n Home | Mountain Home AFB | 83648 | 208-828-2111 | 828-6647 |
| **ILLINOIS** | | | | |
| Belleville | Scott AFB | 62225 | 618-256-1110 | 256-1841 |
| Chicago | O'Hare Air Reserve Facility | 60666 | 312-825-6000 | 825-6000 |
| Glenview | NAS Glenview | 60026 | 630-657-1000 | 657-9195 |
| Glenview | Chicago CG Air Stn | 60026 | 630-657-2145 | 657-2145 |
| Granite City | Charles Melvin Support Center | 62040 | 618-452-4212 | 452-4247 |
| Great Lakes | Naval Training Center | 60088 | 630-688-3939 | 688-3939 |
| Highland Prk | Sheridan Reserve Ctr | 60037 | 630-926-4111 | 926-4111 |
| Rock Island | Rock Island Arsenal | 61299 | 309-782-6001 | 782-6001 |
| **INDIANA** | | | | |
| Crane | Naval Weapons Support Center | 47522 | 812-854-2511 | 854-2511 |
| Edinburgh | Camp Atterbury | 46124 | 812-526-9711 | 526-9711 |

| City | Installation | ZIP Code | Information Number | Locator Number |
|------|-------------|----------|--------------------|-----------------|
| **INDIANA (cont.)** | | | | |
| Indianapolis | Fort B Harrison | 46216 | 317-546-9211 | 542-7197 |
| Indianapolis | Naval Air Warfare Ctr | 46219 | 317-359-8471 | 353-7339 |
| Madison | Jefferson Proving Ground | 47250 | 812-273-7211 | 273-7211 |
| Peru | Grissom Reserve Ctr | 46971 | 317-688-5211 | 688-5211 |
| Terre Haute | Indiana ANG HQ | 47803 | 812-877-5210 | 877-5210 |
| **IOWA** | | | | |
| Des Moines | ANG Base | 50313 | 515-256-8210 | 256-8210 |
| **KANSAS** | | | | |
| Junction City | Fort Riley | 66442 | 913-239-3911 | 239-9868 |
| Leavenworth | Fort Leavenworth | 66027 | 913-684-4021 | 684-3651 |
| Shawnee Mn | 9th MC District | 66204 | 913-236-3306 | 236-3306 |
| Topeka | Forbes Fld ANGB | 66619 | 913-862-1234 | 862-1234 |
| Wichita | McConnell AFB | 67221 | 316-652-6100 | 652-3555 |
| **KENTUCKY** | | | | |
| Fort Knox | Fort Knox | 40121 | 502-624-1181 | 624-1141 |
| Hopkinsville | Fort Campbell | 42223 | 502-798-2151 | 798-7196 |
| Louisville | Naval Ordinance Stn | 40214 | 502-364-5011 | 364-5011 |
| Louisville | Standford Fld ANGB | 40213 | 502-364-9400 | 364-9400 |
| **LOUISIANA** | | | | |
| Bossier City | Barksdale AFB | 71110 | 318-456-2252 | 456-3555 |
| Leesville | Fort Polk | 71459 | 318-531-2911 | 531-1272 |
| New Orleans | CG Support Center | 70117 | 504-271-6262 | 271-6262 |
| New Orleans | CG Air Station | 70143 | 504-393-6005 | 393-6005 |
| New Orleans | Navy Reserve Personnel Center | 70149 | 504-948-5860 | 948-5860 |
| New Orleans | Naval Support Activity | 70142 | 504-948-5011 | 361-2762 |
| Pineville | Camp Beauregard | 71360 | 318-640-2080 | 640-2080 |
| **MAINE** | | | | |
| Augusta | Camp Keyes | 04333 | 207-622-9331 | 622-9331 |
| Bangor | Intl Air Port | 04401 | 207-990-7700 | 990-7700 |
| Brunswick | Naval Air Station | 04011 | 207-921-2214 | 921-2214 |

| City | Installation | ZIP Code | Information Number | Locator Number |
|------|--------------|----------|--------------------|----------------|

## MAINE (cont.)

| City | Installation | ZIP Code | Information Number | Locator Number |
|------|--------------|----------|--------------------|----------------|
| E Machias | Naval Radio Station | 04630 | 207-259-8218 | 259-8218 |
| S Portland | CG Base | 04106 | 207-767-0335 | 767-0335 |
| S Portland | ANG Station | 04106 | 207-772-2873 | 772-2873 |
| S W Harbor | Coast Guard Base | 04679 | 207-244-5517 | 244-5517 |
| Wntr Harbor | Naval Security Group | 04693 | 207-963-5534 | 963-5534 |

## MARYLAND

| City | Installation | ZIP Code | Information Number | Locator Number |
|------|--------------|----------|--------------------|----------------|
| Aberdeen | Aberdeen Proving Ground | 21005 | 410-278-5201 | 278-5138 |
| Aberdeen | Edgewood Arsenal | 21005 | 410-278-5201 | 278-5138 |
| Adelphia | Army Research Laboratories | 20783 | 301-394-2515 | 394-2456 |
| Annapolis | US Naval Academy | 21402 | 410-293-1000 | 293-5001 |
| Baltimore | Fort Ritchie | 21719 | 301-878-1300 | 878-5431 |
| Bethesda | National Naval Medical Center | 20889 | 301-295-4611 | 295-5202 |
| Camp Sprgs | Andrews AFB | 20331 | 301-981-9111 | 981-1110 |
| Curtis Bay | CG Yard | 21226 | 410-789-1600 | 789-1600 |
| Frederick | Fort Detrick | 21702 | 301-619-8000 | 619-2233 |
| Indian Head | Naval Ordinance Stn | 20640 | 301-743-4000 | 743-4000 |
| Odenton | Fort Meade | 20755 | 301-677-6261 | 677-6261 |
| Solomons | Navy Recreation Ctr | 20688 | 410-326-4216 | 326-4216 |

## MASSACHUSETTS

| City | Installation | ZIP Code | Information Number | Locator Number |
|------|--------------|----------|--------------------|----------------|
| Ayer | Fort Devens | 01433 | 508-796-3911 | 796-6046 |
| Bedford | Hanscom AFB | 01731 | 617-377-4441 | 377-5111 |
| Boston | CG Support Center | 02109 | 617-223-3257 | 223-3257 |
| Chicopee | Westover AFB | 01022 | 413-557-1110 | 557-3874 |
| Lexington Pk | Patuxent River NAS | 20670 | 301-826-3000 | 826-3000 |
| Natick | Army R&D Eng Ctr | 01760 | 508-651-4000 | 651-4725 |
| Otis | Cape Cod CGAS | 02542 | 508-968-1000 | 968-1000 |
| Otis | Otis ANG Base | 02542 | 508-968-1000 | 968-1000 |
| Otis | Camp Edwards | 02542 | 508-968-1000 | 968-1000 |
| S Boston | CG Support Activity | 02190 | 617-223-3257 | 223-8179 |
| S Weymouth | Naval Air Station | 02190 | 617-786-2500 | 786-2933 |

| City | Installation | ZIP Code | Information Number | Locator Number |
|---|---|---|---|---|
| **MASSACHUSETTS (cont.)** | | | | |
| Watertown | Army Research Ctr | 02172 | 617-923-5000 | 923-5158 |
| Westfield | Barnes Airport | 01085 | 413-568-9151 | 568-9151 |
| Worcester | Worcester ANGB | 01605 | 508-792-5711 | 799-6963 |
| **MICHIGAN** | | | | |
| Alpena | Collins ANG Base | 49707 | 517-354-6550 | 354-6550 |
| Belle Isle | Detroit CG Base | 48207 | 313-331-3110 | 331-3110 |
| Detroit | Coast Guard Group | 48207 | 313-568-9525 | 568-9525 |
| Grand Haven | Coast Guard Group | 49417 | 616-847-4500 | 847-4517 |
| Grayling | Camp Grayling | 49739 | 517-348-7621 | 348-7621 |
| Gwinn | KI Sawyer AFB | 49843 | 906-372-1110 | 372-2605 |
| Mt Clemens | Selfridge ANG Base | 48045 | 810-307-4011 | 307-4021 |
| Mt Clemens | Detroit CGAS | 48045 | 810-954-4100 | 954-4100 |
| Mt Clemens | Naval Air Reserve Detroit | 48045 | 810-307-4420 | 307-4011 |
| S St Marie | Coast Guard Base | 49783 | 906-635-3217 | 635-3217 |
| Traverse City | CG Air Station | 49684 | 616-922-8214 | 922-8214 |
| Warren | Detroit Arsenal | 48090 | 313-573-1000 | 573-1000 |
| Warren | MI Army Missile Plant | 48089 | 313-374-5000 | 374-5000 |
| **MINNESOTA** | | | | |
| Little Falls | Camp Ripley | 56345 | 612-632-6631 | 632-7425 |
| Minneapolis | Twin City AFRB | 55417 | 612-725-5011 | 725-5011 |
| **MISSISSIPPI** | | | | |
| Bay St Louis | Naval Oceanography | 39529 | 601-688-2211 | 688-2211 |
| Biloxi | Keesler AFB | 39534 | 601-377-1110 | 377-2798 |
| Columbus | Columbus AFB | 39701 | 601-434-7322 | 434-2958 |
| Gulfport | Naval Construction Battalion Center | 39501 | 601-871-2555 | 871-2555 |
| Jackson | Mississippi ANG HQ | 39208 | 601-973-6232 | 973-6232 |
| Hattiesburg | Camp Shelby | 39407 | 601-584-2000 | 584-2000 |
| Jackson | Thompson Field | 39208 | 601-939-3633 | 939-3633 |
| Meridian | Naval Air Station | 39309 | 601-679-2211 | 679-2528 |

| City | Installation | ZIP Code | Information Number | Locator Number |
|------|-------------|----------|-------------------|----------------|
| **MISSOURI** | | | | |
| Kansas City | MC Finance Center | 64197 | 816-926-7652 | 926-7652 |
| Knob Noster | Whiteman AFB | 65305 | 816-687-1110 | 687-1841 |
| Saint Louis | Coast Guard HQ | 63103 | 314-539-5902 | 539-3706 |
| Saint Louis | Army AG Publications Center | 63114 | 314-263-3901 | 263-3901 |
| Saint Louis | Army Reserve Personnel Center | 63132 | 800-325-3770 | |
| Waynesville | Fort Leonard Wood | 65473 | 314-596-0131 | 596-0677 |
| **MONTANA** | | | | |
| Great Falls | Malmstrom AFB | 59402 | 406-731-1110 | 731-4121 |
| **NEBRASKA** | | | | |
| Lincoln | Nebraska ANG HQ | 68524 | 402-471-3241 | 471-3241 |
| Omaha | Offutt AFB | 68113 | 402-294-1110 | 294-5125 |
| **NEVADA** | | | | |
| Fallon | Naval Air Station | 89496 | 702-426-5161 | 426-2709 |
| Indian Sprgs | AF Auxiliary Field | 89018 | 702-652-0201 | 652-8134 |
| Las Vegas | Nellis AFB | 89191 | 702-652-1110 | 652-8134 |
| **NEW HAMPSHIRE** | | | | |
| Newington | Pease ANG Base | 03803 | 603-436-6943 | 436-6943 |
| Portsmouth | Naval Shipyard | 03804 | 207-438-1000 | 438-2208 |
| **NEW JERSEY** | | | | |
| Bayonne | Military Ocean Terminal Command | 07002 | 201-823-5111 | 823-5111 |
| Cape May | CG Training Center | 08204 | 609-898-6900 | 898-6900 |
| Colts Neck | Earle Naval Wpn Sta | 07722 | 908-866-2000 | 866-2000 |
| Dover | Picatinny Arsenal | 07806 | 201-724-4021 | 724-4021 |
| Eatontown | Fort Monmouth | 07703 | 908-532-9000 | 532-9000 |
| Lakehurst | Naval Air Eng Sta | 08733 | 908-323-2011 | 323-2011 |
| Trenton | Naval Warfare Ctr | 08628 | 609-538-6600 | 538-6600 |
| Wrightstown | Fort Dix | 08640 | 609-562-1011 | 562-6051 |
| Wrightstown | McGuire AFB | 08641 | 609-724-1110 | 724-4288 |

| City | Installation | ZIP Code | Information Number | Locator Number |
|------|-------------|----------|-------------------|----------------|
| **NEW MEXICO** | | | | |
| Alamogordo | Holloman AFB | 88330 | 505-475-6511 | 475-7510 |
| Albuquerque | Kirtland AFB | 87117 | 505-846-0011 | 846-0011 |
| Clovis | Cannon AFB | 88101 | 505-784-3311 | 784-3311 |
| Las Cruces | White Sands Missile Range | 88002 | 505-678-2121 | 678-2121 |
| **NEW YORK** | | | | |
| Brooklyn | CG Air Station | 11234 | 718-615-2422 | 615-2423 |
| Brooklyn | Fort Hamilton | 11252 | 718-630-4101 | 630-4101 |
| Buffalo | Coast Guard Group | 14203 | 716-846-4152 | 846-4152 |
| Flushing | Fort Totten | 11359 | 718-352-5700 | 352-5700 |
| Governors Is | Coast Guard Base | 10004 | 212-668-7036 | 668-7036 |
| Newburgh | Stewart Army Sub Pst | 12553 | 914-563-3227 | 563-3227 |
| Newburgh | Stewart ANG Base | 12553 | 914-563-2000 | 563-2000 |
| Niagara Falls | AF Reserve Base | 14304 | 716-236-2000 | 236-2000 |
| Latham | Military Affairs NY | 12110 | 518-786-4520 | 786-4500 |
| Latham | New York ANG HQ | 12110 | 518-786-4502 | 786-4502 |
| Plattsburgh | Plattsburgh AFB | 12903 | 518-565-5000 | 565-5049 |
| Rome | Griffiss AFB | 13441 | 315-330-1110 | 330-1110 |
| Romulus | Seneca Army Depot | 14541 | 607-869-1110 | 869-1110 |
| Roslyn | ANG Station | 11576 | 516-299-5229 | 299-5229 |
| Watertown | Fort Drum | 13602 | 315-772-6900 | 772-5869 |
| Watervliet | Watervliet Arsenal | 12189 | 518-266-5111 | 266-5111 |
| West Point | US Military Academy | 10996 | 914-938-4011 | 938-3388 |
| **NORTH CAROLINA** | | | | |
| Atlantic Bch | Fort Macon CG Base | 28512 | 919-247-4598 | 247-4598 |
| Badin | Badin ANG Station | 28009 | 704-422-2461 | 422-2461 |
| Buxton | Cape Hatteras Coast Guard Group | 27920 | 919-995-5881 | 995-5881 |
| Cherry Point | MC Air Station | 28533 | 919-466-2811 | 466-2026 |
| Elizabeth Cty | CG Air Station | 27909 | 919-338-3941 | 338-3941 |
| Fayetteville | Fort Bragg | 28307 | 910-396-0011 | 396-1461 |
| Fayetteville | Pope AFB | 28308 | 910-394-0001 | 394-4822 |
| Goldsboro | Smr Johnson AFB | 27531 | 919-736-5400 | 736-5584 |

| City | Installation | ZIP Code | Information Number | Locator Number |
|------|-------------|----------|-------------------|----------------|
| **NORTH CAROLINA (cont.)** | | | | |
| Jacksonville | MC Camp Lejeune | 28542 | 910-451-1113 | 451-3074 |
| Jacksonville | New River MCAS | 28545 | 910-451-1113 | 451-6568 |
| Southport | Sunny Point Military Ocean Terminal | 28461 | 910-457-8000 | 457-8000 |
| **NORTH DAKOTA** | | | | |
| Cavalier | Cavalier AFS | 58220 | 701-993-3297 | 993-3297 |
| Fargo | North Dakota ANG HQ | 58102 | 701-237-6030 | 237-6030 |
| Grand Forks | Grand Forks AFB | 58205 | 701-747-3000 | 747-3344 |
| Minot | Minot AFB | 58705 | 701-723-1110 | 723-1841 |
| **OHIO** | | | | |
| Cincinnati | Blue Ash ANG Stn | 45242 | 513-792-2840 | 792-2840 |
| Cleveland | CG Marine Safety Office | 44114 | 216-522-4405 | 522-3929 |
| Cleveland | Navy Finance Ctr | 44199 | 800-321-1080 | 321-1080 |
| Columbus | Rickenbacker ANGB | 43217 | 614-492-8211 | 492-3541 |
| Columbus | Defense Construction Supply Center | 43216 | 614-692-3131 | 692-3131 |
| Dayton | Defense Electronics Supply Center | 45444 | 513-296-6041 | 296-0501 |
| Dayton | Wright-Patterson AFB | 45433 | 513-257-1110 | 257-3231 |
| Newark | Air Force Station | 43057 | 614-522-2171 | 522-2171 |
| Port Clinton | Cp Perry ANG Stn | 43452 | 419-635-4021 | 635-4021 |
| **OKLAHOMA** | | | | |
| Altus | Altus AFB | 73523 | 405-482-8100 | 481-7250 |
| Braggs | Camp Gruber | 74423 | 918-487-6001 | 487-6041 |
| Enid | Vance AFB | 73705 | 405-237-2121 | 249-7791 |
| Lawton | Fort Sill | 73503 | 405-442-8111 | 442-3924 |
| McAlester | Army Ammo Plant | 74501 | 918-421-2524 | 421-2426 |
| Oklahoma Ct | Ok City ANGB | 73159 | 405-736-7711 | 736-7711 |
| Oklahoma Ct | Tinker AFB | 73145 | 405-732-7321 | 732-7321 |
| Tulsa | Tulsa ANG | 74115 | 918-832-8300 | 832-8300 |

| City | Installation | ZIP Code | Information Number | Locator Number |
|------|-------------|----------|--------------------|----------------|
| **OREGON** | | | | |
| Eugene | North Bend CGAS | 97459 | 503-756-9258 | 756-9258 |
| Hermiston | Umatilla Army Depot | 97838 | 503-564-8632 | 564-8632 |
| Klamath Fls | Kingsley Field ANGB | 97603 | 503-885-6365 | 885-6650 |
| Warrenton | Camp Rilea | 97146 | 503-861-4000 | 861-4000 |
| **PENNSYLVANIA** | | | | |
| Annville | Fort Indiantown Gap | 17003 | 717-861-5444 | 861-5444 |
| Annville | PA ANG HQ | 17003 | 717-861-8500 | 861-8500 |
| Carlisle | Carlisle Barracks | 17013 | 717-245-3131 | 245-3839 |
| Chambersbrg | Letterkenny Army Depot | 17201 | 717-267-8111 | 267-8111 |
| Horsham | NAS Willow Grove | 19090 | 610-443-1000 | 443-1000 |
| Mechanicsbrg | Defense Depot | 17055 | 717-790-2000 | 770-6770 |
| Mechanicsbrg | Naval Ships Parts Ctr | 17055 | 717-790-2000 | 790-2000 |
| N Cumberlnd | Defense Distribution | 17070 | 717-770-6011 | 770-6770 |
| Oakdale | Kelley Support Center | 15071 | 412-777-1173 | 777-6770 |
| Philadelphia | 4th MC District | 19112 | 610-897-6303 | 897-6304 |
| Philadelphia | Defense Personnel Support Center | 19101 | 610-737-2000 | 737-2000 |
| Philadelphia | Defense Industrial Supply Center | 19111 | 610-697-2000 | 697-2000 |
| Philadelphia | Naval Aviation Supply Office | 19111 | 610-697-2000 | 697-2000 |
| Philadelphia | Naval Base | 19112 | 610-897-5000 | 897-5000 |
| Philadelphia | USCG Marine Safety Group | 19147 | 610-271-4800 | 271-4800 |
| Tobyhanna | Army Depot | 18466 | 717-895-7000 | 895-7409 |
| Warminster | Naval Air Warfare Center | 18974 | 610-441-2000 | 441-2000 |
| **RHODE ISLAND** | | | | |
| Coventry | Conventry ANG Stn | 02816 | 401-828-7300 | 828-7300 |
| Newport | Naval Edc & Trng Ctr | 02841 | 401-841-2311 | 841-2311 |
| Providence | RI ANG HQ | 02904 | 401-457-4100 | 457-4100 |

| City | Installation | ZIP Code | Information Number | Locator Number |
|------|-------------|----------|--------------------|----------------|
| **SOUTH CAROLINA** | | | | |
| Beaufort | MC Air Station | 29904 | 803-522-7100 | 522-7100 |
| Beaufort | Naval Hospital | 29902 | 803-525-5600 | 525-5582 |
| Charleston | Charleston AFB | 29404 | 803-566-6000 | 566-3282 |
| Charleston | Coast Guard Base | 29401 | 803-724-7600 | 724-7600 |
| Charleston | Naval Base | 29408 | 803-743-4111 | 743-4111 |
| Charleston | Naval Weapons Stn | 29408 | 803-743-4111 | 743-4111 |
| Columbia | Fort Jackson | 29207 | 803-751-7601 | 751-7671 |
| Eastover | McEntire ANGB | 29044 | 803-776-5121 | 776-5121 |
| Parris Island | MC Recruit Depot | 29905 | 803-525-2111 | 525-3358 |
| Sumter | Shaw AFB | 29152 | 803-668-8110 | 668-2811 |
| **SOUTH DAKOTA** | | | | |
| Rapid City | Ellsworth AFB | 57706 | 605-385-1000 | 385-1379 |
| Sioux Falls | Foss Field ANGB | 57117 | 605-333-5700 | 333-5700 |
| **TENNESSEE** | | | | |
| Louisville | McGhee Tyson ANG Base | 37642 | 800-524-5735 | 524-5735 |
| Memphis | Defense Depot | 38114 | 901-775-6011 | 775-6011 |
| Millington | NAS Memphis | 38054 | 901-873-5111 | 873-5770 |
| Tullahoma | Arnold Air Station | 37389 | 615-454-3000 | 454-3000 |
| **TEXAS** | | | | |
| Abilene | Dyess AFB | 79607 | 915-696-0212 | 696-3098 |
| Bastrop | Camp Swift | 78602 | 512-321-2497 | 321-2497 |
| Beaumont | Nederland ANG Stn | 77705 | 409-727-2336 | 727-2336 |
| Corpus Christi | Army Depot | 78419 | 512-939-2413 | 939-2413 |
| Corpus Christi | CG Air Station | 78419 | 512-939-2070 | 939-6213 |
| Corpus Christi | Naval Air Station | 78419 | 512-939-2811 | 939-2384 |
| Dallas | Naval Air Station | 75211 | 214-266-6111 | 266-6640 |
| Del Rio | Laughlin AFB | 78843 | 210-298-3511 | 298-3511 |
| El Paso | Fort Bliss | 79916 | 915-568-2121 | 568-1113 |
| El Paso | Beaumont AMC | 79920 | 915-569-2121 | 568-1113 |
| Fort Worth | Naval Air Stn Reserve | 76127 | 817-782-5000 | 782-5000 |
| Galveston | CG Base | 77553 | 409-766-5623 | 766-5615 |
| Garland | Garland ANG Station | 75046 | 214-276-0521 | 276-0521 |

| City | Installation | ZIP Code | Information Number | Locator Number |
|------|-------------|----------|-------------------|----------------|
| **TEXAS (cont.)** | | | | |
| Houston | Ellington Field ANGB | 77034 | 281-929-2110 | 929-2110 |
| Houston | CG Air Station | 77034 | 281-481-0025 | 481-0025 |
| Ingleside | NS Ingleside | 78362 | 512-776-4200 | 776-4200 |
| Killeen | Fort Hood | 76544 | 817-287-1110 | 287-2137 |
| Kingsville | Naval Air Station | 78363 | 512-595-6136 | 595-6136 |
| La Porte | La Porte ANG Stn | 77571 | 281-471-5111 | 471-5111 |
| Lubbock | Reese AFB | 79489 | 806-885-4511 | 885-3678 |
| San Angelo | El Dorado AFS | 76936 | 915-654-4273 | 654-4246 |
| San Angelo | Goodfellow AFB | 76908 | 915-654-3231 | 654-3410 |
| San Antonio | Brooks AFB | 78235 | 210-536-1110 | 536-1841 |
| San Antonio | Fort Sam Houston | 78234 | 210-221-1211 | 221-3315 |
| San Antonio | Brooke AMC | 78234 | 210-221-6141 | 221-8940 |
| San Antonio | Lackland AFB | 78236 | 210-671-1110 | 671-1841 |
| San Antonio | Kelly AFB | 78241 | 210-925-1110 | 925-1841 |
| San Antonio | Randolph AFB | 78150 | 210-652-1110 | 652-1841 |
| San Antonio | Camp Bullis | 78234 | 210-221-7510 | 221-7510 |
| San Antonio | Camp Stanley | 78269 | 210-221-7403 | 221-7442 |
| Texarkana | Red River Army Dep | 75507 | 903-334-2141 | 334-2726 |
| Wichita Falls | Sheppard AFB | 76311 | 817-676-2511 | 676-1841 |
| **UTAH** | | | | |
| Dugway | Dugway Proving Ground | 84022 | 801-831-2151 | 831-2151 |
| Ogden | Hill AFB | 84056 | 801-777-7221 | 777-1841 |
| Ogden | Defense Distribution Depot | 84407 | 801-399-7011 | 399-7009 |
| Salt Lake Cty | ANG Base | 84116 | 801-595-2000 | 595-2000 |
| Salt Lake Cty | Camp W G Williams | 84065 | 801-524-3669 | 524-3669 |
| Salt Lake Cty | Ft Douglas Res Ctr | 84113 | 801-524-4137 | 524-4137 |
| Tooele | Tooele Army Depot | 84074 | 801-833-3211 | 883-2094 |
| **VIRGINIA** | | | | |
| Alexandria | Cameron Station | 22304 | 540-545-6700 | 545-6700 |
| Alexandria | CG Information Systems Center | 22310 | 540-644-3600 | 644-3600 |

| City | Installation | ZIP Code | Information Number | Locator Number |
|------|-------------|----------|-------------------|----------------|
| **VIRGINIA (cont.)** | | | | |
| Alexandria | Fort Belvoir | 22060 | 540-545-6700 | 805-2043 |
| Arlington | Fort Myer | 22211 | 540-545-6700 | 545-6700 |
| Arlington | Henderson Hall | 22214 | 540-545-6700 | 614-2344 |
| Blackstone | Fort Pickett | 23824 | 804-292-8621 | 292-2266 |
| Bowling Grn | Fort A P Hill | 22427 | 804-633-8710 | 633-8428 |
| Charlottesville | JAG School | 22903 | 804-972-6300 | 972-6300 |
| Chesapeake | Naval Security Group | 23322 | 804-421-8000 | 421-8000 |
| Dahlgren | Naval Surface Warfare Center | 22448 | 540-663-8531 | 663-8531 |
| Hampton | Fort Monroe | 23651 | 804-727-2111 | 727-2111 |
| Hampton | Langley AFB | 23665 | 804-764-9990 | 764-5615 |
| Newport Nws | Fort Eustis | 23604 | 804-878-1212 | 878-5215 |
| Norfolk | NAB Little Creek | 23521 | 804-464-7000 | 464-7000 |
| Norfolk | Naval Station | 23511 | 804-444-0000 | 444-0000 |
| Petersburg | Fort Lee | 23080 | 804-734-1011 | 734-6855 |
| Portsmouth | CG Support Center | 23703 | 804-483-8540 | 483-8586 |
| Portsmouth | Naval Hospital | 23708 | 804-398-5008 | 398-5624 |
| Portsmouth | Norfolk Navy Shipyrd | 23709 | 804-396-3000 | 396-5586 |
| Quantico | MC Air Facility | 22134 | 540-640-2121 | 640-2507 |
| Richmond | Defense General Supply Center | 23297 | 804-279-3861 | 279-3061 |
| Sandston | Virginia ANG HQ | 23150 | 804-236-6000 | 236-6000 |
| Virginia Bch | Fleet Combat Training Center | 23461 | 804-433-6234 | 433-6556 |
| Virginia Bch | Fort Story | 23459 | 804-422-7305 | 422-7682 |
| Virginia Bch | NAS Oceana | 23460 | 804-433-2000 | 433-2000 |
| Warrenton | Vint Hill Farms | 22186 | 540-349-6000 | 349-5864 |
| Williamsburg | Cheatham Annex Naval Supply Center | 23187 | 804-887-4000 | 887-7116 |
| Yorktown | CG Res Tng Ctrr | 23690 | 804-898-3500 | 898-2314 |
| Yorktown | Naval Weapons Stn | 23691 | 804-887-4000 | 887-7661 |
| **WASHINGTON** | | | | |
| Bremerton | NS Puget Sound | 98314 | 360-476-3466 | 476-2515 |
| Everett | Prsnl Spt Dtchmnt | 98207 | 360-304-4200 | 304-3166 |

| City | Installation | ZIP Code | Information Number | Locator Number |
|------|-------------|----------|-------------------|----------------|
| **WASHINGTON (cont.)** | | | | |
| Oak Harbor | NAS Whidbey Island | 98278 | 360-257-2211 | 257-2631 |
| Port Angeles | CG Air Station | 98362 | 360-457-4401 | 457-2217 |
| Seattle | CG Support Center | 98134 | 360-217-6100 | 217-6100 |
| Seattle | NS Puget Sound | 98115 | 360-526-3211 | 304-3166 |
| Seattle | Seattle ANG Base | 98108 | 360-764-5600 | 764-5600 |
| Silverdale | NSB Bangor | 98315 | 360-396-6111 | 396-5733 |
| Spokane | Fairchild AFB | 99011 | 509-247-1212 | 247-5875 |
| Tacoma | Fort Lewis | 98433 | 360-967-1110 | 967-6221 |
| Tacoma | Washington ANG HQ | 98430 | 360-512-8000 | 512-8000 |
| Tacoma | McChord AFB | 98438 | 360-984-1910 | 984-2474 |
| **WEST VIRGINIA** | | | | |
| Charleston | W V ANG HQ | 25311 | 304-341-6316 | 341-6316 |
| Sugar Grove | Naval Security Grp | 26815 | 304-249-6304 | 249-6304 |
| **WISCONSIN** | | | | |
| Cp Douglas | Volk Field ANGB | 54618 | 608-427-3341 | 427-3341 |
| Milwaukee | Coast Guard Group | 53207 | 414-747-7100 | 747-7100 |
| Milwaukee | Mitchell Field | 53207 | 414-482-5000 | 482-5000 |
| Sparta | Fort McCoy | 54656 | 608-388-2222 | 388-2225 |
| **WYOMING** | | | | |
| Cheyenne | F E Warren AFB | 82005 | 307-775-1110 | 775-1841 |
| Guernsey | Camp Guernsey | 82214 | 307-836-2619 | 836-2471 |
| **GUAM** | | | | |
| Yigo | Anderson AFB | 96929 | 671-366-1110 | 366-3247 |
| Agana | Naval Air Station | 96637 | 671-355-1110 | 344-8103 |
| Agana | Naval Hospital | 96637 | 671-355-1110 | 344-9040 |
| Sumay | Naval Station | 96540 | 671-355-1110 | 339-7133 |
| Dededo | Naval Commo Stn | 96919 | 671-355-1110 | 355-5333 |

Country Code: 011. You must dial this before the area code.

| City | Installation | ZIP Code | Information Number | Locator Number |
|------|-------------|----------|-------------------|----------------|
| **PUERTO RICO** | | | | |
| Aguadilla | CGAS Borinquen | 00604 | 809-882-3500 | 882-3500 |
| Ceiba | NAS Roosevelt Rd | 00735 | 809-865-2000 | 865-2000 |
| Sabana Seca | Naval Security Gp | 00749 | 809-795-2255 | 795-0952 |

| City | Installation | ZIP Code | Information Number | Locator Number |
|------|--------------|----------|--------------------|----------------|
| **PUERTO RICO (cont.)** | | | | |
| Salinas | Camp Santiago | 00751 | 809-824-3110 | 824-3110 |
| San Juan | CG Base | 00902 | 809-729-6800 | 729-6800 |
| San Juan | PR ANG HQ | 00902 | 809-723-0395 | 723-0395 |
| San Juan | Fort Buchanan | 00934 | 809-783-2424 | 783-8293 |
| San Juan | Muniz ANGB | 00904 | 809-253-5100 | 253-5100 |

# Air Force, Army, And Fleet (Navy And Coast Guard) Post Offices

The following list of military post office numbers shows their geographical locations.  The Armed Forces World-Wide Locators provide unit locations of military members assigned overseas by their post office numbers only.  By comparing these numbers to the list, you can determine the overseas geographical location of the individual military member.   If you wish to obtain the unit the member is assigned, write to the locator at the APO or FPO.  For example:

Locator
APO AE  09001

To write a letter to an individual, use the following format:

For APOs and FPOs in Europe, use the two-letter code AE.

Sgt. John Doe
Company A, 122 Signal Battalion
Unit 20501, Box 4290
APO AE  09795

For APOs and FPOs in the Pacific area use the two-letter code AP.

> PCCM John Doe
> HI Division, Admin
> USS Nimitz (CVN 88)
> FPO AP  96697

For APOs and FPOs for Central or South America use the two-letter codes AA.

> 1st Lt. John Doe
> Company A, 111 Maintenance Battalion
> APO AA  34002

## APOs And FPOs For Europe:

| | |
|---|---|
| APO AE 09007 | Heidelberg, Germany |
| APO AE 09009 | Ramstein, Germany |
| APO AE 09012 | Ramstein, Germany |
| APO AE 09014 | Heidelberg, Germany |
| APO AE 09021 | Kapaun, Germany |
| APO AE 09028 | Sandhofen, Germany |
| APO AE 09029 | Berchtesgarden, Germany |
| APO AE 09031 | Kitzingen, Germany |
| APO AE 09033 | Schweinfurt, Germany |
| APO AE 09034 | Baumholder, Germany |
| APO AE 09036 | Wurzburg, Germany |
| APO AE 09039 | Frankfurt, Germany |
| APO AE 09042 | Schwetzingen, Germany |
| APO AE 09045 | Kirchgoens, Germany |
| APO AE 09047 | Wertheim, Germany |
| APO AE 09050 | Bad Toelz, Germany |
| APO AE 09053 | Garmisch, Germany |
| APO AE 09054 | Kaiserslautern, Germany |
| APO AE 09056 | Worms, Germany |
| APO AE 09057 | Rhein Main, Germany |
| APO AE 09058 | Worms, Germany |
| APO AE 09059 | Miesau, Germany |
| APO AE 09060 | Frankfurt AMT, Germany |
| APO AE 09063 | Heidelberg, Germany |

| APO AE 09064 | Rhein Main, Germany |
| APO AE 09067 | Kaiserslautern, Germany |
| APO AE 09069 | Bremerhaven, Germany |
| APO AE 09072 | Kerpen, Germany |
| APO AE 09074 | Friedberg, Germany |
| APO AE 09076 | Buldingen, Germany |
| APO AE 09079 | Frankfurt, Germany |
| APO AE 09080 | Bad Godsberg, Germany |
| APO AE 09081 | Schwetzingen, Germany |
| APO AE 09082 | Offenbach, Germany |
| APO AE 09086 | Kaefertal, Germany |
| APO AE 09089 | Babenhausen, Germany |
| APO AE 09090 | Roedelheim, Germany |
| APO AE 09091 | Gelnhausen, Germany |
| APO AE 09094 | Ramstein, Germany |
| APO AE 09095 | Germersheim, Germany |
| APO AE 09096 | Wiesbaden, Germany |
| APO AE 09097 | Rhein Main, Germany |
| APO AE 09098 | Bad Aibling, Germany |
| APO AE 09099 | Heidelberg, Germany |
| APO AE 09100 | Schwetzingen, Germany |
| APO AE 09102 | Heidelberg, Germany |
| APO AE 09103 | Rhinedahlen, Germany |
| APO AE 09104 | Geilenkirchen, Germany |
| APO AE 09107 | Mohringen, Germany |
| APO AE 09110 | Dexheim, Germany |
| APO AE 09111 | Bad Kreuznach, Germany |
| APO AE 09112 | Sorghof, Germany |
| APO AE 09114 | Grafenwohr, Germany |
| APO AE 09123 | Spangdahlem AB, Germany |
| APO AE 09126 | Spangdahlem AB, Germany |
| APO AE 09128 | Vaihingen, Germany |
| APO AE 09130 | Sembach AB, Germany |
| APO AE 09131 | Vaihingen, Germany |
| APO AE 09132 | Bitburg AB, Germany |
| APO AE 09136 | Sembach AB, Germany |
| APO AE 09137 | Goppingen, Germany |
| APO AE 09138 | Pirmasens, Germany |
| APO AE 09139 | Bamberg, Germany |
| APO AE 09140 | Illesheim, Germany |
| APO AE 09142 | Schwabach, Germany |
| APO AE 09146 | Fulda, Germany |
| APO AE 09154 | Stuttgart, Germany |
| APO AE 09156 | Bitburg AB, Germany |
| APO AE 09157 | Augsburg, Germany |

| | |
|---|---|
| APO AE 09164 | Karlsruhe, Germany |
| APO AE 09165 | Hanau, Germany |
| APO AE 09166 | Mannheim, Germany |
| APO AE 09169 | Geissen, Germany |
| APO AE 09172 | Oberammergau, Germany |
| APO AE 09173 | Hohenfels, Germany |
| APO AE 09175 | Darmstadt, Germany |
| APO AE 09177 | Ansbach, Germany |
| APO AE 09178 | Augsburg, Germany |
| APO AE 09180 | Landstuhl, Germany |
| APO AE 09182 | Giebelstadt, Germany |
| APO AE 09183 | Munich, Germany |
| APO AE 09185 | Mainz, Germany |
| APO AE 09186 | Rheinau, Germany |
| APO AE 09189 | Pirmasens, Germany |
| APO AE 09207 | Preum, Germany |
| APO AE 09211 | Darmstadt, Germany |
| APO AE 09212 | Rhein Main AB, Germany |
| APO AE 09213 | Frankfurt, Germany |
| APO AE 09214 | Buchel AB, Germany |
| APO AE 09220 | Wiesbaden, Germany |
| APO AE 09222 | Fuerth, Germany |
| APO AE 09225 | Kitzingen, Germany |
| APO AE 09226 | Schweinfurt, Germany |
| APO AE 09227 | Kaiserslautern, Germany |
| APO AE 09228 | Frankfurt, Germany |
| APO AE 09229 | Kaiserslautern, Germany |
| APO AE 09234 | Rheinberg, Germany |
| APO AE 09235 | Berlin, Germany |
| APO AE 09237 | Frankfurt, Germany |
| APO AE 09242 | Frankfurt, Germany |
| APO AE 09244 | Wurzburg, Germany |
| APO AE 09245 | Munich, Germany |
| APO AE 09250 | Katterbach, Germany |
| APO AE 09252 | Bad Kreuznach, Germany |
| APO AE 09260 | Neubruecke, Germany |
| APO AE 09262 | Idar-Oberstein, Germany |
| APO AE 09263 | Kaiserslautern, Germany |
| APO AE 09264 | Ansbach, Germany |
| APO AE 09266 | Sechkenheim, Germany |
| APO AE 09267 | Ettlingen, Germany |
| APO AE 09275 | Knielingen, Germany |
| FPO AE 09415 | St. Mawgan, England |
| FPO AE 09419 | Edzell, Scotland |
| FPO AE 09420 | Brawdy, Wales |

| | |
|---|---|
| FPO AE 09421 | London, England |
| FPO AE 09422 | Machrihanish, Scotland |
| APO AE 09447 | Newbury, England |
| APO AE 09448 | RAF Burtonwood, England |
| APO AE 09449 | Uxbridge, England |
| APO AE 09456 | RAF Fairford, England |
| APO AE 09459 | Bury-St. Edmunds, Suffolk, England |
| APO AE 09461 | Thetford, England |
| APO AE 09463 | Newbury, England |
| APO AE 09464 | RAF Lakenheath, England |
| APO AE 09465 | Shefford Bedfordshire, England |
| APO AE 09466 | Oxfordshire, England |
| APO AE 09468 | Harrogate, England |
| APO AE 09469 | RAF Alconbury, Cambridgeshire, England |
| APO AE 09470 | Huntingdon, Cambridge, England |
| APO AE 09494 | RAF Croughton, Newhamptonshire, England |
| APO AE 09496 | Fylingdale, Yorkshire, England |
| FPO AE 09498 | London, England |
| FPO AE 09499 | London, England |
| FPO AE 09508 | Guantanamo Bay, Cuba |
| FPO AE 09593 | Guantanamo Bay, Cuba |
| FPO AE 09596 | Guantanamo Bay, Cuba |
| APO AE 09601 | Aviano AB, Italy |
| APO AE 09605 | Brindisi, Italy |
| FPO AE 09609 | Gaeta, Italy |
| APO AE 09610 | Ghedi AB, Italy |
| FPO AE 09612 | LaMaddelena Sardinia, Italy |
| APO AE 09613 | Livorno, Italy |
| FPO AE 09619 | Naples, Italy |
| FPO AE 09620 | Naples, Italy |
| FPO AE 09621 | Naples, Italy |
| FPO AE 09622 | Naples Capodichino, Italy |
| APO AE 09624 | Rome, Italy |
| FPO AE 09625 | Naples, Italy |
| FPO AE 09626 | Naples, Italy |
| FPO AE 09627 | Sigonella, Sicily, Italy |
| APO AE 09628 | Verona, Italy |
| APO AE 09630 | Vicenza, Italy |
| APO AE 09641 | Madrid, Spain |
| APO AE 09642 | Madrid, Spain |
| APO AE 09643 | Moron AB, Spain |
| FPO AE 09644 | Rota, Spain |
| FPO AE 09645 | Rota, Spain |
| APO AE 09647 | Torrejon AB, Spain |

| APO AE 09703 | Brunssum, Netherlands |
| APO AE 09704 | Thule AB, Greenland |
| APO AE 09705 | Shape Casteau, Belgium |
| APO AE 09706 | Kolsas, Norway |
| APO AE 09707 | Oslo, Norway |
| APO AE 09708 | Chievres AB, Belgium |
| APO AE 09713 | Maastricht, Netherlands |
| APO AE 09714 | Brussels City, Belgium |
| APO AE 09715 | The Hague, Netherlands |
| APO AE 09716 | Copenhagen, Denmark |
| APO AE 09717 | Maastricht, Netherlands |
| APO AE 09718 | Rabat, Morocco |
| APO AE 09719 | Soesterberg AB, Netherlands |
| APO AE 09720 | Lages Fld, Azores, Portugal |
| APO AE 09721 | Helsinki, Finland |
| APO AE 09722 | Karup, Denmark |
| APO AE 09723 | Helsinki, Finland |
| APO AE 09724 | Brussels, Belgium |
| APO AE 09725 | AFI Keflavik, Iceland |
| APO AE 09726 | Lisbon, Portugal |
| FPO AE 09727 | Bermuda, West Indies |
| FPO AE 09728 | Keflavik, Iceland |
| FPO AE 09729 | Hofn, Iceland |
| FPO AE 09730 | Argemtia, Newfoundland, Canada |
| FPO AE 09731 | Shelburne, Nova Scotia, Canada |
| APO AE 09732 | North Bay, Canada |
| APO AE 09777 | Paris, France |
| APO AE 09802 | Taif, Saudi Arabia |
| APO AE 09803 | Riyadh, Saudi Arabia |
| APO AE 09804 | Dhahran, Saudi Arabia |
| APO AE 09805 | Al-Jubail, Saudi Arabia |
| APO AE 09808 | Dhahran, Saudi Arabia |
| APO AE 09809 | Khamis Mushayt, Saudi Arabia |
| APO AE 09810 | Tabuk, Saudi Arabia |
| APO AE 09811 | Jidda, Saudi Arabia |
| APO AE 09812 | Islamabad, Pakistan |
| APO AE 09814 | Karachi, Pakistan |
| APO AE 09815 | Mahe, India |
| APO AE 09816 | Balikisir, Turkey |
| APO AE 09819 | Izmir, Turkey |
| APO AE 09821 | Izmir, Turkey |
| APO AE 09822 | Ankara, Turkey |
| APO AE 09823 | Ankara, Turkey |
| APO AE 09824 | Adana, Turkey |
| APO AE 09825 | Diyarbakir, Turkey |

| | |
|---|---|
| APO AE 09827 | Istanbul, Turkey |
| APO AE 09828 | Kinshasa, Congo |
| APO AE 09829 | Khartoum, Sudan |
| APO AE 09830 | Tel Aviv, Israel |
| APO AE 09831 | Nairobi, Kenya |
| APO AE 09832 | El Gorah, Egypt |
| APO AE 09833 | Sharm El Shiek, Egypt |
| FPO AE 09834 | Jafair, Bahrain |
| FPO AE 09835 | Cairo, Egypt |
| FPO AE 09836 | Nicosia, Cypress |
| APO AE 09839 | Cairo, Egypt |
| APO AE 09841 | Athens, Greece |
| APO AE 09842 | Athens, Greece |
| APO AE 09843 | Araxos, Greece |
| FPO AE 09865 | Souda Bay, Crete, Greece |
| APO AE 09866 | Jafair, Bahrain |
| APO AE 09892 | Amman, Jordon |

# Central and South America

| | |
|---|---|
| APO AA 34001 | Howard AFB, Panama |
| APO AA 34002 | Albrook AFS, Panama |
| APO AA 34003 | Quarry Heights, Panama |
| APO AA 34004 | Fort Clayton, Panama |
| APO AA 34005 | Fort Wm. D. Davis, Panama |
| APO AA 34006 | Fort Kobbe, Panama |
| APO AA 34007 | Fort Amador, Panama |
| APO AA 34009 | Albrook AFS, Panama |
| APO AA 34011 | Albrook AFS, Panama |
| APO AA 34021 | Managua, Nicaragua |
| APO AA 34022 | Tegucigalpa, Honduras |
| APO AA 34023 | San Salvador, El Salvador |
| APO AA 34024 | Guatemala City, Guatemala |
| APO AA 34030 | Rio de Janiero, Brazil |
| APO AA 34031 | LIma, Peru |
| APO AA 34032 | La Paz, Bolivia |
| APO AA 34033 | Santiago, Chile |
| APO AA 34034 | Bueno Aires, Argentina |
| APO AA 34035 | Monteviedo, Uraguay |
| APO AA 34036 | Asuncion, Paraguay |
| APO AA 34037 | Caracas, Venezuela |
| APO AA 34038 | Bogota, Colombia |
| APO AA 34039 | Quito, Ecuador |
| APO AA 34040 | San Juan, Puerto Rico |
| APO AA 34041 | Santo Domingo, Dominican Rep |

| | |
|---|---|
| APO AA 34042 | Comayagua, Honduras |
| FPO AA 34050 | Punta Borinquen, Puerto Rico |
| FPO AA 34051 | Roosevelt Roads, Puerto Rico |
| FPO AA 34053 | Sabana Seca, Puerto Rico |
| FPO AA 34054 | Antigua, Antilles |
| FPO AA 34058 | Andros Island, The Bahamas |
| FPO AA 34059 | Fort Amador, Panama |
| FPO AA 34060 | Galetta Island, Panama |
| FPO AA 34061 | Rodman, Panama |

## Pacific area:

| | |
|---|---|
| APO AP 96201 | Kimpo, Korea |
| APO AP 96202 | Kimpo AB, Korea |
| APO AP 96203 | Yongsan, Korea |
| APO AP 96204 | Yongsan, Korea |
| APO AP 96205 | Yongsan, Korea |
| APO AP 96206 | Yongsan, Korea |
| APO AP 96207 | Yongsan, Korea |
| APO AP 96208 | Chunchon, Korea |
| APO AP 96212 | Taegu, Korea |
| APO AP 96214 | Kim Hae, Korea |
| APO AP 96218 | Taegu, Korea |
| APO AP 96220 | Cheju-Do, Korea |
| APO AP 96224 | Tongduchon-ni, Korea |
| APO AP 96251 | Yong-Tae-Ri, Korea |
| APO AP 96257 | Uijongbu, Korea |
| APO AP 96258 | Uijongbu, Korea |
| APO AP 96259 | Pusan, Korea |
| APO AP 96260 | Waegwan, Korea |
| APO AP 96264 | Kunsan AB, Korea |
| APO AP 96266 | Osan AB, Korea |
| APO AP 96267 | Osan AB, Korea |
| FPO AP 96269 | Chinhae, Korea |
| APO AP 96271 | Pyongtaek, Korea |
| APO AP 96276 | Seoul, Korea |
| APO AP 96278 | Song Tansi, Korea |
| APO AP 96283 | Bupyeong, Korea |
| APO AP 96284 | Bupyeong, Korea |
| APO AP 96297 | Wongju, Kangwon-Do, Korea |
| FPO AP 96306 | Atsugi, Japan |
| FPO AP 96310 | Iwakuni, Japan |
| FPO AP 96313 | Kami Seya, Japan |
| APO AP 96319 | Misawa AB, Honshu, Japan |
| FPO AP 96321 | Sasebo, Japan |

| | | |
|---|---|---|
| FPO AP 96322 | Sasebo, Japan |
| APO AP 96323 | Yokota AB, Japan |
| APO AP 96325 | Yokota AB, Japan |
| APO AP 96326 | Yokota AB, Honshu, Japan |
| APO AP 96328 | Yokota AB, Honshu, Japan |
| APO AP 96330 | Yokota AB, Honshu, Japan |
| APO AP 96336 | Tokyo, Honshu, Japan |
| APO AP 96337 | Tokyo, Honshu, Japan |
| APO AP 96338 | Tokyo, Honshu, Japan |
| APO AP 96339 | Camp Zama, Honshu, Japan |
| APO AP 96343 | Tokyo, Honshu, Japan |
| FPO AP 96347 | Yokohama, Japan |
| FPO AP 96348 | Yokohama, Japan (Housing Area) |
| FPO AP 96349 | Yokosuka, Japan (FLT ACT) |
| FPO AP 96350 | Yokosuka (NAVHOSP), Japan |
| FPO AP 96362 | Cmp Kuwae (NRMC), Okinawa, Japan |
| APO AP 96364 | Kadena AB, Okinawa, Japan |
| APO AP 96365 | Kadena AB, Okinawa, Japan |
| APO AP 96367 | Kadena AB, Okinawa, Japan |
| APO AP 96368 | Kadena AB, Okinawa, Japan |
| FPO AP 96370 | Kadena AB, Okinawa, Japan |
| FPO AP 96372 | Futema, Okinawa, Japan |
| FPO AP 96373 | Kawasaki, Okinawa, Japan |
| APO AP 96374 | Makiminato, Okinawa, Japan |
| APO AP 96375 | Makiminato, Okinawa, Japan |
| APO AP 96376 | Makiminato, Okinawa, Japan |
| FPO AP 96377 | Tengan, Okinawa, Japan |
| APO AP 96378 | Zukeran, Okinawa, Japan |
| APO AP 96379 | Zukeran, Okinawa, Japan |
| APO AP 96440 | Manila, Luzon, Philippines |
| FPO AP 96464 | Diego Garcia, Is, Diego Garcia |
| FPO AP 96505 | Adak, (NAVCOMMSTA) Alaska |
| FPO AP 96506 | Adak, Alaska |
| APO AP 96508 | Fort Greely, Big Delta, Alaska |
| APO AP 96509 | Clear Mews AFS, Alaska |
| APO AP 96512 | Shemya AFB, Alaska |
| APO AP 96513 | King Salmon AFS, Alaska |
| FPO AP 96516 | Midway Islands |
| APO AP 96518 | Wake Island |
| APO AP 96520 | Djakarta, Indonesia |
| FPO AP 96521 | Hong Kong, BCC |
| FPO AP 96522 | Hong Kong, BCC |
| FPO AP 96531 | Christchurch, New Zealand |
| FPO AP 96534 | Singapore |
| FPO AP 96539 | Guam, (NAS) Marianas Islands |

| | |
|---|---|
| FPO AP 96540 | Guam, (NAVSTA) Marianas Islands |
| APO AP 96541 | Andersen AFB, Guam |
| APO AP 96542 | Andersen AFB, Guam |
| APO AP 96543 | Agana, Guam |
| APO AP 96546 | Bangkok, Thailand |
| APO AP 96548 | Alice Springs, Australia |
| APO AP 96549 | Canberra A.C.T., Australia |
| APO AP 96551 | Melbourne Victor, Australia |
| APO AP 96552 | Woomera, Australia |
| APO AP 96553 | Sydney, Australia |
| APO AP 96554 | Sydney, Australia |
| APO AP 96555 | Kwajalein, Marshall Isand |
| APO AP 96556 | Pohakuloa, Hawaii |
| APO AP 96558 | Pohakuloa, Hawaii |
| FPO AP 96598 | Amundsen-Scott, Antarctica |
| FPO AP 96599 | McMurdo Station, Antarctica |

## US Coast Guard Fleet Post Offices

| Ship's Name | Hull Number | ZIP Code |
|---|---|---|
| USCG Basswood | WLB 388 | AP 96661-3901 |
| USCG Boutwell | WHEC 719 | AP 96661-3902 |
| USCG Eagle | WIX 327 | AE 09568-3906 |
| USCG Escape | WMEC 6 | AA 34091-3946 |
| USCG Galveston Is | WPB 1349 | AP 96450-1056 |
| USCG Jarvis | WHEC 725 | AP 96669-3912 |
| USCG Mallow | WLB 396 | AP 96672-3913 |
| USCG Mellon | WHEC 717 | AP 96698-3914 |
| USCG Midgett | WHEC 726 | AP 96698-3915 |
| USCG Monhegan | WPB 1305 | AA 34051-3823 |
| USCG Morgenthau | WHEC 722 | AP 96672-3916 |
| USCG Munro | WHEC 724 | AP 96672-3917 |
| USCG Nantucket | WPB 1316 | AA 34051-3823 |
| USCG Nunivak | WPB 1306 | AA 34051-3823 |
| USCG Polar Sea | WAGB 11 | AP 96698-3919 |
| USCG Polar Star | WAGB 10 | AP 96698-3920 |
| USCG Rush | WHEC 723 | AP 96677-3921 |
| USCG Sassafras | WLB 401 | AP 96678-3922 |
| USCG Sherman | WHEC 720 | AP 96678-3923 |
| USCG Tahoma | WMEC 908 | AE 09588-3938 |
| USCG Thetis | WMEC 910 | AA 34093-3942 |
| USCG Vashon | WPB 1308 | AA 34051-3823 |

# US Navy Fleet Post Offices and Homeports

The following pages contain active navy ships, their hull number, fleet post office (ZIP code) and their home port.

The following codes designate the assigned homeport.

0. No homeport assigned
2. Alameda, CA
3. Concord, CA
4. Long Beach, CA
5. Oakland, CA
6. San Diego, CA
8. Vallejo, CA
9. Groton, CT
10. New London, CT
12. Mayport, FL
13. Kings Bay, GA
14. Pearl Harbor, HI
15. Pascagoula, MS
16. Portsmouth, NH
17. Earle, NJ

18. New York, NY
19. Philadelphia, PA
21. Charleston, SC
23. Ingleside, TX
24. Little Creek, Norfolk, VA
25. Norfolk, VA
26. Bangor, WA
27. Bremerton, WA
29. Tacoma, WA
30. Gaeta, Italy
31. La Maddalena, Italy
32. Sasebo, Japan
33. Yokosuka, Japan
34. Guam, Marianas Islands

## US Navy FPOs and Homeports

| Ship's Name | Hull Number | ZIP Code | Home Port |
|---|---|---|---|
| Able | TAGOS 20 | None Assigned | 0 |
| Acadia | AD 42 | AP 96647-2530 | 6 |
| Advantage | TAK 9652 | None Assigned | 0 |
| Alabama | SSBN 731 | AP 96698-2108 | 26 |
| Alaska | SSBN 732 | AP 96698-2111 | 26 |
| Alatna | TAOG 81 | None Assigned | 0 |
| Albany | SSN 753 | AE 09564-2409 | 25 |
| Albuquerque | SSN 706 | AE 09564-2386 | 9 |
| Alexandria | SSN 757 | AE 09564-2413 | 9 |
| Algol | TAKR 287 | None Assigned | 0 |
| Altair | TAKR 291 | None Assigned | 0 |

## US Navy FPOs and Homeports (cont.)

| Ship's Name | Hull Number | ZIP Code | Home Port |
|---|---|---|---|
| America | CV 66 | AE 09531-2790 | 25 |
| American Cormorant | TAK 2062 | None Assigned | 0 |
| American Explorer | TAOT 165 | None Assigned | 0 |
| American Kestrel | TAK 9651 | None Assigned | 0 |
| American Merlin | TAK 9302 | None Assigned | 0 |
| American Osprey | TAOT 5075 | None Assigned | 0 |
| Anchorage | LSD 36 | AP 96660-1724 | 6 |
| Anderson Jr, James, Pfc | TAK 3002 | None Assigned | 0 |
| Annapolis | SSN 760 | AE 09564-2416 | 9 |
| Antares | TAKR 294 | None Assigned | 0 |
| Antietam | CG 54 | AP 96660-1174 | 4 |
| Antrim | FFG 20 | AA 34090-1476 | 15 |
| Anzio | CG 68 | AE 09564-1188 | 25 |
| Apache | TATF 172 | None Assigned | 0 |
| Archerfish | SSN 678 | AE 09564-2358 | 9 |
| Ardent | MCM 12 | AA 34090-1932 | 23 |
| Arkansas | CGN 41 | AP 96660-1168 | 2 |
| Asheville | SSN 758 | AP 96660-2414 | 6 |
| Ashland | LSD 48 | AE 09564-1736 | 24 |
| Aspro | SSN 648 | AP 96660-2334 | 14 |
| Assertive | TAGOS 9 | None Assigned | 0 |
| Assurance | TAGOS 5 | None Assigned | 0 |
| Atlanta | SSN 712 | AE 09564-2392 | 25 |
| Audacious | TAGOS 11 | None Assigned | 0 |
| Augusta | SSN 710 | AE 09564-2390 | 9 |
| Austin | LPD 4 | AE 09564-1707 | 25 |
| Austral Rainbow | TAK 1005 | None Assigned | 0 |
| Avenger | MCM 1 | AA 34090-1921 | 23 |
| Bainbridge | CGN 25 | AE 09565-1161 | 25 |
| Baltimore | SSN 704 | AE 09565-2384 | 25 |
| Banner | TAK 5008 | None Assigned | 0 |
| Barry | DDG 52 | AE 09565-1270 | 25 |
| Bates, William H | SSN 680 | AP 96661-2360 | 14 |
| Batfish | SSN 681 | AA 34090-2361 | 21 |
| Baugh, William B, Pfc | TAK 3001 | None Assigned | 0 |
| Beaufort | ATS 2 | AP 96661-3218 | 32 |
| Belknap | CG 26 | AE 09565-1149 | 30 |
| Bellatrix | TAKR 288 | None Assigned | 0 |

## US Navy FPOs and Homeports (cont.)

| Ship's Name | Hull Number | ZIP Code | Home Port |
|---|---|---|---|
| Belleau Wood | LHA 3 | AP 96623-1610 | 32 |
| Bergall | SSN 667 | AP 96661-2347 | 25 |
| Big Horn | TAO 198 | None Assigned | 0 |
| Billfish | SSN 676 | AA 34090-2356 | 21 |
| Birmingham | SSN 695 | AP 96661-2375 | 14 |
| Blue Ridge | LCC 19 | AP 96628-3300 | 33 |
| Bluefish | SSN 675 | AA 34090-2355 | 21 |
| Bobo, John P, 2nd Lt | TAK 3008 | None Assigned | 0 |
| Boise | SSN 764 | AE 09565-2420 | 25 |
| Bold | TAGOS 12 | None Assigned | 0 |
| Bolivar, Simon | SSBN 641 | AA 34090-2060 | 21 |
| Bolster | ARS 38 | AP 96661-3201 | 4 |
| Bonnyman, Alex, 1st Lt | TAK 3003 | None Assigned | 0 |
| Boone | FFG 28 | AA 34093-1484 | 12 |
| Boston | SSN 703 | AE 09565-2383 | 9 |
| Bradley, Robert G | FFG 49 | AA 34090-1503 | 21 |
| Bremerton | SSN 698 | AP 96661-2378 | 14 |
| Briscoe | DD 977 | AE 09565-1215 | 25 |
| Brunswick | ATS 3 | AP 96661-3219 | 32 |
| Buffalo | SSN 715 | AP 96661-2395 | 14 |
| Buffalo Soldier | TAK 9301 | None Assigned | 0 |
| Bunker Hill | CG 52 | AP 96661-1172 | 33 |
| Burke, Arleigh | DDG 51 | AE 09565-1269 | 25 |
| Butte | AE 27 | AE 09565-3005 | 17 |
| Button, William R, Sgt | TAK 3012 | None Assigned | 0 |
| Buyer | TAK 2033 | None Assigned | 0 |
| Cable, Frank | AS 40 | AA 34086-2615 | 21 |
| California | CGN 36 | AP 96662-1163 | 27 |
| Callaghan | DDG 994 | AP 96662-1266 | 6 |
| Callaghan, Wm M, Adm | TAKR 1001 | None Assigned | 0 |
| Camden | AOE 2 | AP 98799-3013 | 27 |
| Canopus | AS 34 | AA 34087-2595 | 13 |
| Capable | TAGOS 16 | None Assigned | 0 |
| Cape Adventurer | TAK 5005 | None Assigned | 0 |
| Cape Agent | TAK 5015 | None Assigned | 0 |
| Cape Aide | TAK 5006 | None Assigned | 0 |
| Cape Alava | TAK 5012 | None Assigned | 0 |
| Cape Alexander | TAK 5010 | None Assigned | 0 |

## US Navy FPOs and Homeports (cont.)

| Ship's Name | Hull Number | ZIP Code | Home Port |
|---|---|---|---|
| Cape Ambassador | TAK 5007 | None Assigned | 0 |
| Cape Ann | TAK 5009 | None Assigned | 0 |
| Cape Archway | TAK 5011 | None Assigned | 0 |
| Cape Avinof | TAK 5013 | None Assigned | 0 |
| Cape Blanco | TAK 5060 | None Assigned | 0 |
| Cape Bon | TAK 5059 | None Assigned | 0 |
| Cape Borda | TAK 5058 | None Assigned | 0 |
| Cape Bover | TAK 5057 | None Assigned | 0 |
| Cape Breton | TAK 5056 | None Assigned | 0 |
| Cape Canaveral | TAK 5040 | None Assigned | 0 |
| Cape Canso | TAK 5037 | None Assigned | 0 |
| Cape Carthage | TAK 5042 | None Assigned | 0 |
| Cape Catawba | TAK 5074 | None Assigned | 0 |
| Cape Catoche | TAK 5043 | None Assigned | 0 |
| Cape Chalmers | TAK 5036 | None Assigned | 0 |
| Cape Clear | TAK 5039 | None Assigned | 0 |
| Cape Cod | AD 43 | AP 96649-2535 | 6 |
| Cape Cod | TAK 5041 | None Assigned | 0 |
| Cape Decision | TAKR 5054 | None Assigned | 0 |
| Cape Diamond | TAKR 5055 | None Assigned | 0 |
| Cape Domingo | TAKR 5053 | None Assigned | 0 |
| Cape Douglas | TAKR 5052 | None Assigned | 0 |
| Cape Ducato | TAKR 5051 | None Assigned | 0 |
| Cape Edmont | TAKR 5069 | None Assigned | 0 |
| Cape Farewell | TAK 5073 | None Assigned | 0 |
| Cape Fear | TAK 5061 | None Assigned | 0 |
| Cape Flattery | TAK 5070 | None Assigned | 0 |
| Cape Florida | TAK 5071 | None Assigned | 0 |
| Cape Gibson | TAK 5051 | None Assigned | 0 |
| Cape Girardeau | TAK 2039 | None Assigned | 0 |
| Cape Henry | TAKR 5067 | None Assigned | 0 |
| Cape Horn | TAKR 5068 | None Assigned | 0 |
| Cape Hudson | TAKR 5066 | None Assigned | 0 |
| Cape Inscription | TAKR 5076 | None Assigned | 0 |
| Cape Intrepid | TAKR 11 | None Assigned | 0 |
| Cape Isabel | TAKR 5062 | None Assigned | 0 |
| Cape Jacob | TAK 5029 | None Assigned | 0 |
| Cape John | TAK 5022 | None Assigned | 0 |

## US Navy FPOs and Homeports (cont.)

| Ship's Name | Hull Number | ZIP Code | Home Port |
|---|---|---|---|
| Cape Johnson | TAK 5075 | None Assigned | 0 |
| Cape Juby | TAK 5077 | None Assigned | 0 |
| Cape Lambert | TAKR 5077 | None Assigned | 0 |
| Cape Lobos | TAKR 5078 | None Assigned | 0 |
| Cape May | TAK 5063 | None Assigned | 0 |
| Cape Mendocino | TAK 5064 | None Assigned | 0 |
| Cape Mohican | TAK 5065 | None Assigned | 0 |
| Cape Nome | TAK 1014 | None Assigned | 0 |
| Cape St George | CG 71 | AE 09566-1191 | 25 |
| Cape Washington | TAKR 9961 | None Assigned | 0 |
| Cape Wrath | TAKR 9962 | None Assigned | 0 |
| Capella | TAKR 293 | None Assigned | 0 |
| Caron | DD 970 | AE 09566-1208 | 25 |
| Carr | FFG 52 | AA 34090-1506 | 21 |
| Catawba | TATF 168 | None Assigned | 0 |
| Cavalla | SSN 684 | AP 96662-2364 | 14 |
| Champion | MCM 4 | AA 34090-1924 | 23 |
| Chancellorsville | CG 62 | AP 96662-1182 | 6 |
| Chandler | DDG 996 | AP 96662-1268 | 6 |
| Chanticleer | ASR 7 | None Assigned | 0 |
| Chattahoochee | TAOG 82 | None Assigned | 0 |
| Chesapeake | TAOT 5084 | None Assigned | 0 |
| Chicago | SSN 721 | AP 96662-2401 | 6 |
| Chief | MCM 14 | AA 34090-1934 | 23 |
| Chosin | CG 65 | AP 96662-1185 | 14 |
| Cimarron | AO 177 | AP 96662-3018 | 14 |
| Cincinnati | SSN 693 | AE 09566-2373 | 25 |
| City Of Corpus Christi | SSN 705 | AE 09566-2385 | 9 |
| Clark | FFG 11 | AE 09566-1469 | 25 |
| Cleveland | LPD 7 | AP 96662-1710 | 6 |
| Columbus | SSN 762 | AP 96662-2418 | 14 |
| Comet | TAKR 7 | None Assigned | 0 |
| Comfort | TAH 20 | None Assigned | 0 |
| Comstock | LSD 45 | AP 96662-1733 | 6 |
| Concord | TAFS 5 | None Assigned | 0 |
| Conolly | DD 979 | AE 09566-1217 | 25 |
| Constellation | CV 64 | AP 96635-2780 | 6 |
| Copeland | FFG 25 | AP 96662-1481 | 6 |

## US Navy FPOs and Homeports (cont.)

| Ship's Name | Hull Number | ZIP Code | Home Port |
|---|---|---|---|
| Cornhusker State | TACS 6 | None Assigned | 0 |
| Coronado | AGF 11 | AP 96662-3330 | 6 |
| Courier | TAK 5019 | None Assigned | 0 |
| Cowpens | CG 63 | AP 96662-1183 | 6 |
| Crommelin | FFG 37 | AP 96662-1492 | 14 |
| Curtiss | TAVB 4 | None Assigned | 0 |
| Curts | FFG 38 | AP 96662-1493 | 33 |
| Cushing | DD 985 | AP 96662-1223 | 14 |
| Cyclone | PC 1 | AE 09566-1960 | 24 |
| Dale | CG 19 | AA 34090-1143 | 12 |
| Dallas | SSN 700 | AE 09567-2380 | 9 |
| Davis, Rodney M | FFG 60 | AP 96663-1514 | 33 |
| De Grasse, Comte | DD 974 | AE 09566-1212 | 25 |
| Defender | MCM 2 | AA 34090-1922 | 23 |
| Del Monte | TAK 5049 | None Assigned | 0 |
| Del Valle | TAK 5050 | None Assigned | 0 |
| Del Viento | TAK 5026 | None Assigned | 0 |
| Denebola | TAKR 289 | None Assigned | 0 |
| Denver | LPD 9 | AP 96663-1712 | 6 |
| Detroit | AOE 4 | AE 09567-3015 | 17 |
| Devastator | MCM 6 | AA 34090-1926 | 23 |
| Dewert | FFG 45 | AA 34090-1499 | 21 |
| Dextrous | MCM 13 | AA 34090-1933 | 23 |
| Deyo | DD 989 | AA 34090-1227 | 21 |
| Diamond State | TACS 7 | None Assigned | 0 |
| Diehl, Walter S | TAO 193 | None Assigned | 0 |
| Dixon | AS 37 | AP 96648-2605 | 6 |
| Dolphin | AGSS 555 | AP 96663-4000 | 6 |
| Doyle | FFG 39 | AA 34090-1494 | 12 |
| Drum | SSN 677 | AP 96663-2357 | 6 |
| Dubuque | LPD 8 | AP 96663-1711 | 32 |
| Duluth | LPD 6 | AP 96663-1709 | 6 |
| Duncan | FFG 10 | AP 96663-1468 | 6 |
| Edenton | ATS 1 | AE 09568-3217 | 24 |
| Effective | TAGOS 21 | None Assigned | 0 |
| Eisenhower, Dwight D | CVN 69 | AE 09532-2830 | 25 |
| Elliot | DD 967 | AP 96664-1205 | 6 |
| Elrod | FFG 55 | AA 34091-1509 | 21 |

## US Navy FPOs and Homeports (cont.)

| Ship's Name | Hull Number | ZIP Code | Home Port |
|---|---|---|---|
| Empire State | TAP 1001 | None Assigned | 0 |
| Enterprise | CVN 65 | AE 09543-2810 | 25 |
| Equality State | TACS 8 | None Assigned | 0 |
| Ericsson, John | TAO 194 | None Assigned | 0 |
| Essex | LHD 2 | AP 96643-1661 | 6 |
| Estocin | FFG 15 | AE 09569-1473 | 25 |
| Fahrion | FFG 22 | AA 34091-1478 | 21 |
| Fairfax County | LST 1193 | AE 09569-1814 | 24 |
| Fife | DD 991 | AP 96665-1229 | 33 |
| Finback | SSN 670 | AE 09569-2350 | 25 |
| Fitch, Aubrey | FFG 34 | AA 34091-1490 | 12 |
| Flatley | FFG 21 | AA 34091-1477 | 15 |
| Fletcher | DD 992 | AP 96665-1230 | 14 |
| Flickertail State | TACS 5 | None Assigned | 0 |
| Flint | AE 32 | AP 96665-3008 | 3 |
| Florida | SSBN 728 | AP 96698-2099 | 26 |
| Flying Fish | SSN 673 | AE 09569-2353 | 25 |
| Ford | FFG 54 | AP 96665-1508 | 4 |
| Forrestal | CV 59 | None Assigned | 0 |
| Fort Fisher | LSD 40 | AP 96665-1728 | 6 |
| Fort Mchenry | LSD 43 | AP 96665-1731 | 6 |
| Foster, Paul F | DD 964 | AP 96665-1202 | 4 |
| Franklin, Benjamin | SSBN 640 | None Assigned | 0 |
| Franklin, Benjamin | SSN 642 | None Assigned | 0 |
| Frederick | LST 1184 | AP 96665-1805 | 6 |
| Gallery | FFG 26 | AA 34091-1482 | 15 |
| Gary | FFG 51 | AP 96666-1505 | 6 |
| Gates, Thomas S | CG 51 | AE 09570-1171 | 25 |
| Gato | SSN 615 | AE 09570-2326 | 10 |
| Gem State | TACS 2 | None Assigned | 0 |
| Georgia | SSBN 729 | AP 96698-2102 | 26 |
| Germantown | LSD 42 | AP 96666-1730 | 32 |
| Gettysburg | CG 64 | AA 34091-1184 | 12 |
| Gladiator | MCM 11 | AA 34091-1931 | 23 |
| Gompers, Samuel | AD 37 | AP 96641-2515 | 2 |
| Gopher State | TACS 4 | None Assigned | 0 |
| Grand Canyon State | TACS 3 | None Assigned | 0 |
| Grapple | ARS 53 | AE 09570-3223 | 24 |

## US Navy FPOs and Homeports (cont.)

| Ship's Name | Hull Number | ZIP Code | Home Port |
|---|---|---|---|
| Grasp | ARS 51 | AE 09570-3220 | 24 |
| Grayling | SSN 646 | AA 34091-2332 | 21 |
| Green Harbour | TAK 2064 | None Assigned | 0 |
| Green Mountain State | TACS 9 | None Assigned | 0 |
| Green Valley | TAK 2049 | None Assigned | 0 |
| Groton | SSN 694 | AE 09570-2374 | 9 |
| Groves, Stephen W | FFG 29 | AA 34091-1485 | 15 |
| Gruman, Leroy | TAO 195 | None Assigned | 0 |
| Guadalcanal | LPH 7 | AE 09562-1635 | 25 |
| Guadalupe | TAO 200 | None Assigned | 0 |
| Guam | LPH 9 | AE 09563-1640 | 25 |
| Guardian | MCM 5 | AA 34091-1925 | 23 |
| Gulf Banker | TAK 5044 | None Assigned | 0 |
| Gulf Farmer | TAK 5045 | None Assigned | 0 |
| Gulf Merchant | TAK 5046 | None Assigned | 0 |
| Gulf Shipper | TAK 2035 | None Assigned | 0 |
| Gulf Trader | TAK 2036 | None Assigned | 0 |
| Gunston Hall | LSD 44 | AE 09573-1732 | 24 |
| Gurnard | SSN 662 | AP 96666-2342 | 6 |
| Hall, John L | FFG 32 | AA 34091-1488 | 15 |
| Halyburton | FFG 40 | AA 34091-1495 | 21 |
| Hammerhead | SSN 663 | AE 09573-2343 | 25 |
| Hampton | SSN 767 | AE 09573-2423 | 25 |
| Hancock, John | DD 981 | AA 34091-1219 | 12 |
| Harlan County | LST 1196 | AE 09573-1817 | 24 |
| Hauge Jr, Louis J, Cpt | TAK 3000 | None Assigned | 0 |
| Hawes | FFG 53 | AA 34091-1507 | 21 |
| Hawkbill | SSN 666 | AP 96667-2346 | 14 |
| Hayler | DD 997 | AE 09573-1231 | 25 |
| Helena | SSN 725 | AP 96667-2405 | 14 |
| Heron | MHC 52 | AA 34091-1951 | 23 |
| Hewitt | DD 966 | AP 96667-1204 | 33 |
| Higgins, Andrew J | TAO 190 | None Assigned | 0 |
| Hill, Harry W | DD 986 | AP 96667-1224 | 6 |
| Hoist | ARS 40 | AE 09573-3203 | 24 |
| Holland | AS 32 | AP 96642-2585 | 34 |
| Honolulu | SSN 718 | AP 96667-2398 | 14 |
| Houston | SSN 713 | AP 96667-2393 | 6 |

## US Navy FPOs and Homeports (cont.)

| Ship's Name | Hull Number | ZIP Code | Home Port |
|---|---|---|---|
| Hue City | CG 66 | AA 34091-1186 | 12 |
| Humpreys, Joshua | TAO 188 | None Assigned | 0 |
| Hunley | AS 31 | AE 09559-2580 | 25 |
| Hurricane | PC 3 | AP 96667-1962 | 6 |
| Implicit | MSO 455 | AP 98799-1912 | 29 |
| Inchon | LPH 12 | AE 09529-1655 | 25 |
| Independence | CV 62 | AP 96618-2760 | 33 |
| Indianapolis | SSN 697 | AP 96668-2377 | 14 |
| Indomitable | TAGOS 7 | None Assigned | 0 |
| Ingersoll | DD 990 | AP 96668-1228 | 14 |
| Ingraham | FFG 61 | AP 96668-1515 | 4 |
| Invincible | TAGOS 10 | None Assigned | 0 |
| Jackson, Henry M | SSBN 730 | AP 96698-2105 | 26 |
| Jackson, Stonewall | SSBN 634 | AA 34091-2048 | 21 |
| Jacksonville | SSN 699 | AE 09575-2379 | 25 |
| James, Reuben | FFG 57 | AP 96669-1511 | 14 |
| Jarrett | FFG 33 | AP 96669-1489 | 4 |
| Jason | AR 8 | AP 96644-2560 | 6 |
| Jefferson City | SSN 759 | AP 96669-2415 | 6 |
| Jones, John Paul | DDG 53 | AP 96669-1271 | 6 |
| Juneau | LPD 10 | AP 96669-1713 | 6 |
| Kaiser, Henry J | TAO 187 | None Assigned | 0 |
| Kalamazoo | AOR 6 | AE 09576-3028 | 25 |
| Kamehameha | SSN 642 | AP 96670-2063 | 14 |
| Kanawha | TAO 196 | None Assigned | 0 |
| Kansas City | AOR 3 | AP 96670-3025 | 5 |
| Kauffman | FFG 59 | AE 09576-1513 | 25 |
| Kearsarge | LHD 3 | AE 09534-1662 | 25 |
| Kennedy, John F | CV 67 | AE 09538-2800 | 19 |
| Kentucky | SSBN 737 | AA 34091-4990 | 13 |
| Key West | SSN 722 | AE 09576-2402 | 25 |
| Keystone State | TACS 1 | None Assigned | 0 |
| Kidd | DDG 993 | AE 09576-1265 | 25 |
| Kilauea | AE 26 | None Assigned | 0 |
| Kilauea | TAE 26 | None Assigned | 0 |
| Kinkaid | DD 965 | AP 96670-1203 | 6 |
| Kiska | AE 35 | AP 96670-3011 | 3 |
| Kittiwake | ASR 13 | AE 09576-3208 | 25 |

## US Navy FPOs and Homeports (cont.)

| Ship's Name | Hull Number | ZIP Code | Home Port |
|---|---|---|---|
| Kitty Hawk | CV 63 | AP 96634-2770 | 6 |
| Klakring | FFG 42 | AA 34091-1497 | 21 |
| Kocak, Matej, Sgt | TAK 3005 | None Assigned | 0 |
| L Y Spear | AS 36 | AE 09547-2600 | 25 |
| La Jolla | SSN 701 | AP 96671-2381 | 6 |
| La Moure County | LST 1194 | AE 09577-1815 | 24 |
| La Salle | AGF 3 | AE 09577-3320 | 25 |
| Lake | TAK 5016 | None Assigned | 0 |
| Lake Champlain | CG 57 | AP 96671-1177 | 6 |
| Lake Erie | CG 70 | AP 96671-1190 | 14 |
| Land, Emory S | AS 39 | AE 09545-2610 | 25 |
| Leahy | CG 16 | None Assigned | 0 |
| Leftwich | DD 984 | AP 96671-1222 | 14 |
| Lenthall, John | TAO 189 | None Assigned | 0 |
| Leyte Gulf | CG 55 | AA 34091-1175 | 12 |
| Lincoln, Abraham | CVN 72 | AP 96612-2872 | 2 |
| Lopez, Baldomero, 1st Lt | TAK 3010 | None Assigned | 0 |
| Los Angeles | SSN 688 | AP 96671-2368 | 8 |
| Louisville | SSN 724 | AP 96671-2404 | 6 |
| Loyal | TAGOS 22 | None Assigned | 0 |
| Lummus, Jack, 1st Lt | TAK 3011 | None Assigned | 0 |
| Madison, James | SSBN 627 | None Assigned | 0 |
| Mars | TAFS 1 | None Assigned | 0 |
| Maryland | SSBN 738 | AA 34092-2129 | 13 |
| Mauna Kea | AE 22 | AP 96672-3001 | 3 |
| Mccain, John S | DDG 56 | AP 96672-1274 | 14 |
| Mcclusky | FFG 41 | AP 96672-1496 | 33 |
| Mcinerney | FFG 8 | AA 34092-1466 | 12 |
| Mckee | AS 41 | AP 96621-2620 | 6 |
| Memphis | SSN 691 | AE 09578-2371 | 16 |
| Mercy | TAH 19 | None Assigned | 0 |
| Merrill | DD 976 | AP 96672-1214 | 6 |
| Merrimack | AO 179 | AE 09578-3020 | 25 |
| Meteor | TAKR 9 | None Assigned | 0 |
| Miami | SSN 755 | AE 09578-2411 | 9 |
| Michigan | SSBN 727 | AP 96698-2096 | 26 |
| Minneapolis-St Paul | SSN 708 | AE 09578-2388 | 25 |
| Mission Buenaventura | TAOT 1012 | None Assigned | 0 |

## US Navy FPOs and Homeports (cont.)

| Ship's Name | Hull Number | ZIP Code | Home Port |
|---|---|---|---|
| Mission Capistrano | TAOT 5005 | None Assigned | 0 |
| Mississippi | CGN 40 | AE 09578-1167 | 25 |
| Mobile Bay | CG 53 | AP 96672-1173 | 33 |
| Mohawk | TATF 170 | None Assigned | 0 |
| Monongahela | AO 178 | AE 09578-3019 | 25 |
| Monsoon | PC 4 | AP 96672-1963 | 6 |
| Monterey | CG 61 | AA 34092-1181 | 12 |
| Montpelier | SSN 765 | AE 09578-2421 | 25 |
| Moore, John A | FFG 19 | AP 96672-1475 | 6 |
| Moosebrugger | DD 980 | AA 34092-1218 | 21 |
| Morison, Samuel Eliot | FFG 13 | AA 34092-1471 | 21 |
| Mount Baker | AE 34 | AA 34092-3010 | 21 |
| Mount Hood | AE 29 | AP 96672-3007 | 3 |
| Mount Vernon | LSD 39 | AP 96672-1727 | 6 |
| Mount Vernon | TAOT 3009 | None Assigned | 0 |
| Mount Whitney | LCC 20 | AE 09517-3310 | 25 |
| Narragansett | TATF 167 | None Assigned | 0 |
| Narwhal | SSN 671 | AA 34092-2351 | 21 |
| Nashville | LPD 13 | AE 09579-1715 | 25 |
| Nassau | LHA 4 | AE 09557-1615 | 25 |
| Navajo | TATF 169 | None Assigned | 0 |
| Nebraska | SSBN 739 | AA 34092-2132 | 13 |
| Nevada | SSBN 733 | AP 96698-2114 | 26 |
| New Orleans | LPH 11 | AP 96627-1660 | 6 |
| New York City | SSN 696 | AP 96673-2376 | 14 |
| Newport | LST 1179 | None Assigned | 0 |
| Newport News | SSN 750 | AE 09579-2406 | 25 |
| Niagara Falls | AFS 3 | AP 96673-3032 | 34 |
| Nicholas | FFG 47 | AA 34092-1501 | 21 |
| Nicholson | DD 982 | AA 34092-1220 | 21 |
| Nimitz | CVN 68 | AP 98780-2820 | 27 |
| Nitro | AE 23 | AE 09579-3002 | 17 |
| Nodaway | TAOG 78 | None Assigned | 0 |
| Norfolk | SSN 714 | AE 09579-2394 | 25 |
| Normandy | CG 60 | AE 09579-1180 | 25 |
| Northern Light | TAK 284 | None Assigned | 0 |
| O'bannon | DD 987 | AA 34092-1225 | 21 |
| O'brien | DD 975 | AP 96674-1213 | 33 |

## US Navy FPOs and Homeports (cont.)

| Ship's Name | Hull Number | ZIP Code | Home Port |
|---|---|---|---|
| Obregon, Eugene A, Pfc | TAK 3006 | None Assigned | 0 |
| Ogden | LPD 5 | AP 96674-1708 | 6 |
| Ohio | SSBN 726 | AP 96698-2093 | 26 |
| Oklahoma City | SSN 723 | AE 09581-2403 | 25 |
| Oldendorf | DD 972 | AP 96674-1210 | 6 |
| Olympia | SSN 717 | AP 96674-2397 | 14 |
| Omaha | SSN 692 | AP 96674-2372 | 14 |
| Ortolan | ASR 22 | AA 34092-3212 | 21 |
| Osprey | MHC 51 | AA 34092-1950 | 21 |
| Parche | SSN 683 | AP 96675-2363 | 26 |
| Pargo | SSN 650 | AE 09582-2336 | 10 |
| Pasadena | SSN 752 | AP 96675-2408 | 6 |
| Patriot | MCM 7 | AA 34092-1927 | 23 |
| Patriot State | TAP 1000 | None Assigned | 0 |
| Pecos | TAO 197 | None Assigned | 0 |
| Peleliu | LHA 5 | AP 96624-1620 | 6 |
| Pennsylvania | SSBN 735 | AA 34092-2120 | 13 |
| Pensacola | LSD 38 | AE 09582-1726 | 24 |
| Permit | SSN 594 | None Assigned | 0 |
| Perry, Oliver Hazard | FFG 7 | AE 09582-1465 | 18 |
| Persistent | TAGOS 6 | None Assigned | 0 |
| Peterson | DD 969 | AE 09582-1207 | 25 |
| Philadelphia | SSN 690 | AE 09582-2370 | 16 |
| Philip, George | FFG 12 | AP 96675-1470 | 6 |
| Philippine Sea | CG 58 | AA 34092-1178 | 12 |
| Phillips, Franklin J, Pvt | TAK 3004 | None Assigned | 0 |
| Phoenix | SSN 702 | AE 09582-2382 | 25 |
| Pigeon | ASR 21 | None Assigned | 0 |
| Pintado | SSN 672 | AP 96675-2352 | 14 |
| Pioneer | MCM 9 | AA 34092-1929 | 23 |
| Pioneer Commander | TAK 2016 | None Assigned | 0 |
| Pioneer Contractor | TAK 2018 | None Assigned | 0 |
| Pioneer Crusader | TAK 2019 | None Assigned | 0 |
| Pittsburgh | SSN 720 | AE 09582-2400 | 9 |
| Platte | AO 186 | AA 34092-3022 | 25 |
| Pless, Stephen W, Maj | TAK 3007 | None Assigned | 0 |
| Pogy | SSN 647 | AP 96675-2333 | 6 |
| Polk, James K | SSN 645 | AA 34092-2072 | 25 |

## US Navy FPOs and Homeports (cont.)

| Ship's Name | Hull Number | ZIP Code | Home Port |
|---|---|---|---|
| Pollux | TAKR 290 | None Assigned | 0 |
| Ponce | LPD 15 | AE 09582-1717 | 25 |
| Port Royal | CG 73 | AP 96675-1193 | 14 |
| Portland | LSD 37 | AE 09582-1725 | 24 |
| Portsmouth | SSN 707 | AP 96675-2387 | 6 |
| Potomac | TAOT 181 | None Assigned | 0 |
| Powhatan | TATF 166 | None Assigned | 0 |
| Prevail | TAGOS 8 | None Assigned | 0 |
| Pride | TAK 5017 | None Assigned | 0 |
| Princeton | CG 59 | AP 96675-1179 | 6 |
| Providence | SSN 719 | AE 09582-2399 | 9 |
| Puffer | SSN 652 | AP 96675-2338 | 6 |
| Puget Sound | AD 38 | AE 09544-2520 | 25 |
| Puller, Lewis B | FFG 23 | AP 96675-1479 | 6 |
| Radford, Arthur W | DD 968 | AE 09586-1206 | 25 |
| Ray, David R | DD 971 | AP 96677-1209 | 4 |
| Reclaimer | ARS 42 | AP 96677-3205 | 14 |
| Recovery | ARS 43 | AE 09586-3206 | 24 |
| Regulus | TAKR 292 | None Assigned | 0 |
| Reid | FFG 30 | AP 96677-1486 | 6 |
| Rentz | FFG 46 | AP 96677-1500 | 6 |
| Rhode Island | SSBN 740 | AA 34092-2135 | 13 |
| Rickover, Hyman G | SSN 709 | AE 09586-2309 | 25 |
| Rivers, L Mendel | SSN 686 | AA 34092-2366 | 21 |
| Roanoke | AOR 7 | AP 96677-3029 | 27 |
| Roberts, Samuel B | FFG 58 | AE 09586-1512 | 25 |
| Rodgers, John | DD 983 | AA 34092-1221 | 21 |
| Roosevelt, Theodore | CVN 71 | AE 09599-2871 | 25 |
| Rushmore | LSD 47 | AP 96677-1735 | 6 |
| Sacramento | AOE 1 | AP 96678-3012 | 27 |
| Safeguard | ARS 50 | AP 96678-3221 | 14 |
| Saipan | LHA 2 | AE 09549-1605 | 25 |
| Salt Lake City | SSN 716 | AP 96678-2396 | 6 |
| Salvor | ARS 52 | AP 96678-3222 | 14 |
| San Bernardino | LST 1189 | AP 96678-1810 | 32 |
| San Diego | TAFS 6 | None Assigned | 0 |
| San Francisco | SSN 711 | AP 96678-2391 | 14 |
| San Jacinto | CG 56 | AE 09587-1176 | 25 |

## US Navy FPOs and Homeports (cont.)

| Ship's Name | Hull Number | ZIP Code | Home Port |
|---|---|---|---|
| San Jose | TAFS 7 | None Assigned | 0 |
| San Juan | SSN 751 | AE 09587-2407 | 9 |
| Sand Lance | SSN 660 | AE 09587-2340 | 21 |
| Santa Barbara | AE 28 | AA 34093-3006 | 21 |
| Santa Fe | SSN 763 | AE 09587-2419 | 9 |
| Saratoga | CV 60 | AE 09543-2740 | 12 |
| Saturn | TAFS 10 | None Assigned | 0 |
| Savannah | AOR 4 | AE 09587-3026 | 25 |
| Scan | TAK 5018 | None Assigned | 0 |
| Scott | DDG 995 | AE 09587-1267 | 25 |
| Scout | MCM 8 | AA 34093-1928 | 23 |
| Scranton | SSN 756 | AE 09687-2412 | 25 |
| Seahorse | SSN 669 | AA 34093-2349 | 21 |
| Seattle | AOE 3 | AE 09587-3014 | 17 |
| Sentry | MCM 3 | AA 34093-1923 | 23 |
| Shasta | AE 33 | AP 96678-3009 | 3 |
| Shenandoah | AD 44 | AE 09551-2540 | 25 |
| Shiloh | CG 67 | AP 96678-1187 | 6 |
| Shoshone | TAOT 151 | None Assigned | 0 |
| Shreveport | LPD 12 | AE 09587-1714 | 25 |
| Sides | FFG 14 | AP 96678-1472 | 6 |
| Simon Lake | AS 33 | AE 09536-2590 | 31 |
| Simpson | FFG 56 | AE 09587-1510 | 25 |
| Sioux | TATF 171 | None Assigned | 0 |
| Sirius | TAFS 8 | None Assigned | 0 |
| Sirocco | PC 6 | AE 09587-1965 | 25 |
| South Carolina | CGN 37 | AE 09587-1164 | 25 |
| Southern Cross | TAK 285 | None Assigned | 0 |
| Spadefish | SSN 668 | AE 09587-2348 | 25 |
| Spartanburg County | LST 1192 | AE 09587-1813 | 24 |
| Spica | TAFS 9 | None Assigned | 0 |
| Sprague, Clifton | FFG 16 | AE 09587-1474 | 18 |
| Springfield | SSN 761 | AE 09587-2417 | 9 |
| Spruance | DD 963 | AA 34093-1201 | 12 |
| Squall | PC 7 | AP 96678-1966 | 6 |
| Stalwart | AGOS 1 | None Assigned | 0 |
| Stalwart | TAGOS 1 | None Assigned | 0 |
| Stark | FFG 31 | AA 34093-1487 | 12 |

## US Navy FPOs and Homeports (cont.)

| Ship's Name | Hull Number | ZIP Code | Home Port |
|---|---|---|---|
| Stuart, Jeb | TAK 9204 | None Assigned | 0 |
| Stump | DD 978 | AE 09587-1216 | 25 |
| Sturgeon | SSN 637 | None Assigned | 0 |
| Sunbird | ASR 15 | AE 09587-3210 | 9 |
| Sunfish | SSN 649 | AE 09587-2430 | 25 |
| Supply | AOE 6 | AE 09587-3037 | 25 |
| Suribachi | AE 21 | AE 09587-3000 | 17 |
| Tarawa | LHA 1 | AP 96622-1600 | 4 |
| Tautog | SSN 639 | AP 96679-2331 | 14 |
| Taylor | FFG 50 | AA 34093-1504 | 21 |
| Tempest | PC 2 | AE 09588-1961 | 24 |
| Tenacious | TAGOS 17 | None Assigned | 0 |
| Tennessee | SSBN 734 | AA 34093-2117 | 13 |
| Thach | FFG 43 | AP 96679-1498 | 33 |
| Thorn | DD 988 | AA 34093-1226 | 21 |
| Ticonderoga | CG 47 | AE 09588-1158 | 25 |
| Tippecanoe | TAO 199 | None Assigned | 0 |
| Tisdale, Mahlon S | FFG 27 | AP 96679-1483 | 6 |
| Topeka | SSN 754 | AP 96679-2410 | 6 |
| Tortuga | LSD 46 | AE 09588-1734 | 24 |
| Trenton | LPD 14 | AE 09588-1716 | 25 |
| Trepang | SSN 674 | AA 34093-2354 | 21 |
| Tripoli | LPH 10 | AP 96626-1645 | 6 |
| Truxtun | CGN 35 | AP 98799-1162 | 27 |
| Tunny | SSN 682 | AP 96679-2362 | 14 |
| Turner, Richmond K | CG 20 | AA 34093-1144 | 21 |
| Typhoon | PC 5 | AE 09588-1964 | 25 |
| Underwood | FFG 36 | AA 34093-1491 | 12 |
| Vallejo, Mariano G | SSBN 658 | AA 34093-2087 | 21 |
| Valley Forge | CG 50 | AP 96682-1170 | 6 |
| Vandergrift | FFG 48 | AP 96682-1502 | 6 |
| Vella Gulf | CG 72 | AE 09590-1192 | 25 |
| Vicksburg | CG 69 | AA 34093-1189 | 12 |
| Victorious | TAGOS 19 | None Assigned | 0 |
| Vincennes | CG 49 | AP 96682-1169 | 6 |
| Vinson, Carl | CVN 70 | AP 96629-2840 | 2 |
| Virginia | CGN 38 | None Assigned | 0 |
| Vulcan | AR 5 | None Assigned | 0 |

## US Navy FPOs and Homeports (cont.)

| Ship's Name | Hull Number | ZIP Code | Home Port |
|---|---|---|---|
| Wabash | AOR 5 | AP 96683-3027 | 4 |
| Wadsworth | FFG 9 | AP 96683-1467 | 6 |
| Warrior | MCM 10 | AA 34093-1930 | 23 |
| Washington, George | CVN 73 | AE 09550-2873 | 25 |
| Wasp | LHD 1 | AE 09556-1660 | 25 |
| West Virginia | SSBN 736 | AA 34093-2123 | 13 |
| Whale | SSN 638 | AE 09591-2330 | 9 |
| Whidbey Island | LSD 41 | AE 09591-1729 | 24 |
| White Plains | AFS 4 | AP 96683-3033 | 34 |
| Wichita | AOR 1 | None Assigned | 0 |
| Wilbur, Curtis | DDG 54 | AP 96683-1272 | 6 |
| Willamette | AO 180 | AP 96683-3021 | 14 |
| Williams, Dewayne T, Pfc | TAK 3009 | None Assigned | 0 |
| Williams, Jack | FFG 24 | AA 34093-1480 | 12 |
| Wright | TAVB 3 | None Assigned | 0 |
| Yellowstone | AD 41 | AE 09512-2525 | 25 |
| Yorktown | CG 48 | AE 09594-1159 | 25 |
| Young, John | DD 973 | AP 96686-1211 | 6 |
| Yukon | TAO 202 | None Assigned | 0 |

# Paternity Suits, Child Support And Overseas Marriages

For any of these matters, write to the Commanding Officer of the unit to which the active duty member is assigned. Be sure to include full name, rank, SSN and organization, if known.

If the person involved is on active duty in the Army, you may obtain assistance by writing to:

Army Community and Family Support Center
ATTN: CSSC-SSA                    (703) 325-9390
2461 Eisenhower Ave          FAX (703) 325-6327
Alexandria, VA 22331-0521

## American Red Cross

The American Red Cross, under federal statute, and in accordance with regulations of the armed forces, usually has one or more representatives at each military installation to deal with families of military members concerning family emergencies.

To locate a member of the armed forces (who is on active duty or active duty for training) due to an emergency in their family, such as a death or serious illness, do not contact the military, but call your local Red Cross chapter. They are listed in the telephone book. Tell the Red Cross representative the nature of the emergency and the name, rank, and service of the military member. The Red Cross will immediately verify the matter and forward a message via Red Cross channels for notification purposes to the military member. Upon request of the member, the verified information can be passed to the military authorities to assist them to make a decision regarding emergency leave. Both the Red Cross and military have guidelines under which they work. While it is not a necessity for the military to have a Red Cross verification in order to grant leave in emergency situations, they normally request it. The American Red Cross is the best way to contact a military member when there is a crisis at home. For more information regarding Red Cross services contact your local Red Cross office.

## To Locate Military Personnel Through Banks, Credit Unions And Insurance Companies

As a service to their members and customers many banks, credit unions and insurance companies (automobile, life and home owners) will forward letters to their customers. If you know the financial institution of the person you are looking for, this is an excellent way to locate them. Before you attempt this, you should contact the institution first to ensure that they will forward your letter. Some of these institutions provide this service for their members and customers only. There are several large national insurance companies and associations that do all or most of their business with members of the armed forces. Many of their customers continue this business relationship after they separate or retire from the military.

Base information telephone operators can normally give you the name and number of banks and credit unions that have offices on their base. See Base and Post Locator Directory in this chapter for the appropriate telephone numbers.

## Active Military Owes You Money

If the person you are looking for owes you money and is on active duty with any of the armed forces, you should find out to what organization he is assigned, then write a letter to the commanding officer of his unit. Include all facts concerning the indebtedness, (i.e., amount, date, purchase, loan, the amount and dates he has made payments and current amount due, etc.).

The military does not look favorably on delinquency or avoidance of payment of legitimate debts by service members. You will receive a reply from the commanding officer who will advise you what payments you may expect. You will most likely receive such a reply within two to three weeks.

Collection agencies cannot legally write to an individual's commanding officer asking for their assistance; however, they can prepare a letter for their client to an individual's commanding officer using the client's letterhead and signed by the client requesting assistance. The letter may state that payments be made directly to the collection agency.

## To Locate Someone
## On Active Duty Rapidly

The Nationwide Locator can provide the current reported home address of anyone who is on active duty, if you provide the individual's Social Security number. The Social Security number will be processed immediately and the individual's current address will be returned to you by mail or fax within 24 hours of receipt. The fee for this service is $30.00. For additional information, see Appendix B.

The Nationwide Locator            FAX (210) 828-4667
Post Office Box 39903
San Antonio, TX  78218

# Chapter Three

# How To Locate Members Of The Reserve And National Guard

*The armed forces operate locators which will provide the unit of assignment or forward a letter to members of the reserve and National Guard. Members assigned to the inactive reserve and Individual Ready Reserve (IRR) are not assigned to a unit and the locators will only forward a letter to the members home address. (See Chapter Two for procedure).*

## To Locate Members Of The Air Force Reserve And Air National Guard

The Air Force locator will forward only one letter per each request and will not provide overseas unit of assignment of active members or reserve or Air National Guard units on active duty. Requests for more than one address per letter will be returned without action. Include self-addressed stamped envelope with request for unit assignment. If the individual is separated from the Air Force they will tell you.

USAF World-Wide Locator   Recording (210) 652-5774
AFMPC-RMIQL                          (210) 652-5775
55 C Street West, Room 50
Randolph AFB, TX  78150-4752
($3.50 research fee)

# To Locate Members Of
# The Civil Air Patrol

The Civil Air Patrol is an official auxiliary organization of the US Air Force. Its members are civilian, but many are former and retired military. The uniform and insignias of rank are similar to the Air Force. Send inquires to:

Civil Air Patrol (MSPM)              (205) 953-7748
105 S Hansell St                      (205) 953-4262
Maxwell AFB, AL  36112-6332

# To Locate Members Of The Army
# Reserve And Inactive Reserve

Army Reserve Personnel Center
ATTN:  DARP-PAS-EVS
9700 Page Blvd
St. Louis, MO  63132-5100
(no research fee)

# To Locate Members Of
# The Army National Guard

To locate personnel assigned to the National Guard Bureau call (202) 697-2943 (Army) and (202) 697-9751 (Air Force).

To locate members of the Army National Guard you must write to the appropriate state Adjutant General (Senior military officer of the National Guard in each state). There is no research fee.

## The State Adjutants General

ALABAMA
Adjutant General
PO Box 3711
Montgomery, AL  36109-0711
(334) 271-7200
FAX (334) 271-7386

ALASKA
Adjutant General
PO Box 5800
Ft Richardson, AK 99505-5800
(907) 428-6003
FAX (907) 420-6019

ARIZONA
Adjutant General
5636 E Mcdowell Rd
Phoenix, AZ 65008-3495
(802) 267-2710
FAX (602) 267-2688

ARKANSAS
Adjutant General
Camp Robinson
N Little Rock, AR 72110
(501) 791-5000
FAX (501) 791-5009

CALIFORNIA
Adjutant General
PO Box 269101
Sacramento, CA  95826-9101
(916) 854-3500
FAX (916) 854-3192

COLORADO
Adjutant General
6848 S Revere Parkway
Englewood, CO  80112-6710
(303) 397-3023
FAX (303) 397-3003

CONNECTICUT
Adjutant General
380 Broad St
Hartford, CT  08105-3795
(203) 524-4953
FAX (203) 548-3207

DELAWARE
Adjutant General
First Regiment Rd
Wilmington, DE  19808-2191
(302) 324-7001
FAX (302) 324-7061

DISTRICT OF COLUMBIA
Commanding General
2001 E Capitol St
Washington, DC  20003-1719
(202) 433-5220
FAX (202) 433-5105

FLORIDA
Adjutant General
State Arsenal Box 1008
St Augustine, FL  32084-1008
(904) 823-0364
FAX (904) 823-0152

GEORGIA
Adjutant General
PO Box 17965
Atlanta, GA  30318-0965
(404) 624-6001
FAX (404) 624-6633

GUAM
Adjutant General
822 E Harmon Ind Pk Rd
Tamuning, GU  96911-4421
(011) 671-647-0264
FAX (011) 671-647-2800

HAWAII
Adjutant General
3949 Diamond Head Rd
Honolulu, HI  96818-4495
(808) 734-2195
FAX (808) 732-2015

IDAHO
Adjutant General
PO Box 45
Boise, ID  83707-0045
(208) 389-5242
FAX (208) 389-6179

ILLINOIS
Adjutant General
1301 N Macarthur Blvd
Springfield, IL  62702-2398
(217) 785-3500
FAX (217) 785-3736

INDIANA
Adjutant General
2002 S Holt Rd
Indianapolis, IN  46241-4839
(317) 247-3274
FAX (317) 247-3540

IOWA
Adjutant General
7700 Nw Beaver Dr
Johnston, IA  50131-1902
(515) 242-5011
FAX (515) 242-5578

KANSAS
Adjutant General
2800 Sw Topeka Blvd
Topeka, KS  66611-1287
(913) 266-1001
FAX (913) 266-1059

KENTUCKY
Adjutant General
Boone National Guard Ctr
Frankfort, KY  40601-6168
(502) 564-8558
FAX (502) 564-6394

LOUISIANA
Adjutant General
Hq Bldg Jackson Barracks
New Orleans, LA  70146-0330
(504) 278-6211
FAX (504) 277-6366

MAINE
Adjutant General
Camp Keyes
Augusta, ME  04333-0033
(207) 626-4225
FAX (207) 626-4509

MARYLAND
Adjutant General
5th Regiment Armory
Baltimore, MD  21201-2266
(410) 578-6097
FAX (410) 576-6161

MASSACHUSETTS
Adjutant General
25 Haverhill Rd Camp Guild
Reading, MA  01667-1999
(617) 944 0500 X2320

MICHIGAN
Adjutant General
2500 S Washington Ave
Lansing, MI  48013-5101
(517) 483-5507
FAX (517) 483-5822

MINNESOTA
Adjutant General
20 W 12th St
St Paul, MN  56155
(612) 298-4666
FAX (612) 296-4541

MISSISSIPPI
Adjutant General
PO Box 5027
Jackson, MS  39296-5027
(601) 973-6232
FAX (601) 973-6251

MISSOURI
Adjutant General
1717 Industrial Dr
Jefferson City, MO 85101
(314) 751-9710
FAX (314) 751-9929

MONTANA
Adjutant General
PO Box 4789
Helena, MT 59604-4788
(406) 444-6910
FAX (406) 444-6973

NEBRASKA
Adjutant General
1300 Military Rd
Lincoln, NE 68508-1090
(402) 473-1114
FAX (402) 473-1400

NEVADA
Adjutant General
2525 S Carson St
Carson City, NV 89701-5502
(702) 887-7302
FAX (702) 887-7278

NEW HAMPSHIRE
Adjutant General
#1 Airport Rd
Concord, NH 03301-5353
(803) 225-1200
FAX (803) 225-1257

NEW JERSEY
Adjutant General
Eggert Crossing Rd Cn 340
Trenton, NJ 08625-0340
(609) 292-3888 X7
FAX (609) 530-7087

NEW MEXICO
Adjutant General
PO Box 4277
Santa Fe, NM 87502-4277
(505) 473-2402
FAX (505) 473-2489

NEW YORK
Adjutant General
330 Old Niskayuna Rd
Latham, NY 12110-2224
(518) 788-4502
FAX (518) 786-4509

NORTH CAROLINA
Adjutant General
4105 Reedy Creek Rd
Raleigh, NC 27607-6410
(919) 664-6101
FAX (919) 664-6400

NORTH DAKOTA
Adjutant General
PO Box 5511 Fraine Bks
Mismarck, ND 58502-5511
(701) 224-5102
FAX (701) 224-5180

OHIO
Adjutant General
2825 W Granville Rd
Columbus, OH  43235-2712
(614) 889-7070
FAX (614) 889-7074

OKLAHOMA
Adjutant General
3501 Military Circle Ne
Oklahoma City, OK 73111
(405) 425-8201
FAX (405) 425-8289

OREGON
Adjutant General
1776 Militia Way Ne
Salem, OR  97309-5047
(503) 945-3981
FAX (503) 378-3962

PENNSYLVANIA
Adjutant General
Dept Of Military Affairs
Annville, PA  17003-5002
(717) 865-8500 X1
FAX (717) 865-8314

PUERTO RICO
Adjutant General
PO Box 3786
San Juan, PR  00904-3786
(809) 724-1295
FAX (809) 723-6360

RHODE ISLAND
Adjutant General
1051 N Main St
Providence, RI  02904-5717
(401) 457-4100
FAX (401) 457-4338

SOUTH CAROLINA
Adjutant General
1 National Guard Rd
Columbia, SC  28201-3117
(803) 746-4217
FAX (803) 748-4329

SOUTH DAKOTA
Adjutant General
2823 W Main
Rapid City, SD  57702 8186
(605)) 399-6702
FAX (605) 399-6677

TENNESSEE
Adjutant General
PO Box 41502
Nashville, TN  37204-1501
(816) 532-3001
FAX (815) 532-3358

TEXAS
Adjutant General
PO Box 5218
Austin, TX  78783-5218
(512) 465-5006
FAX (512) 465-5578

UTAH
Adjutant General
PO Box 1776
Praper, UT 84020-1776
(801) 576-3900
FAX (801) 576-3575

VERMONT
Adjutant General
Bldg #1 Camp Johnson
Colchester, VT 05446
(802) 864-1124
FAX (802) 864-1425

VIRGINIA
Adjutant General
501 E Franklin St
Richmond, VA 23218-2317
(804) 775-9102
FAX (804) 344-4151

VIRGIN ISLANDS
Adjutant General
Fab Alexander Hamilton Arprt
St Croix, VI 00850-2380
(808) 776-4916
FAX (809) 776-5770

WASHINGTON
Adjutant General
Camp Murray
Tacoma, WA 98430-5000
(206) 581-1950
FAX (206) 581-8497

WEST VIRGINIA
Adjutant General
1703 Coonskin Dr
Charleston, WV 25311-1085
(304) 341-6316
FAX (304) 341-6466

WISCONSIN
Adjutant General
3020 Wright St
Madison, WI 53708-6111
(608) 241-6352
FAX (608) 241-6496

WYOMING
Adjutant General
PO Box 1709
Cheyenne, WY 62003-1709
(307) 772-6234
FAX (307) 772-6910

## State Guard

Several states have State Guard or Defense Organizations, which are not a part of the National Guard, but are volunteer military units that come under the jurisdiction of the State Adjutant General of the appropriate state. You must contact each state Adjutant General separately for information on their members. (See previous list for address.) Address your letter to

The Adjutant General, State of _____. There is no research fee.

**The following states have State Guard organizations:**

| | |
|---|---|
| Alaska | New Mexico |
| Alabama | Nevada |
| Arizona | New York |
| California | Ohio |
| Colorado | Oklahoma |
| Florida | Oregon |
| Georgia | Pennsylvania |
| Illinois | Puerto Rico |
| Indiana | Rhode Island |
| Louisiana | South Carolina |
| Massachusetts | Tennessee |
| Maryland | Texas |
| Montana | Utah |
| Michigan | Virginia |
| Mississippi | Vermont |
| North Carolina | Washington |
| New Hampshire | West Virginia |

For additional information, contact:

State Defense Force Association of US
213 Congress, Suite 339　　　　　　(512) 266-2350
Austin, Texas 78701

# To Locate Members Of
# The Coast Guard Reserve

The Coast Guard will provide assignment and unit telephone number of reserve personnel when requested by telephone. A $5.20 search fee is charged to provide a written verification of unit assignment.

Commandant                              (202) 267-0547
U S Coast Guard                    FAX (202) 267-4553
Locator Service (G-RFM-3)
2100 2nd Street, SW
Washington, DC  20593-0001

## To Locate Members Of
## The Coast Guard Auxiliary

The US Coast Guard Auxiliary, which has 40,000 members, is a non-military organization created by Congress to assist the Coast Guard to promote boating efficiency and safety.  Members of this organization wear uniforms and insignias similar to the US Coast Guard.  For additional information, contact:

Commandant (G-C) USCG              (202) 267-1077
2100 Second Street, SW             FAX (202) 267-4158
Washington, DC  20593-0001

## To Locate Members Of The Marine
## Corps Selected Reserve

Commandant                              (703) 640-3942
Marine Corps (MMSB-10)
Locator Service
400 7th St SW
Quantico, VA  22134-5030
(no research fee)

# To Locate Members Of The Marine Corps Individual Ready Reserve And Fleet MC Reserve/Inactive Reserve

Marine Corps Reserve Support Center
10950 El Monte                          (913) 491-7502
Overland Park, KS  66211-1408
(no research fee)

# To Locate Members Of The Navy Active Reserve

Chief of Naval Personnel                (703) 694-5011
Bureau of PersonneL                     (703) 694-3155
2 Navy Annex
Washington, DC  20370-5021
(3.50 research fee)

# To Locate Members Of The Navy Individual Ready Reserve (IRR) And Inactive Reserve

Navy Reserve Personnel Center           (800) 535-2699
4400 Dauphin Street                     (504) 948-5400
New Orleans, LA  70149                   (504) 948-5404
(no research fee)
(Do not put a return address on letter to be forwarded)

## To Locate Members Of Reserve And National Guard Through The Department Of Veterans Affairs

Members of the reserves and National Guard who have served on active duty in the armed forces are considered veterans. They may have applied for veterans benefits. Also numerous members of the reserve components are eligible for educational benefits under the Montgomery Act which is administered by the Department of Veterans Affairs (VA). These individuals may also be contacted through the VA (see Chapter Five for details).

## To Locate Someone In The Reserve Or National Guard Rapidly

The Nationwide Locator can provide the current reported home address of anyone who is in the reserve of National Guard, if you provide the individual's Social Security number. The Social Security number will be processed immediately and the individual's current address will be returned to you by mail or fax within 24 hours of receipt. The fee for this service is $30.00. For additional information, see Appendix B.

The Nationwide Locator          FAX (210) 828-4667
Post Office Box 39903
San Antonio, TX  78218

# Chapter Four

# How To Locate
# Retired Members

*This chapter describes how to locate retired members through the Armed Forces World-Wide Locators and other agencies.*

The Armed Forces World-Wide Locators will forward letters to retired members of the armed forces. These include members who have retired from active duty, the reserve or National Guard. Reserve and National Guard members do not become eligible for retired pay until age 60 and are usually members of the inactive reserve until that time. They may be located through the reserve (see Chapter Three).

# Retired From The Air Force: Active Duty, Reserve Or National Guard

This locator will forward only one letter per each request. Requests for more than one address per letter will be returned without action.

USAF World-Wide Locator
HQ AFMPC-RMIQL          Recording (210) 652-5774
55 C Street West, Room 50          (210) 652-5775
Randolph AFB, TX  78150-4752

# Retired From The Army: Active Duty, Reserve Or National Guard

Army Reserve Personnel Center
ATTN:  DARP-VSE-VS          (314) 538-3798
9700 Page Blvd
St. Louis, MO  63132-5200
($3.50 research fee)

# Retired From The Coast Guard: Active Duty Or Reserve

Commandant  G-PMP-2
Retired Military Affairs Branch          (202) 267-6641
US Coast Guard          FAX (202) 267-4823
2100 2nd St SW
Washington, DC  20593
(no search fee)

# Retired From The Marine Corps: Active Duty Or Reserve

US Marine Corps                     (703) 614-1901
MMSR-6 2 Navy Annex          FAX (703) 614-4400
Washington, DC  20380-1775
($3.50 research fee)

# Retired From The Navy: Active Duty Or Reserve

CO NRPC                              (800) 535-2699
4400 Dauphin Street              (504) 948-5400
New Orleans, LA  70149-7800                ext 5404
(no search fee)                  FAX  (504) 942-6934
Do not put a return address on letter to be forwarded.

# Retired National Oceanic And Atmospheric Administration Personnel

Commissioned Personnel Center
NCI N009 (CTC)                      (800) 224-NOAA
1315 F West Ave Rm 12100          (301) 713-3453
Silversprings, MD  20910        FAX  (301) 713-4140
(no search fee)

# Retired US Public Health Service Personnel

US Public Health Service            (202) 619-0146
Department of Health and Human Services
330 Independence Ave SW Room 1040
Washington, DC  20201        FAX  (202) 619-1851
(no search fee)                      (800) 638-8744

## To Locate Retired Members
## Through Defense Finance And
## Accounting Services

If a locator is unable to identify the person you are
looking for, you may be able to get some assistance from
the appropriate office of the Defense Finance and
Accounting Service (phone numbers listed below). These
centers maintain files of all retired military members
(active duty, reserve and National Guard) and Survivor
Benefit Plan annuitants (widows, widowers and some
dependent children). They can reveal the names and
rank/rates of retired members and annuitants to third
parties.   They can also forward letters to the retired
members and annuitants in a similar manner as retired
locators.  There is no fee for this service.

| | |
|---|---|
| Army | (800) 428-2290 |
| Air Force retired pay accounts | (800) 321-1080 |
| Air Force SBP annuitants | (800) 435-3396 |
| Marine Corps | (800) 645-2024 |
| Navy retired pay accounts | (800) 321-1080 |
| Navy SBP annuitants | (800) 435-3396 |
| Coast Guard & NOAA | (800)-772-8724 |

## To Locate Widows / Widowers
## Of Military Retirees

If you wish to contact a widow/widower of military
personnel who retired from the armed forces (active duty,
reserve and National Guard), it may be possible to have a
letter forwarded.   If the widow/widower is receiving
survivor's benefits from a particular service, the address
may be contained in the files of the individual service.
Not all widows/widowers receive these benefits, therefore

their address will not be listed. If the person is a recipient of these benefits, the Privacy Act prohibits releasing their address, but the service may forward a letter as they will for retirees. For more information, contact the appropriate finance center. The addresses and telephone numbers are listed in the preceding section.

## To Locate Divorced Spouses Of Active And Retired Members

Some former spouses of active duty and retired military members who have not remarried may be eligible for some military privileges, such as commissary, exchange and medical benefits as well as a portion of the former spouse's retired pay. Normally these spouses were married at least twenty years to someone who was on active duty at least fifteen years. You may have a letter forwarded to them in the same manner as mentioned for military members. Call or write to determine if the individual is listed in the Defense Enrollment Eligibility Reporting System (DEERS) automated files. The DEERS files contain the names and addresses of all former spouses and dependents of active duty and retired personnel eligible for military benefits.

The DEERS files also contains the names and addresses of all retired members.

DEERS Support Office
2511 Garden Road, Suite 260          (800) 538-9552
ATTN: Field Support                   CA (800) 334-4162
Monterey, CA 93940            AK, HI (800) 527-5602

## Retirement Services Officers

Most major military installations have retirement services/retiree activity officers who assist retirees of all military services in providing information on retired benefits and services. These officers deal closely with the retired military population and may be able to provide some assistance in locating retired members in their service areas. Call the base/post information operator for their telephone number (see Chapter Two).

## To Determine The Social Security Number Of A Retired Officer

The Social Security number of many retired officers and warrant officers may be obtained from the Officer's Registers that were published by the various armed forces between 1968 and 1980. See the Library section of Chapter Seven for complete details.

## To Locate Someone Who Is Retired Rapidly

The Nationwide Locator will provide the current reported home address of anyone who is retired if you provide the individual's Social Security number. The Social Security number will be immediately processed and the individual's current address returned by mail or fax within 24 hours upon receipt. The fee for this service is $30.00. For additional information, see Appendix B.

The Nationwide Locator                 FAX (210) 828-4667
Post Office Box 39903
San Antonio, TX  78218

# Chapter Five

# How To Locate Veterans Of The Armed Forces And Former Members Of The Reserve And National Guard

*This chapter explains how to locate veterans and former members of the reserve and National Guard through the Departments of Veterans Affairs (VA), the National Personnel Records Center, veterans organizations, military reunion organizations and private organizations.*

## Department Of Veterans Affairs

The Department of Veterans Affairs (formerly the Veterans Administration) will forward a letter in a similar manner as the armed forces (see Chapter Two). Before attempting to have a letter forwarded, it is recommended that you call the VA. You may call 1-800-827-1000 and you will automatically be connected with the VA Regional Office closest to you.   Tell the VA counselor that you wish to verify that a veteran is listed in their files before you mail any correspondence.   Give the individual's full name and service number, social security number or VA file or claim number, if known.   If you do not have this information the VA can sometimes identify veterans with either their date of birth, city and state that the person entered the service, branch of service, middle name or possibly the name alone, if the person has a unique name.   If the individual's name is listed in the files, ask for their VA claim number.

If the Regional Office cannot find the individual in their file, then contact the VA Insurance Office in Philadelphia at:

Department of Veterans Affairs          (800) 669-8477
PO Box 13399
Philadelphia, PA  19101

For veterans who have been separated for less than five years, contact:

Office of Service Group Life Insurance
213 Washington Street          (800) 419-1473
Newark, NJ  07102-2999

These offices have insurance information in their files which is not readily available in the regional offices files.

The VA does not have addresses of all veterans listed in their files; only those individuals who have at some time applied for VA benefits, such as educational assistance, medical care, disability compensation, pensions, home loans, and VA insurance.   The address in their file is the address given when the veteran last obtained or applied for VA benefits.

To have a letter forwarded, place your correspondence in an unsealed, stamped envelope without your return address. Put the veteran's name and VA file number on the front of the envelope. Next prepare a short fact sheet and state that you request the VA forward this letter to the veteran. Tell them you were given the VA claim number by their Regional Office. Also include all other pertinent information to ensure they can identify the veteran. Include as much information as you can such as name, service number, SSN, date of birth, city and state entered service, etc. Next, place this letter and the fact sheet in a larger envelope and mail to the VA Regional Office you spoke with, or where that office instructed you to send it. If they cannot identify the individual, they will return your letter to you. They will also inform you if the letter is undeliverable by the Post Office.

The VA is very cooperative in providing assistance in locating veterans. There are over 27 million living veterans. Of these, approximately 90,000 are veterans of World War I, more than nine million are veterans of World War II, almost five million are veterans of the Korean War and more than eight million are veterans of the war in Vietnam. The remaining five million are non-war veterans.

For additional information, contact the nearest VA Regional Office by dialing 1-800-827-1000. You will automatically be connected with the VA Regional Office closest to you. You may also contact the appropriate VA Regional Office through the addresses and telephone numbers listed on the following pages.

ALABAMA
VA Regional Office
474 S Court St
Montgomery, AL 36104
(205) 262-7781

ALASKA
VA Regional Office
2925 Debarr Rd
Anchorage, AK 99508-2989
(907) 257-4700

ARIZONA
VA Regional Office
3225 N Central Ave
Phoenix, AZ 85012
(602) 263-5411

ARKANSAS
VA Regional Office
Bldg 65 Ft Roots
N Little Rock, AR 72115
(501) 370-3800

CALIFORNIA
VA Regional Office
11000 Wilshire Blvd
Los Angeles, CA 90024
(213) 479-4011

CALIFORNIA
VA Regional Office
2022 Camino Del Rio N
San Diego, CA 92108
(619) 297-8220

CALIFORNIA
VA Regional Office
1301 Clay St
Oakland, CA 94612
(510) 637-1325

COLORADO
VA Regional Office
44 Union Blvd
Denver, CO 80225
(303) 980-1300

CONNECTICUT
VA Regional Office
450 Main St
Hartford, CT 06103
(203) 278-3230

DELAWARE
VA Regional Office
1601 Kirkwood Hwy
Wilmington, DE 19805
(302) 998-0191

DISTRICT OF COLUMBIA
VA Regional Office
941 N Capitol St NE
Washington, DC 20421
(202) 872-1151

FLORIDA
VA Regional Office
144 1st Ave S
St Petersburg, FL 33701
(813) 898-2121

GEORGIA
VA Regional Office
730 Peachtree St NE
Atlanta, GA 30365
(404) 881-1776

HAWAII
VA Regional Office
300 Ala Moana Blvd
Honolulu, HI 96850
(808) 541-1000

IDAHO
VA Regional Office
805 W Franklin St
Boise, ID 83702
(208) 334-1010

ILLINOIS
VA Regional Office
536 S Clark St
Chicago, IL 60680
(312) 663-5510

INDIANA
VA Regional Office
575 N Pennsylvania St
Indianapolis, IN 46204
(317) 226-5566

IOWA
VA Regional Office
210 Walnut St
Des Moines, IA 50309
(515) 284-0219

KANSAS
VA Regional Office
5500 E Kellogg
Wichita, KS 67218
(316) 682-2301

KENTUCKY
VA Regional Office
545 S Third St
Louisville, KY 40202
(502) 584-2231

LOUISIANA
VA Regional Office
701 Loyola Ave
New Orleans, LA 70113
(504) 589-7191

MAINE
VA Regional Office
Rte 17 E
Togus, ME 04330
(207) 623-8000

MARYLAND
VA Regional Office
31 Hopkins Plaza
Baltimore, MD 21201
(410) 685-5454

MASSACHUSETTS
VA Regional Office
JFK Fed Bldg Gov Cen
Boston, MA 02203
(617) 227-4600

MICHIGAN
VA Regional Office
477 Michigan Ave
Detroit, MI 48226
(313) 964-5110

MINNESOTA
VA Regional Office
Fed Bldg Ft Snelling
St Paul, MN 55111
(612) 726-1454

MISSISSIPPI
VA Regional Office
100 W Capitol St
Jackson, MS 39269
(601) 965-4873

MISSOURI
VA Regional Office
1520 Market St
St Louis, MO 63103
(314) 342-1171

MONTANA
VA Regional Office
Williams St & Hwy 12W
Ft Harrison, MT 59636
(406) 447-7975

NEBRASKA
VA Regional Office
5631 S 48th St
Lincoln, NE 68516
(402) 437-5001

NEVADA
VA Regional Office
1201 Terminal Way
Reno, NV 89520
(702) 329-9244

NEW HAMPSHIRE
VA Regional Office
275 Chestnut St
Manchester, NH 03101
(603) 666-7785

NEW JERSEY
VA Regional Office
20 Washington Pl
Newark, NJ 07102
(201) 645-2150

NEW MEXICO
VA Regional Office
500 Gold Ave SW
Albuquerque, NM 87102
(505) 766-3361

NEW YORK
VA Regional Office
111 W Huron St
Buffalo, NY 14202
(716) 846-5191

NEW YORK
VA Regional Office
252 7th Ave & 24th St
New York City, NY 10001
(212) 620-6901

NORTH CAROLINA
VA Regional Office
251 N Main Street
Winston-Salem, NC  27155
(919) 748-1800

NORTH DAKOTA
VA Regional Office
2101 Elm St
Fargo, ND  58102
(701) 239-3777

OHIO
VA Regional Office
1240 E 9th St
Cleveland, OH  44199
(216) 621-5050

OKLAHOMA
VA Regional Office
125 S Main St
Muskogee, OK  74401
(918) 687-2500

OREGON
VA Regional Office
1220 SW 3rd Ave
Portland, OR  97204
(503) 221-2431

PENNSYLVANIA
VA Regional Office
5000 Wissahickon Ave
Philadelphia, PA  19101
(215) 438-5225

PENNSYLVANIA
VA Regional Office
1000 Liberty Ave
Pittsburgh, PA  15222
(412) 281-4233

PHILIPPINES
VA Regional Office
1131 Roxas Blvd
APO AP  96440
(810) 521-7521

PUERTO RICO
VA Regional Office
GPO Box 364867
San Juan, PR  00936
(809) 766-5141

RHODE ISLAND
VA Regional Office
380 Westminster Mall
Providence, RI  02903
(401) 273-4910

SOUTH CAROLINA
VA Regional Office
1801 Assembly St
Columbia, SC  29201
(803) 765-5861

SOUTH DAKOTA
VA Regional Office
2501 W 22nd St
Sioux Falls, SD  57117
(605) 336-3496

TENNESSEE
VA Regional Office
110 9th Ave S
Nashville, TN 37203
(615) 736-5251

TEXAS
VA Regional Office
8900 Lakes At 610 Dr
Houston, TX 77054
(713) 664-4664

TEXAS
VA Regional Office
1400 N Valley Mills Dr
Waco, TX 76799
(817) 772-3060

UTAH
VA Regional Office
125 S State St
Salt Lake City, UT 84147
(801) 524-5960

VERMONT
VA Regional Office
N Hartland Rd
White River Jun, VT 05001
(802) 296-5177

VIRGINIA
VA Regional Office
210 Franklin Rd SW
Roanoke, VA 24011
(703) 982-6440

WASHINGTON
VA Regional Office
915 2nd Ave
Seattle, WA 98174
(206) 624-7200

WEST VIRGINIA
VA Regional Office
640 4th Ave
Huntington, WV 25701
(304) 529-5720

WISCONSIN
VA Regional Office
5000 W National Ave B-6
Milwaukee, WI 53295
(414) 383-8680

WYOMING
VA Regional Office
2360 E Pershing Blvd
Cheyenne, WY 82001
(307) 778-7396

## Mailing From A Roster, Muster Roll or List

The VA Records Processing Center in St. Louis, Missouri (do not confuse this office with the National Personnel Records Center which is also located in St Louis, MO) is responsible for research of large groups of veterans so people can forward letters such as a military unit reunion notifications or to secure statements to substantiate VA disability claims. They can work with copies of unit rosters, muster rolls and compiled lists which contains names and service numbers. Anyone may use this service whether or not they are a veteran. There are two ways to obtain information from the VA Records Processing Center.

First, you can submit a list of veterans names and service numbers (see section on unit and ship rosters in Chapter Six) or one of the following if you do not have a service number to help identify the veteran:

• Social Security number
• VA file or claim number
• date of birth
• place of entry into service (city and state)
• middle name
• name only (if veteran has a unique name)
• branch of service

Include a check or money order for $2.00 for each name to be researched, made payable to the Department of Veterans Affairs (personal checks are acceptable). The center will research the names and provide the following information:

• VA file or claim number
• VA folder location (VA Regional Office)
• If the veteran is deceased and date of death, if known.
• If the VA does not have a record, they will notify you of this. (veteran has never applied for VA benefits.)
• If they cannot identify the veteran from the information provided.

The information will be returned to you along with instructions on how to have letters forwarded to these veterans.  The letters should be submitted with the VA claim number listed along with the name on an unsealed envelope, with sufficient postage to cover mailing costs and with no return address.   Letters involving debt collections will not be forwarded.

The VA cannot assure that the veteran will either receive or respond to this correspondence.   If the letter is returned to the VA by the Post Office as undeliverable, the inquirer will be notified approximately five weeks after the letter is mailed.

The VA file number is sometimes referred to as the VA claim number and, in some cases, may be the same as the veteran's Social Security number.  Since June 1974, the VA has used Social Security numbers as VA Claim numbers.   Claim number in this category will have the letter "C" followed by the nine digit SSN without any dashes or spaces.

The second way to use this center's service is by sending the letters, names and payments together.   The center will do the necessary research and forward the letters. This process usually takes up to two weeks to complete; however, in peak periods it may take four to six weeks. Attempts to contact this office for status of this request may delay its processing.  This is one of the most efficient offices in the VA system.  Send rosters and payment or rosters, letters and payment to:

VA Records Processing Center
PO Box 5020
St. Louis, MO  63115

## Obtaining Essential Information
## From The VA By Telephone

There is a great deal of identifying information you may be able to obtain from the Department of Veterans Affairs (VA) over the telephone. Call any VA Regional Office and tell them you want to forward a letter to a veteran if they have his address on file (even if this is not your intent). Tell them there is no reason for you to send the letter if they do not have an address for the veteran. Ask if they can identify the veteran from the information you have. They can normally identify a veteran if you can provide any of the following: name and date of birth, Social Security number, service number, or VA claim number. In some cases, they can also identify the veteran by name only if the name is not too common. This is done by a surname search on their computer. It helps if you know an approximate date of birth or year of birth, service he was in, and dates of services.

If the VA Regional Office can identify the veteran, you may be able to obtain some of the following information: service number, date of birth, VA claim number, if the veteran went to college on the GI bill, the name of the college he attended and the dates attended. The VA must tell you the location of the veteran's file, whether it is in a Regional Office or in storage in a records holding area.

If the address is not over three or four years old, the veteran is probably living within 300 miles of the VA Regional Office where the file is located. Check with telephone information operators in cities within this radius. If you do a surname search with the Nationwide Locator against the National Telephone Directory file, you will most likely get his current address. If you are able to obtain a date of birth, then you can do a driver license or date of birth search.  With the veteran's service number, you may be able to obtain a copy of the military records which also has the veteran's date of birth, place of entry, separation from the service and other valuable information.  Also, with either his service number or his VA claim number, you can in some cases obtain his Social Security number (see paragraph below).

If the VA counselor you are dealing with is not cooperative and tells you they cannot give any information because of the Privacy Act, then discontinue your conversation.  Call again and you will get another counselor who will probably be more helpful.  Be persistent and courteous and you will sooner or later obtain some important identifying information that will enable you to locate the person you are seeking.

## To Obtain A Veteran's SSN Through The VA

You may be able to obtain a SSN for a veteran if the veteran applied for benefits after April 1973 and you provide the veteran's name, service number or DOB. Send a check in the amount of two dollars payable to Department of Veterans Affairs.  State in your letter that you want the veteran's VA Claim number (do not ask for the veterans SSN). If the number returned is nine digits then it is the veterans SSN. Mail request to:

VA Records Processing Center
PO Box 5020
St. Louis, MO 63115

# The National Personnel Records Center

The National Personnel Records Center (NPRC) will forward correspondence to veterans to their last known address (address in their military records when the individual separated from active duty or when the veteran's reserve commitment was completed) only in limited situations. These include:

- requestor's VA or Social Security benefits are dependent on contacting the veteran.
- veteran to be contacted will have veterans benefits affected.
- forwarding is in veteran's/next of kin's interest e.g., estate settlement.
- veteran's who may have fathered children.
- financial institution's legitimate effort to collect a debt.

A search fee of $3.50 is applicable only when the forwarding of correspondence is not in the veteran's interest, e.g. debt collection.  Make checks payable to "Treasurer of the US".

The NPRC will place the letter to be forwarded in another envelope and will add the individual's name and last known address.  In the event the letter is not delivered, it will be returned to the NPRC and you will not be informed.

If a person writes to the NPRC for assistance in locating a veteran and the reason does not fall into any of the above categories, then the writer will be informed to contact the nearest VA Regional Office (for requests of fewer than five names) or the VA Records Processing Center (for requests of five or more names).  Requests should have the name, SSN, service number or VA claim number. See preceding sections for details.

In July 1973 a fire at the NPRC destroyed about 80% of the records for Army personnel discharged between November 1, 1912 and January 1, 1960. About 75% of the records for Air Force personnel with surnames from Hubbard through "Z" who were discharged between September 25, 1947 and January 1, 1964 were also destroyed. Some alternate information may be obtained from records of the state Adjutants General and state "Veterans Service" offices. There are currently over 50 million military records at the NPRC.

National Personnel Records Center
9700 Page Blvd
St. Louis, MO 63132

# To Locate Former Members
# Of The US Coast Guard

In addition to the information provided in previous chapters, the Coast Guard will forward letters to former members of the Coast Guard at their last known address. There is no fee for this service. Send letters to:

Commandant (G-PIM-2)                    (202) 267-1340
US Coast Guard
2100 2nd Street, SW
Washington, DC  20593-0001

## Selective Service Records

The classification records of individuals who were registered for the draft under the Selective Service Act and information from ledger books are available to the public. These classification records list name, date of birth, draft classification, date to report for induction and in some cases date of separation. Records were maintained from 1940 to 1975. These records are maintained at various federal records centers (by state and county). All requests for information, if available, must be made through:

National Headquarters              (703) 235-2202
Selective Service System       FAX (703) 235-2245
1550 Wilson Blvd  STE 601
Arlington, VA  22209-2426

# To Locate Civil Service Employees

Thousands of former (veterans) and retired military are employed by the federal Civil Service because of military experience and hiring preference.

The Office of Personnel Management operates a centralized service that will locate most federal civil service employees except those employed by the judicial and congressional offices, US Postal Service, TVA, General Accounting Office, FBI, DCA and other intelligence agencies.

The only information that is permitted to be released is the name and address of the individual's employing agency, the location of his actual place of employment or the address of the agency's personnel office. The latter will provide address of work site if their policy permits.

To make the search you need to submit the person's name and social security number. Allow two weeks for replies to written requests. Telephone requests will only be taken for one or two names.

US Office of Personnel Management     (202) 606-2133
1900 E Street, NW
Room 7494
Washington, DC  20415

The following are the telephone numbers of the major federal agency's personnel offices that are not included in the above search:

| | |
|---|---|
| US Public Health Service | (301) 443-3087 |
| Central Intelligence Agency | (703) 351-2028 |
| Federal Bureau of Investigations | (202) 324-3000 |
| US Postal Service | (202) 268-2000 |
| National Oceanic and Atmospheric | |
|    Administration | (301) 443-8910 |
| Government Accounting Office | (202) 512-4500 |
| Tennessee Valley Authority | (202) 898-2999 |
| Congressional employees | (202) 224-3121 |
| Employees of Federal Courts | (202) 273-2777 |

You may locate Civil Service personnel or non-appropriated fund civilian personnel (civilian who works for military clubs, messes and exchanges) who are employed at military bases by calling the appropriate base assistance operator and asking for the telephone number of the Civilian Locator. (See Base/Post Locator, Chapter Two, for telephone numbers). These locators will provide work assignment and work telephone number. The Army World-Wide Locator also provides work address for all civilians assigned to the Army (see Chapter Two).

# To Locate Current And Former Merchant Mariners

The Merchant Marines is a civil organization and refers to the nations commercial shipping industry. It is not an armed or uniformed service of the United States. However, many merchant mariners and officers are members of the Navy, Coast Guard, and Army reserves. Graduates of the US Merchant Marine Academy at Kings Point, New York are appointed officers in the US Navy Reserve. You may locate them through the appropriate military reserve. The US Coast Guard registers all merchant seamen and will forward a letter to the last known address of the mariner. There is no charge for this service. The letter must be placed in an envelope with a stamp and no return address and mailed to:

Commandant                          (202) 267-0234
US Coast Guard (G-MVP-6)      FAX (202) 267-4570
2100 Second Street, SW
Washington, DC  20593-0001

or contact the following:

US Merchant Marine                   (310) 519-9545
Veterans of World War II
PO Box 629
San Pedro, CA  90731

or

American Merchant Marine Veterans     (813) 549-1010
4720 SE 15th Ave, Ste 202
Cape Coral, FL 33904-9600

In January 1988, a federal court decision awarded veteran status to all merchant seamen who served in

World War II (December 7, 1941 to August 15, 1945), so you may attempt to contact members of this group of merchant mariners through the Department of Veterans Affairs.

Merchant mariners must apply for a military discharge (DD 214) before than can apply for veterans benefits. This status does not qualify them for membership in some veterans organizations such as the VFW.

# Veterans, Military, And Patriotic Organizations

Veterans, military, and patriotic organizations can help in locating veterans and providing information about reunions of former military organizations. The service and assistance varies with each organization. Most have magazines or newsletters which publish names of veterans that people are trying to locate and dates that military unit reunions are being held.

The addresses and telephone numbers of the majority of the national organizations are listed below. When you contact them list as much information as you know such as: names, aliases, date of birth, dates of service, rank, service or SSN (see sample letter following this section). All listed organizations (except The American Legion) will provide locator service and/or will forward letters to present and former members. Usually there are no fees required for these services.

| Name/Address | Telephone Number | No. of Members |
|---|---|---|
| Air Force Association<br>1501 Lee Highway<br>Arlington, VA 22209-1198 | (703) 247-5810 | 200,000 |
| Air Force Sergeants Association<br>PO Box 50<br>Temple Hills, MD 20748 | (301) 899-3500 | 162,000 |
| American Defenders of Bataan<br>and Corregidor, Inc.<br>PO Box 12052<br>New Bern, NC 28561 | (919) 637-4033 | 5,484 |
| American Ex-Prisoners of War<br>3201 East Pioneer Parkway # 40<br>Arlington, TX 76010 | (817) 649-2979 | 33,000 |
| American GI Forum of the US<br>1017 N Main Suite 200<br>San Antonio, TX 78212 | (210) 223-4088 | 143,000 |
| American Legion, The<br>PO Box 1055<br>Indianapolis, IN 46206 | (317) 635-0411 | 3,100,000 |
| American Retirees Assn.<br>2009 N 14th Street # 300<br>Arlington, VA 22201 | (703) 527-3065 | 800 |
| American Military Retirees Assn.<br>68 Clinton St.<br>Plattsburg, NY 12901 | (518) 563-9479 | 14,000 |

| Name/Address | Telephone Number | No. of Members |
|---|---|---|
| American Red Cross<br>17th and D Street NW<br>Washington, DC 20006 | (202) 639-3586 | N/A |
| American Veterans Committee<br>6309 Bannockburn Drive<br>Bethesda, MD 20817 | (301) 320-6490 | 15,000 |
| American Veterans of WWII<br>  Korea and Vietnam (AMVETS)<br>4647 Forbes Boulevard<br>Lanham, MD 20706 | (301) 459-9600 | 250,000 |
| Army and Air Force Mutual Aid<br>  Association<br>Fort Myer<br>Arlington, VA 22211 | (703) 522-3060 | 55,000 |
| Army and Navy Union, USA<br>1391 Main Street<br>Lakemore, OH 44250 | (216) 456-7312 | 11,850 |
| Association of the US Army<br>2425 Wilson Blvd<br>Arlington, VA 22201 | (703) 841-4300<br>FAX (703) 243-2589<br>(800) 336-4570 | 150,000 |
| Blinded Veterans Association<br>477 H Street, NW<br>Washington, DC 20001 | (202) 371-8880 | 7,460 |
| Catholic War Veterans USA, Inc.<br>419 N Lee Street<br>Alexandria, VA 22314 | (703) 549-3622 | 35,000 |

| Name/Address | Telephone Number | No. of Members |
|---|---|---|
| Congressional Medal of Honor Society of the USA USS Intrepid Museum 12th Ave at West 46th St New York, NY 10036 | (212) 582-5355 | 210 |
| Disabled American Veterans 3725 Alexandria Pike Cold Springs, KY 41076 | (606) 441-7300 | 1,127,000 |
| Fleet Reserve Association 125 N West Street Alexandria, VA 22314 | (703) 683-1400 | 150,000 |
| Gold Star Wives of America 540 N Lombardy Arlington, VA 22203 | (703) 527-7706 | 11,000 |
| Italian American War Veterans of the US 122 Mather Street Syracuse, NY 13203 | (315) 479-8315 | 10,000 |
| Jewish War Veterans USA 1811 R Street, NW Washington, DC 20009 | (202) 265-6280 | 100,00 |
| Marine Corps Association PO Box 1775 Quantico, VA 22134 | (703) 640-6161 | 110,000 |
| Marine Corps League 8626 Lee Highway, Suite 201 Fairfax, VA 22031 | (703) 207-9588 | 34,000 |

| Name/Address | Telephone Number | No. of Members |
|---|---|---|
| Marine Corps Reserve Officers Association 201 N Washington Street, # 206 Alexandria, VA 22314 | (703) 548-7607 | 5,000 |
| Military Chaplains Assn of USA PO Box 42660 Washington, DC 20015 | (202) 574-2423 | 1,500 |
| Military Order of the Purple Heart of the USA, Inc. 5413-B Backlick Road Springfield, VA 22151 | (703) 642-5360 | 24,000 |
| Military Order of the World Wars 435 N Lee Street Alexandria, VA 22314 | (703) 683-4911 | 18,000 |
| National Amputation Foundation 12-45 150th Street Whitestone, NY 11357 | (718) 767-0596 | 2,500 |
| National Association for Uniformed Services 5535 Hempstead Way Springfield, VA 22151-4094 | (703) 750-1342 | 55,000 |
| National Association of Atomic Veterans PO Box 4424 Salem, MA 01970 | (800) 955-1186 FAX (508) 740-9267 | 4,000 |
| National Association of Fleet Tug Sailors 2905 Aurora Lane St Cloud, MN 56303 | (612) 252-1977 | 3,000 |

| Name/Address | Telephone Number | No. of Members |
|---|---|---|
| National Guard Association of the United States 1 Massachusetts Avenue, NW Washington, DC  20001 | (202) 789-0031 | 51,000 |
| National League of Families of American Prisoners and Missing in Southeast Asia 1001 Connecticut Ave NW Suite 219 Washington, DC  20036-5504 | (202) 223-6846 | 3,600 |
| National Military Family Assn 6000 Stephenson Avenue # 304 Alexandria, VA  22304-3526 | (703) 823-6632 | 6,000 |
| Naval Enlisted Reserve Assn 6703 Farragut Avenue Falls Church, VA  22042 | (703) 534-1329 | 16,000 |
| Naval Reserve Association 1619 King Street Alexandria, VA  22314 2703 | (703) 548-5800 | 24,000 |
| Navy League of the US 2300 Wilson Blvd Arlington, VA  22201 | (703) 528-1775 | 73,000 |
| Navy Mutual Aid Association Arlington Annex  Room G-070 Washington, DC  20370 | (703) 614-1638 | 77,000 |
| Non-Commissioned Officers Association 10635H IH35 North San Antonio, TX  78233 | (210) 653-6161 | 160,000 |

| Name/Address | Telephone Number | No. of Members |
|---|---|---|
| Paralyzed Veterans of America<br>801 18th Street NW<br>Washington, DC 20006 | (202) 872-1300 | 14,000 |
| Pearl Harbor Survivors<br>Association, Inc.<br>Drawer 2598<br>Lancaster, CA 93539 | (805) 948-1851 | 10,750 |
| Polish Legion of American<br>Veterans of USA<br>5413-C Backlick Road<br>Springfield, VA 22151 | (703) 354-2771 | 16,000 |
| Regular Veterans<br>Association of the US, Inc.<br>2470 Cardinal Loop B/217<br>Del Valley, TX 78617 | (512) 389-2288 | 18,000 |
| Reserve Officers Association<br>of the United States<br>One Constitution Ave, NE<br>Washington, DC 20002 | (202) 646-7715 | 128,000 |
| Retired Enlisted Association<br>1111 S Abilene Court<br>Aurora, CO 80012 | (303) 752-0660 | 54,000 |
| Retired Officers Association<br>201 N Washington Street<br>Alexandria, VA 22314 | (703) 549-2311 | 363,000 |
| Uniformed Service Disabled<br>Retirees<br>5909 Alta Monte NE<br>Albuquerque, NM 97110 | (505) 881-4568 | 2,000 |

| Name/Address | Telephone Number | No. of Members |
|---|---|---|
| US Army Warrant Officer Assn<br>462 Herndon Parkway, # 207<br>Herndon, VA 22070 | (703) 742-7727 | 4,000 |
| US Coast Guard CPO<br>(and Enlisted) Association<br>5520 G Hempstead Way<br>Springfield, VA 22151 | (703) 941-0395 | 9,000 |
| US Naval Home<br>(USN, USMC, USCG)<br>1800 Beach Dr<br>Gulfport, MS 38507-1587 | (800)-332-3527 | 500 |
| US Soldiers & Airmen's Home<br>3700 N Capitol St NW<br>Washington, DC 20317-0001 | (800) 422-9988<br>(202) 722-3337 | 1,700 |
| US Submarine Vets of WWII<br>862 Chatham Avenue<br>Elmhurst, IL 60126 | (708) 834-2718 | 8,000 |
| Veterans of the<br>Battle of the Bulge<br>PO Box 11129<br>Arlington, VA 22210-2129 | (703) 979-5270 | 6,900 |
| Veterans of Foreign<br>Wars of the US<br>406 W 34th Street<br>Kansas City, MO 64111 | (816) 756-3390 | 2,300,000 |
| Veterans of the<br>Vietnam War, Inc.<br>760 Jumper Road<br>Wilkes-Barre, PA 18702-8033 | (800) VIETNAM | 32,500 |

| Name/Address | Telephone Number | No. of Members |
|---|---|---|
| Veterans of World War I of the USA, Inc. 941 N Capitol St, Room 1201-C Washington, DC 20002 | (202) 208-1388 | 20,000 |
| Vietnam Helicopter Pilots Association 7 W 7th Street, Suite 1940 Cincinnati, OH 45202 | (513) 721-8472 | 5,000 |
| Vietnam Veterans of America, Inc. 1224 M Street, NW Washington, DC 20005 | (202) 628-2700 | 43,000 |
| Women's Army Corps Veterans Association PO Box 5577 Fort McClellan, AL 36205 | (205) 820-4019 | 3,400 |
| Women World War Veterans Morgan Hotel 237 Madison Avenue New York, NY 10016 | (212) 684-6728 | 40,000 |

## SAMPLE LETTER

December 7, 1995


Veteran Organization
111 Some Street
Sometown, USA  54321

Ladies/Gentlemen:

The purpose of this letter is to ask your assistance in locating my brother, John Paul Smith.  I have not seen or heard from him in five years.  It is extremely important that I contact him.

John was born on January 1, 1939.  He served in the US Navy from 1959 to 1964 as a Chief Petty Officer.  He was a member of the Naval Reserve from 1964 to 1968.  In 1968 he was appointed a Warrant Officer in the Transportation Corps of the US Army.

I would appreciate it if you would check your files and determine if he was or is a member of your organization.  If so, please advise me of his current address. If your policy prohibits giving out his address, please forward this letter to him.

If you do not have any records of his membership, would you please include a notice in your magazine or newsletter stating that I am trying to locate him or anyone who knows his location.

I learned about the services your organization provides in the book *How To Locate Anyone Who Is Or Has Been In The Military: Armed Forces Locator Directory.*

Thank you for your assistance.

Sincerely,


Mary Smith

# Military Reunion Associations

## Air Force and Army Air Force Associations

2nd Air Div Association
PO Drawer B
Ipswich, MA  01938

8th AF Association
711 S Smith Ave
St Paul, MN  55107
(800) 833-1942

11th Air Force Reunion
615 Stedman Street
Ketchikan, AK  99901
(907) 225-2121

Flying Tigers of the 14th
Air Force Assn
4847 Drumcliff Dr
Canton, OH  44708
(216) 477-0442

15th AF Association
PO Box 6325
March AFB, CA  92518

Bombardiers, Inc.
500 Jackson St #1407
Daphne, AL  36526
(334) 626-3920

CBI Hump Pilots Association
11010 Prairie Hills Drive, S
Popular Buff, MO  63902
(314) 785-2420

Hymalayan Flyers
PO Box 458
Omaha, NE  68144

Order of Daedalians, Inc.
PO Box 249
Randolph AFB, TX  78148
(210) 945-2111

Society of AF Retired Nurses
PO Box 681026
San Antonio, TX  78268
(210) 494-1096

Women AF Service Pilots
4300 Caledonia Way
Los Angeles, CA  90065

## Army Associations

11th Airborne Div Association
125 Lexington Dr
Clarksville, TN  37042-3651
(615) 552-7761

17th Airborne Div Association
825 Newberry
Bolling Green, KY  42103

82nd Airborne Div Assn
5459 Northcutt Place
Dayton, OH  45414
(513) 898-5977

101st Airborne Div Assn
PO Box 586
Sweetwater, TN  37874
(615) 337-4103

Society of the 173rd
Airborne Brigade
PO Box 27822
Washington, DC  20038

1st Armored Div Association
PO Box 211609
Augusta, GA  30917
(706) 860-6467

2nd Armored Div Assn
8053 Highpoint Blvd
Brooksville, FL  34613
(904) 596-6834

3rd Armored Div Association
PO Box 61743
Phoenix, AZ  85082
(602) 840-0398

4th Armored Div Association
1823 Shady Drive
Farrell, PA  16121
(412) 342-6058

5th Armored Div Association
13344 Luthman Road
Minster, OH  45865
(419) 628-4032

6th Armored Div Association
PO Box 5011
Louisville, KY  40205

7th Armored Div Association
23218 Springbrook Drive
Farmington Hills, MI  48024
(810) 476-0777

8th Armored Div Association
12834 Paintbrush Drive
Sun City W, AZ  85375
(602) 584-5967

10th Armored Div Association
Box 213
Bay Port, MI  48720
(517) 656-3551

11th Armored Div Association
2328 Admiral Street
Aliquippa, PA  15001
(412) 375-6295

12th Armored Div Association
1706 N Second St
Seward, NE  68434
(402) 643-4625

13th Armored Div Association
3702 Pennsylvania Ave
Charleston, WV  25302-4635
(304) 343-8288

14th Armored Div Association
42 Vestal Ave
Binghamton, NY  13903
(607) 724-1958

16th Armored Div Association
Box 15
Columbus, OH  43216
(201) 891-7433

1st Cavalry Div Association
302 North Main Street
Copperas Cove, TX  76522
(800) 234-9313

9th & 10th Cav Regiments
2602 Agnes
Kansas City, MO  64127
(816) 924-8192

11th Armored Cav Regiment
PO Box 999
Ft Knox, KY  40121
(502) 351-5738

11th Armored Cavalry Vets of
Vietnam and Cambodia
1602 Lorrie Drive
Richardson, TX  75080
(214) 235-6542

Society of the 1st Division
5 Montgomery Avenue
Erdenheim, PA  19038-8283
(215) 836-4841

2nd (Indian Head) Div Assn
PO Box 460
Buda, TX  78610
(512) 295-5324

Society of the 3rd Inf Division
163 Lyman Street
Westboro, MA  01581-2619
(508) 366-7029

National 4th Inf Div Assn
161 Vista Hermosa Circle
Sarasota, FL  34242
(708) 852-6507

Society of the 5th Division
2S 645 Ave Vendome
Oak Brook, IL  60521

Natl Association 6th Inf Dvsn
5649 South 39th Ave
Minneapolis, MN 55417
(612) 727-2326

7th Inf Div Association
7303 H Street
Little Rock, AR 72205
(501) 663-4622

10th Mt Div Association
5350 Yellowstone Street
Littleton, CO 80123
(303) 795-6508

24th Inf Div Association
120 Maple St Room 207
Springfield, MA 01103
(413) 733-3194

26th Div Vet Association
74 Argyle Street
Melrose, MA 02176
(617) 825-2626

27th Inf Div Association
20 Tyler St
Troy, NY 12180
(518) 272-5585

28th Inf Division Association
14th and Calder
Harrisburg, PA 17103-1297
(717) 787-6705

29th Inf Division Association
835 Dexter Rd NW
Roanoke, VA 24019
(703) 366-6575

30th Inf Division Association
13645 Whippet Way East
Delray Beach, FL 33484
(407) 499-5261

31st Inf Division Association
Route 1 Box 300
Ragely, LA 70657
(318) 855-7314

32nd Div Vet Association
615 Appletree Dr
Holland, MI 49423
(616) 396-6332

34th Inf Division Association
3113 Aspen Ave
Richmond, VA 23228
(804) 262-2084

35th Inf Division Association
PO Box 5004
Topeka, KS 66605
(913) 266-5516

36th Inf Div Association
394 Fenwick Dr
San Antonio, TX 7239-2419
(210) 656-7000

37th Div Vet Association
183 E Mound St Rm 103
Columbus, OH 43215
(614) 228-3788

38th Inf Div Association
3912 W Minnesota St
Indianapolis, IN 46241-4064
(317) 247-3447

40th Inf Div Association
210 Highland Avenue
Maybrook, NY  12543
(914) 427-2320

41st Inf Div Association
POB 2277
Beaverton, OR  90705-2277
(503) 646-7890

42nd (Rainbow Div) Vets
7430 Windmill Ln
Garland, TX  75044
(214) 495-6039

45th Div Association
PO Box 182
Pinetta, FL  32350
(904) 929-4026

63rd Inf Div Association
19W 565 Deerpath
Lemont, IL  60439
(312) 739-2449

65th Inf Div Association
123 Dorchester Road
Buffalo, NY  14213
(716) 886-2960

66th Inf Div Association
167 Jefferson Ave
Bahwah, NJ  07065
(908) 381-4216

70th Inf Div Association
5825 Horron
Mission, KS  66262
(913) 722-2024

71st Div Vets Association
6545 W 11th Street
Indianapolis, IN  46214
(317) 241-3730

75th Div Vets Association
4105 75th St
Des Moines, IA  50322-2251
(515) 278-0081

77th Inf Div Association
346 Broadway Rm 816
New York, NY  10013

78th Div Vets Association
1221 Brinkerton Rd
Greensburg, PA  15601
(412) 834-6651

80th Div Vets Association
20 Woodleigh Ct
Youngstown OH  44511
(216) 792-8089

81st Inf Div Reunion
713 N Bermuda St
Weslaco, TX  78596
(210) 968-6316

83rd Inf Div Association
3749 Stalheber Road
Hamilton, OH  45013
(513) 863-2199

86th Inf Div Association
5328 E Calle Redondo
Phoenix, AZ  85018
(602) 840-5783

87th Inf Div Association
2374 N Dundee Court
Highland, MI 48357
(810) 887-9005

88th Inf Div Association
PO Box 925
Havertown, PA 19083
(215) 533-9170

89th Inf Division Society
PO Box 489
Donnelly, ID 83615
(208) 325-8396

90th Inf Div Association
POB 730
Southhill, VA 29370

91st Inf Div Association
7822 16th Street, NW
Washington, DC 20012
(202) 726-6241

92nd Inf Div Association
834 Neal Avenue
Salina, KS 67401
(913) 827-9566

94th Inf Div Association
609 Dogwood Dr.
Downingtown, PA 19335
(215) 363-7826

95th Inf Div Association
8032 S 86th Ct
Justice, IL 60458
(708) 458-3047

96th Inf Div Association
7634 Field Street
Detroit, MI 48228
(313) 271-5778

98th Inf Div Association
PO Box 5894 Biltmore Sta
Ashville, NC 28813
(704) 274-4500

99th Inf Div Association
9675 Mockingbird Ln
Sebastian, FL 32976
(407) 664-4665

100th Inf Div Association
51 Ninth Ave
Carbondale, PA 18407
(717) 282-2285

102nd Inf Div Association
4 Pinion Pine Ln
Littleton, CO 80127-3502
(303) 979-4425

103rd Inf Div Association
8260 Moreland Road
Jerome, MI 49249
(517) 688-9249

104th Inf Div Association
721 Bryon Ave
New York, NY 11010
(516) 481-3804

106th Inf Div Association
448 Monroe Trace
Kennesaw, GA 30144
(404) 928-3207

196th Light Infantry Brigade
PO Box 531
Phoenix, OR  97535
(503) 535-7104

199th Light Infantry Brigade
PO Box 199
McLean, VA  22101
(703) 448-0199

Americal Div Vet Association
PO Box 1381
Boston, MA  02104
(508) 535-6793

Army Aviation Association
49 Richmondville Ave
Westport, CT  06880
(203) 226-8184

Retired Army Nurse
Corps Assn
PO Box 39235
San Antonio, TX  78218
(210) 824-0329

Society of Daughters of
the US Army
2410 Nemeth Ct
Alexandria, VA  22306
(703) 768-4357

## Marine Corps Associations

1st Marine Div Association
PO Box 220840
Chantilly, VA  22022-6840
(703) 803-3195

2nd Marine Div Association
21500 Lasen St, # 168
Chatsworth, CA  91311
(818) 341-0504

3rd Marine Div Association
7622 Highland Street
Springfield, VA  22150
(703) 451-3844

4th Marine Div Association
PO Box 430180
Kissimmee, FL  34743
(407) 348-5004

5th Marine Div Association
13016 155th Ave SE
Renton, WA  98056
(206) 255-5849

6th Marine Div Association
4857 Beacon St
Orlando, FL  32808
(407) 298-3056

Beirut Veterans of America
1410 Springfield Pike, # 31B
Wyoming, OH  452115
(513) 948-0058

The Chosin Few
4585 Orchard Ave
Ogden, UT  84403
(801) 479-8018

Edison's Raiders Association
(1st Raider Bn)
PO Box 980
Washington, DC  20044

Marine Corps Aviation Assn
PO Box 296
Bldg 715
Quantico, VA  22134
(800) 336-0291

Marine Corps Combat
Correspondents Assoc
1035 Hazen Drive
San Marcos, CA  92069
(619) 744-5423

MC Reserve Officers Assn
201 N Washington St # 206
Alexandria, VA  22314
(703) 548-7607

Marine Drill Instructor Assn
PO Box 400084 MCRD
San Diego, CA  92140
(619) 420-1809

Marine Military Academy
320 Iwo Jima
Harlingen, TX  78550

Retired Marine Corps
Musicians Association
100 Domain Drive
Exeter, NH  03833

US Marine Raider Assn
3005 Ridge Creek St
Las Vegas, NV  89117-0685
(702) 255-0601

Women Marine Association
PO Box 387
Quantico, VA  22131 0387
(703) 356-1527

World War II
  Marine Parachute Units
PO Box 1972
La Jolla, CA  92038

## Navy and Coast Guard Associations

Coast Guard SEA Veterans
Mid-America
18 Golf Road
Clarendon Hills, IL  60514

Destroyer-Escort Sailors Asn
PO Box 680085
Orlando, FL  32868-0085
(407) 877-7671

National LSM Association
PO Box 575
Raynham, MA  02768

Navy Seabee Vets
Box 190
Forest Hill, LA  71430

Patrol Frigate Sailors Assn
5272 Dorris Drive
Arnold, MO  63010

PT Boats, Inc.
PO Box 38070
Germantown, TN  38183
(901) 775-8410

Tin Can Sailors, Inc.
PO Box 100
Somerset, MA  02726

US LST Association
PO Box 167438
Oregon, OH  43616
(800) 228-5870

US Navy Armed Guard WWII
7115 Dunn Road
Cincinnati, OH  45230
(513) 231-3181

US Navy Memorial Founadt'n
Box 48817
Arlington, VA  22209-8728

US Coast Guard
Combat Vets Association
6858 Lafayette Rd.
Medina, OH  44256

WAVES National
444 Moore Rd
Pine Mountain, GA  31822
(706) 663-8253

## All Services Associations

Alliance of Women Veterans
3200 E South Street, # 710
Long Beach, CA  90805

American Gold Star Mothers
2128 Leroy Place NW
Washington, DC  20008
(202) 265-0991

China-Burma-India Veterans
Association, Inc.
1469 Magellan Circle
Orlando, FL  32818
(407) 298-4580

Counterparts Advisors in VN
100 Red Oak Circle
Temple, TX  76502
(817) 773-6520

Assn of Ex-POW of
  the Korean War
PO Box 120993
Arlington, TX  76012
(817) 460-4919

Korean War Veterans Assn
209 Country Club Dr
Rehoboth Beach, DE  19971
(302) 227-3675

Korean War Veterans
Memorial Trust Fund
8656 Park Lane # 2008
Dallas, TX  75231

Ntnl Assn for Black Veterans
3330 W Wev
Milwaukee, WI  53208
(414) 342-5000

Ntnl Assn of Military Widows
4023 25th Road N
Arlington, VA  22207
(703) 527-4565

National Assn of
  Radiation Survivors
PO Box 278
Liveoak, CA  95953
(800) 798-5102

National Congress
  Puerto Rican Vets
304 Park Avenue S
New York, NY  10010
(212) 260-3000, Ext. 353

National Incarcerated
  Veterans
PO Box 37
Atmore, AL  36503

Uniformed Service
  Disabled Retirees
5909 Alta Monte NE
Albuquerque, NM  87110

Uniformed Services Assn
1304 Vincent Place
McLean, VA  22101

Vietnam Helicopter Pilots
3700 Filmore
Virginia Beach, VA  23452

Women's Overseas
  Service League
11419 Whisper Valley
San Antonio, TX  78230
(210) 492-1205

The addresses of many reunion associations change periodically with the election of  new officers or reunion organizers.  To obtain the current address of any of the above reunion organizations or of the over 6,000 other reunion organizations, contact:

National Reunion Registry
  and Press Service
PO Box 355
Bulverde, TX  78163-0355

(210) 438-4177
FAX (210) 438-4114

## To Locate Former Air Force And Army Air Force Pilot Cadets

The Aviation Cadet Alumni Association was formed as a no-dues, non-profit endeavor to provide ex-cadets with current addresses of their former classmates.  Former Air Force and Army Air Force Cadets are invited to submit their flying class, primary, basic and advanced schools.  The association currently has approximately 30,000 names and addresses of former pilots representing classes from 1922 to 1962 (with a few latter ones).  Printouts of individual classes are available to participants who send their flight class, primary, basic and advanced schools along with a self-addressed stamped envelope to the address below:

Robert C. White
54 Seton Trail
Ormond Beach, FL  32176

## Veterans Association For Service Activities Abroad

Veterans Association for Service Activities Abroad (VASAA) was organized to locate and assist, if possible, families of former allies who were anxious to be reunited with relatives in the United States.  VASAA also has an extensive project to locate all veterans who are members of the Church of Jesus Christ of Latter Day Saints (Mormons).  These veterans may have served in any branch of the armed forces of their respective countries and during any period of time, whether on active duty or in reserve or National Guard status.  It has contacts with many organizations in the United States and foreign countries.  Since 1984, through United Nations programs,

VASAA has assisted numerous families to be reunited with relatives, bringing refugees from camps in Southeast Asia or from Vietnam, Ethiopia, Iran, and Europe.

VASAA                  (801) 278-7674
PO Box 17815      24-hour # (801) 840-2033
Salt Lake City, Utah 84117-0815

# Women In Military Service For America

The Women in Military Service Memorial Foundation seeks women veterans to include in its computer database. Authorized by Congress in 1986, the Memorial, to be built with private donations, will be located at the main entrance of Arlington National Cemetery. It will include a computer registry with the names and service histories of as many of the nations 1.8 million women veterans as possible. The data base will also include photographs of women in uniform and their own narratives of their most memorable experiences, if provided to the memorial. You can assist the Memorial by identifying women veterans for inclusion in the Register. When completed, the Memorial will become another resource for locating veterans, specifically women veterans. The foundation has registered approximately 100,000 military women. The organization does not release the addresses of individuals registered with the memorial, but can, on a limited basis, forward correspondence. There is no cost for this service, but donations are accepted For information on registration and how to donate:

Women in Military Service For America
    Memorial Foundation, Inc.      (800) 222-2294
5510 Columbia Pike St # 302      (703) 533-1155
Arlington, VA 22204      FAX (703) 931-4208

## Army Quartermaster Roll Call

The Army Quartermaster Roll Call preserves veterans' names, places of birth, dates of service, units of assignment and highest ranks or grades held in the U.S. Army Quartermaster Museum at Fort Lee, VA, home of the Quartermaster Corps.

The Roll Call's goal is "to be the only place in the world that preserves for public viewing, for all time, the names of the members of the Quartermaster Corps past, present and future."

For more information, write to:

The Army Quartermaster Roll Call
PO Box A
Fort Lee, VA 23801

## To Locate Former Military Doctors

Two medical directories that list the names and current addresses of physicians are recommended to disabled veterans who are trying to substantiate a claim and need to locate the physicians who treated them for their service-connected disabilities.

They are The Directory of Medicine Specialists, by Marquis Who's Who, and The American Medical Directory, by the American Medical Association.

Both references list a doctor's medical specialty and type of practice. The Directory of Medical Specialists also provides biographical information, such as military service, including a physicians service period, branch of military service, and former rank.

This biographical information can be particularly helpful to disabled veterans who can't remember their doctors first names.  Both directories can usually be found in large public libraries.  Another source that disabled veterans might find useful in locating physicians is the American Medical Associations computer data file in Chicago.  Veterans can request the address of a physician by writing to:

Data Release          Recording (312) 464-5199
American Medical Accooiation
515 N State St
Chicago, IL  60610

## To Locate Veterans To Substantiate VA Claims

In order to substantiate claims for disability through the VA, you may need to locate other veterans you served with in order to obtain statements concerning injuries and wounds.  You should do the following:

1.  Obtain the assistance of a Veteran Service Officer of an accredited national veterans organizations (e.g. The American Legion, VFW, Disabled American Veterans, AMVETS etc.).  They can help obtain rosters from the National Personnel Records Center, the Archives or the appropriate military service and assistance from the Department of Veterans Affairs. There is no fee for their services, nor do you need to be a member of their organization.  See your local telephone book for the listings of local veterans organizations.

2.  Obtain copies of your entire military personnel and medical records and rosters of the unit in which you

served when the disability occurred from the National Personnel Records Center. (Do not mention VA Claim on your request for medical records.) (See Chapter Six.)

3. Prepare letters to all the veterans listed on the rosters and send letters to the VA Records Processing Center for forwarding. Even if some of the individuals were unaware of the event, they may know the addresses of other former members of the unit. (See Chapter Five.)

4. To locate officers and warrant officers, obtain service number, date of birth or Social Security number from appropriate officers register. Have The Nationwide Locator do Social Security traces for all Social Security numbers located. For officers with service numbers, forward letters through the VA or do driver's license or date of birth search with name and date of birth.

5. For those veterans that the VA does not have an address and is unable to forward letters, send names of veterans to the Nationwide Locator and obtain addresses with the National Surname Search. (See Chapter Seven.)

6. Determine if your unit has a reunion group. Check with all reunion registries listed in Chapter Eight. If a reunion group is located, ask for the address of individuals desired or ask that your letters be forwarded to them.

7. Publish notices in all appropriate veterans organization magazines and newsletters as listed in Chapter Five.

8. Send letters to all appropriate veterans organizations and request that they check their membership for the

veterans you are seeking. Request that they provide you with their address or forward your letters.

9. Obtain dates of birth of remaining veterans from VA or from individual military records from the National Personnel Record Center and do driver license and date of birth searches. (See Chapters Six and Nine.)

10. For remaining veterans that are not located, contact local veterans organizations, mayors, newspapers, police chiefs, postmasters, high schools and churches in their home town, if known. (See Chapter Seven.)

11. To obtain address of doctors that treated your injury, (See Chapter Five.)

12. Send letters to the Social Security Administration and the Internal Revenue Service for forwarding. (See Chapter Seven.)

# Special Information For People Searching For Birth Parents

To locate a birth parent for someone who was placed for adoption may, in many instances, seem like an impossible task. But this is not always true.

Numerous birth parents who were in the military have been located, with the use of the information in this book, by individuals on their own. In addition, the author has located many other birth parents through personal searches.

In every search, it is extremely important to gather as much information as possible. But in searches for birth parents, it is vital to gather every scrap of so called relevant and irrelevant information. This information must be obtained from adoption agencies, hospitals, doctors, attorneys, friends, family neighbors and anyone who may have any information concerning your birth parents. Sometimes a small bit of information may be the thing it takes to solve a case. Records must be searched as well as newspaper files. Try to find old letters, photographs, phone and address books, medical information, etc. This information is especially valuable if the birth parent or one of his relatives was ever in the military.

There are 27 million living military veterans. That is one tenth of the population of the United States. The military has records on everyone who is or was in the service. Individual military records show when and where an individual was assigned, as well as other identifying information. Most of these records still exist and are located in the National Personnel Records Center, the Department of Veterans Affairs, military and civilian libraries, historical organizations and/or military reunion organizations. These records consist of unit rosters, muster rolls of ship's members, officers registers, morning reports, ships logs, troop lists, unit year books, photographs, lists of old Army and Air Force Post Offices as well as Fleet Post Offices, etc. All of these are excellent sources of information. There are also military records that show where units were stationed, where ship home ports were and where the ships traveled.

Birth parents have been located with such sketchy information as just a first or a last name. In other cases, birth parents have been located without a name, but with a unit, a ship, a military base, a picture, rank, military job, old letters, names of friends etc. Birth parents with common names like Joe Smith have been located in a short period of time.

Each birth parent search is different and, as a result, there is no set pattern or course on how to proceed on any particular search.

Persistence is the most important factor in a birth parent search. There is always information, but it may take many attempts to obtain the desired information. Never give up! If you persevere you will ultimately find the person you are looking for.

It is recommended that you read this book carefully and, if you have any question regarding so called impossible searches for birth parents who are or were in the military, write to the author for advice and assistance. It is importance to point out that this book cannot explain every search method nor every source of information, but there are many books that will assist you in your search.

## Someone May Be Looking For You!

If you are a veteran there is a good chance that someone you served with or your reunion organization is actively seeking you. If you do not belong to a reunion organization or a veterans organization you should consider joining one. These organizations are made up of veterans who have contributed time, money and effort to promote issues that benefit all veterans. By becoming a member of an organization you will make it easier for your unit reunion organizers and others to find you.

## To Locate A Veteran Rapidly

The Nationwide Locator can provide the current reported home address of a veteran if you can provide the individual's Social Security number. The Social Security number will be immediately processed upon receipt and the current address returned by mail or fax within 24 hours. The fee for this service is $30.00.

The Nationwide Locator can perform a date of birth search. If you provide the first and last name, approximate date or year of birth and Social Security number (if known), we will provide all matching names, city and state of residence. May be able to provide street address and phone number. The fee for this service is $75.00.

The Nationwide Locator can also do a surname search from the National Telephone Directory file. If you provide the first name, middle initial and last name, you will receive a list of names, addresses and listed telephone numbers of everyone in the nation with a matching name. The fee for this service is $30.00.

For additional information, see Appendix B.

The Nationwide Locator          FAX (210) 828-4667
PO Box 39903
San Antonio, TX  78218

# Chapter Six

# How To Obtain Military Records, Unit And Ship Rosters, Organizational Records And Histories

*This chapter describes how you can obtain individual military records, unit records and unit histories. These records are an important source of information in any search of a former military member, for a military reunion or for a family history.*

## Military Records Of Current, Retired And Former Members Of The Military

Current and former members of the military (or next of kin if deceased) can obtain copies of their complete military personnel and medical records. (Next of kin may be grandson, great-grand daughter, etc. in the case of military members who have been dead for several years.) A request should be made on a Standard Form 180 or by typewritten letter if the form is not available. There is usually no fee this type of request. It should be sent to the appropriate address listed at the end of this section. No reason is required for requesting the records, but all requests citing medical emergencies and VA claims are processed first. Requests by current and former military members or their next of kin should not cite the Freedom of Information Act.

To ensure that all documents in the file are provided, the request should state, in Section II Item 1, the exact items being requested. For example: "provide all information in my military personnel file to include unit orders, awards and commendations, any derogatory information, efficiency reports and ratings, promotion orders, assignment and reassignment orders, photographs and qualification records". Be sure to list any other documents the member remembers being in his records. Only those items specifically named will be provided.

To obtain a complete copy of health records, the veteran should state that he needs them for review by his physician. If he needs information relating to a specific illness or injury while in the military, he should ask for those documents pertaining to that illness or injury. Also, if inpatient (hospitalization) records are needed, he should furnish the approximate dates of hospitalization and the name or number of the hospital as these records are filed separately from the individual's military records at the National Personnel Records Center.

Due to the Freedom of Information Act, anyone (civilian or military) may receive limited information from the military personnel records of current, former and deceased members of the military. The following information (if available) can be provided.

- Rank/grade
- Name
- Duty status
- Date of rank
- Service number
- Date of birth
- Dependents (including name, sex and age)
- Gross salary
- Geographical location of duty assignments
- Future assignments (approved)
- Unit or office telephone number
- Source of commission (officers)
- Military and civilian education level
- Promotion sequence number
- Awards and decorations
- Official photograph
- Record of court-martial trials (unless classified)
- City/town, state of last known residence; date of that address
- Places of induction and separation

Place of birth, date and location of death and place of burial of deceased veterans can also be released.

Because of recent changes to the Freedom of Information Act regulations, the armed forces may not provide date of birth, official photo, records of courts marshall of members on active duty or in the reserve or National Guard.

Because of the Privacy Act, the general public will not be provided with medical information, Social Security number or present address of any current or former living member of the military.

A Standard Form 180 (SF 180) is at the back of this book (see Appendix C). This form or a photo copy may be used. If possible, this form should be enlarged to 8 1/2 x 11 inches. Additional copies of this form may be obtained from most veterans organization, military installations or from the National Personnel Records Center. For the latter you may call any of the three telephone numbers listed below and leave a message with your address on their recorder. A SF 180 will be mailed to you.

| | |
|---|---|
| Army | (314) 538-4261 |
| Air Force | (314) 538-4243 |
| Navy, USMC, USCG | (314) 538-4141 |

Request for records should be mailed to the following addresses:

# Air Force

Air Force officers and enlisted personnel on active duty:

Air Force Military Personnel Center
Military Personnel Records Division
550 C St West
Randolph AFB, TX  78150

Current enlisted member of the Air Force National Guard:

The Adjutant General
(of the appropriate state)
see Chapter Three for addresses

Air Force reserve:

Air Reserve Personnel Center
6760 East Irvington Place
Denver, CO 80280-1800

Discharged, deceased and retired Air Force:

National Personnel Records Center
9700 Page Boulevard
St. Louis, MO 63132 5100

# Army

Reserve and living retired members of the Army:

US Army Reserve Personnel Center
ATTN: ARPC-SFR
9700 Page Boulevard
St. Louis, MO 63132-5200

Army officers on active duty:

USA PERSCOM
ATTN: TAPC-PDI-MSR
200 Stoval Street
Alexandria, VA 22332-0400

Army enlisted personnel on active duty:

US Army Enlisted Records
and Evaluation Center
Ft. Benjamin Harrison, IN 46249

Army National Guard officers not on active duty:

Army National Guard Personnel Center
Columbia Pike Office Building
5600 Columbia Pike
Falls Church, VA  22041

Army National Guard enlisted members not on active duty:

The Adjutant General
(of the appropriate state)
see Chapter Three for addresses

Discharged and deceased Army members:

National Personnel Records Center
9700 Page Boulevard
St. Louis, MO  631325100

Army officers separated before July 1, 1917 and enlisted members separated before November 1, 1912:

General Reference Branch (NNRG)
National Archives and Records Administration
Washington, DC  20408

# Coast Guard

Active and reserve Coast Guard members:

Commandant
US Coast Guard
2100 2nd Street, SW
Washington, DC  20593

Deceased Discharged and retired members of the Coast Guard:

National Personnel Records Center
9700 Page Boulevard
St. Louis, MO 63132-5100

Coast Guard officers separated before January 1, 1929 and Coast Guard enlisted personnel separated before January 1, 1915:

General Reference Branch (NNRG)
National Archives and Records Administration
Washington, DC 20408

## Marine Corps

Active and Selected Marine Corps Reserve members:

Commandant of the Marine Corps (MMRB)
US Marine Corps
Washington, DC 20380

Individual Ready Reserve and Fleet Marine Corps reserve:

Marine Corps Reserve Support Center
10950 El Monte
Overland Park, KS 66211

Discharged, deceased and retired members of the Marine Corps:

National Personnel Records Center
9700 Page Boulevard
St. Louis, MO 63132-5100

Members of the Marine Corps separated before January 1, 1905:

General Reference Branch (NNRG)
National Archives and Records Administration
Washington, DC  20408

# Navy

Active officers and enlisted personnel of the Navy:

Commander
Naval Military Personnel Command
ATTN: NMPC-036
Washington, DC  20370

Discharged, deceased and reserve members of the Navy:

National Personnel Records Center
9700 Page Boulevard
St. Louis, MO  63132-5100

Navy offices separated before January 1, 1903 and enlisted members separated before January 1, 1886:

General Reference Branch (NNRG)
National Archives and Records Administration
Washington, DC  20408

Include as much information as is known about the individual, such as service number, name and service dates, date of birth, branch of service, etc.  In Section II Paragraph 1, put "request all releasable information under Freedom of Information Act" or include this statement if your request is made in a letter.  No fees are charged for Freedom of Information requests by the National Personnel Records Center.  Other agencies may charge a small research and copying fee. Requests may take from four to six months to be processed. The National Personnel Records Center receives approximately 200,000 letters and requests per month.

In July 1973, a fire at the National Personnel Records Center destroyed about 80 percent of the records for Army personnel discharged between November 1, 1912 and January 1, 1960. About 75 percent of the records for Air Force personnel with surnames from Hubbard through "Z" who were discharged between September 25, 1947 and January 1, 1964 were also destroyed. Statements of service and some other information may be obtained for these individuals from final pay vouchers. Also some alternate information may be obtained from records of the state Adjutants General and state veteran service officers. There are currently over 50 million military records at the National Personnel Records Center.

# Records From The Department Of Veterans Affairs

The Department of Veterans Affairs (VA) only has records for veterans who have filed claims. These records usually include identifying information about the veteran such as date of birth, date of death, addresses of spouse and children or parents, etc. Information of a genealogical nature for deceased veterans may be released to anyone if its disclosure will not be detrimental to the memory of the veteran and not prejudicial to the interest of any living person. Requests should be made in writing to any VA Regional office. See Chapter Five for addresses.

# Records Maintained By The National Archives

The following is a list of military computer records maintained by the National Archives. These records are available in either computer formats or in printouts.

- Repatriated Korean Conflict Prisoners of War File
- Repatriated American Prisoners of War File (VA), World War II, Korea, Vietnam
- Korean Conflict Casualty Files
- Southeast Asia Combat Area Casualties Data Base
- Korean War Casualty File - US Army
- Casualty Information System, 1961-81

See Chapter Ten for more details concerning the above casualty reports. All requests for copies of records must be received in writing and be accompanied by full payment. For fee and information requirements, contact:

Center for Electronic Records (NSX)
National Archives and Records Administration
8601 Adelphi Road                    (301) 713-6630
College Park, MD  20740-6001

# Unit Rosters And Ship Muster Rolls

Anyone can obtain copies of a unit roster or ship muster roll (list of personnel) or organizational records by requesting them from the National Personnel Records Center, the National Archives or the appropriate armed force. If the roster is needed to support a VA claim, there is usually no cost. You may obtain such records at a minimum cost of $8.30 (deposit) an hour plus a searching cost of $13.25 per hour if your request is for matters other than VA claims. Reunion requests receive low priority and will take more time to process. You may also make a "Freedom of Information Act Request" for a roster and there is no fee charged by the National Personnel Records Center and usually a small fee by the armed forces.

If you are planning a reunion or need the service number of an individual, a roster/muster roll is the place to start. The roster/muster roll will have name, rank and service number (if prior to July 1, 1969 for Army and Air Force, July 1, 1972 for Navy and Marine Corps and October 1, 1974 for Coast Guard) but Social Security numbers will be removed. Be sure to state in your letter the date of the roster/muster roll requested (e.g., May 1940) and that this is a "Freedom of Information Act Request" (do not mention reunions on this request). The National Personnel Records Center has copies of the following:

- US Army Morning Reports and Personnel rosters from November 1, 1912 to 1974 and all subsequent reports (including SIDPERS reports) after Morning Reports were discontinued. All rosters for Army and Army Air Force units for the years 1944, 45 and 46 were destroyed.

- US Air Force Morning Reports from September 1947 to June 30, 1966 when Morning Reports were discontinued. The Air Force did not prepare unit rosters.

- US Navy Muster Rolls from 1939 through 1966 (ships only).

Many of these rosters and muster rolls are taken from microfilm and the quality can be very poor because of age or fire damage. It is advisable to request rosters for several months before and after actual date needed. Unit rosters and ship muster rolls usually contain the names, rank and service numbers of assigned members. Prior to World War I, these usually contained name and rank only.

National Personnel Records Center
9700 Page Blvd                    Army (314) 538-4261
St Louis, MO  63132        Air Force (314) 538-4243
                      USN,USMC,USCG (314) 538-4141

Staff Daily Journals, After Action Reports and Operational Reports (lessons learned) from World War II, the Korean War and the Vietnam War are available from:

Washington National Records Center (NNRR)
Military Reference Branch
4205 Suitland Road
Washington, DC  20409

US Navy Muster Rolls from 1967 to 1975 are available from:

Bureau of Naval Personnel (PERS-093)
Arlington Annex, Federal Building 2, Room 4531
Washington, DC  20370-5000

Muster rolls for US Navy ships from 1800 to 1966 are available from the National Archives. The muster rolls through 1860 are contained within bound volumes and can be copied only as microfilm. The muster rolls from 1860 through 1879 are in the form of large sheets which can be copied as oversized electrostatic copies for $1.80 per sheet. The muster rolls from 1879 through 1900 are in volumes which were compiled on an annual basis (microfilm copies only). The muster rolls from 1900 through 1939 are also in bound volumes, with each volume containing from one to several ships' muster rolls for a limited time period (microfilm copies only).

The Records of the Bureau of Naval Personnel, Record Group 24, have 16mm positive microfilm copies of the muster rolls for US Navy ships from 1940 through 1966. Muster rolls list only the names of enlisted personnel and do not contain current addresses of former naval personnel or their survivors.

Some of the rolls do include the original place of enlistment. These rolls can be reproduced only as microfilm copies for $0.33 per foot of microfilm. Paper copies are not available, nor can less than a full roll of microfilm be reproduced. A number of images may be illegible due to the poor quality of the original microfilm which was transferred by the Department of the Navy. The original paper muster rolls were destroyed by the Department of the Navy after filming.

The muster rolls from 1940 through 1949 are arranged so that one ship is on each roll of microfilm. After 1949, ships and shore activities were assigned activity numbers, and the muster rolls were microfilmod oo that each role contains several activities for a limited time period, usually 2 years.

Do not send any money with information requests. Each requester will be provided an order form with the appropriate information listed, to use in ordering copies. All requests for information or copies of these records should be directed to:

General Reference Branch
National Archives and Records Administration
Room 13W
Washington, DC  20408

The National Archives also has custody of deck logs of US Navy ships from 1800 through 1945. The logs from the 19th century through 1930 are in bound volumes. Only microfilm copies of such records are offered as the process of making paper copies can permanently damage the bindings. The current fee for microfilm copies is $0.33 per image, which corresponds to a page of text.

The deck logs after 1930 can be taken apart, and electrostatic (paper) copies can be made for $0.25 per page. It is estimated that most logs of this time period comprise approximately 45 pages per month, although larger ships such as battleships and carriers comprise approximately 55 pages per month. The deck logs of this time period include a monthly roster of officers which lists name of officer, rank, and his next of kin.

For information on these deck logs, contact the National Archives at the address listed above.

US Navy muster rolls from 1976 to the present are available from:

Enlisted Personnel Management Center
Code 312
New Orleans, LA 70159

US Marine Corps unit diaries from the Vietnam War to the present are held by the US Marine Corps Headquarters. The records of the above period are not open to visiting researchers, however, interested persons may write to that office to request no more than three rosters for specific months and years.

Records Service Section
Headquarters USMC/MMSB-10
Building 2008, Room 203
Quantico, VA 22134-5002

Marine Corps After Action Reports and all unit historical records prior to 1963 are available from:

Washington National Records Center (NNRR)
Military Reference Branch
4205 Suitland Road
Washington, DC  20409

Marine Corps After Action Reports and all unit historical records after 1963 are available from:

Commandant
US Marine Corps
Headquarters USMC/HDH
Building 2008
Quantico, VA  22134-5002

The Reference Section of the Marine Corps Historical Center holds on microfilm muster rolls (1807 to 1949) and unit diaries (1950 to pre-Vietnam) which contain rosters. These records are arranged by month and year, and list the officers and enlisted Marines within a unit.  They were either submitted at the company level of command, or the battalion/squadron lovol of command.  The above records are open to researchers.  Interested persons may write to request one muster roll or unit diary roster for a specific month and year.

Marine Corps Historical Center      (202) 433-3483
Reference Section
Building 58
Washington Navy Yard
Washington, DC  20374-0580

# US Coast Guard Muster Rolls

US Coast Guard muster rolls are primarily those for vessels operated by the Revenue Cutter Service, which predated the establishment of the United States Coast Guard. The muster rolls are arranged alphabetically by the name of the vessel, and then chronologically, chiefly from the 1840s to about 1915. Some are a combination muster roll and payroll. The information usually shown is the name and rank of each officer on the vessel and names and ranks of enlisted men. Many entries show, for enlisted men, the place of birth, place of enlistment, salary information, and explanation of periods of absence during the month. Verification of the service of an enlisted man cannot be made without knowing the name of the vessel on which he served and his approximate period of service on the vessel. Most muster rolls are oversize one page documents and are copied for $1.50 per page.

The records do not include a name index to the muster rolls by name of enlisted man, but this information is available for line and engineer officers from about 1870 to the early 1900s. We also have muster rolls and/or payrolls up to the early 1930s for some shore units of the Coast Guard. No listing exists at present showing the holdings of muster rolls for shore units.

National Archives and Records Administration
Civil Reference Branch
Washington, DC  20408

US Coast Guard Muster Rolls from 1914 to the present for vessels, districts, life boat stations, miscellaneous units, and recruiting stations are available from:

National Archives and Records Administration
Civil Reference Branch
Washington, DC 20408

# Rosters For National Guard Units During World War II

Rosters of National Guard units that served on active duty during World War II, in some cases, may be obtained from the appropriate state Adjutant General's offioo, otate military hislui ical offlce, state military museum, National Guard association or from the appropriate military reunion organization. Rosters are also available from the National Personnel Records Center. See Chapter Five for addresses of state Adjutant General's offices.

# Unit Yearbooks

Numerous military organizations prepared yearbooks that include pictures and rosters of individuals assigned to the unit. Additionally, most Coast Guard and Navy ships prepared cruise books. During and immediately after World War II, many units prepared yearbooks which included names and photos of members who were assigned, those that were killed in action, and members who received awards. Many yearbooks also contain group pictures of members of their units and ships.

# Ship Passenger Manifests

Passenger manifests are lists of names of individuals (civilian or military) who were passengers on Navy or merchant marine ships. Passenger manifests prior to

1941 are maintained by the National Records Center in Washington, DC. The manifests for the period 1942-1955 were apparently destroyed. The manifests for 1956 to the present are maintained by the National Personnel Records Center. For fee and information requirements, contact:

National Records Center
National Archives and Records Administration
Washington, DC  20408

or

National Personnel Records Center
Attn:  Organizational Records Branch
9700 Page Boulevard
St. Louis, MO  63132-5100

# Partial Unit Rosters

Veterans of the Vietnam War operates a computerized locator service called "FIND-A-VET" for Vietnam veterans. Hundreds of veterans have been located through this service. A unit search will list all members of that unit who are in their computer files. To register or request a search (individual or unit) send a $1.00 donation.

Veterans of the Vietnam War, Inc.     (800) 843-8626
760 Jumper Road                        (717) 825-7215
Wilkes-Barre, PA  18702-8033     FAX (717) 825-8223

Seaweeds Ship's History sells histories of all US Navy, US Army Transports, most US Coast Guard and Liberty ships. They have partial, up to date crew rosters of the ships. They also have lists of sunken US ships. Lists are free with the purchase of a ship's history or $1.00 without an order. Include a self-addressed stamped envelope:

Seaweeds Ship's History          (304) 652-1525
PO Box 154-MIE                      phone or FAX
Sisterville, WV 26175               (800) 732-9333

## Military Historical Organizations

The following military historical organizations can be of great help in providing unit and ship historical information. While most cannot help in searches for individuals, many have names of unit and ship commanders, officer's registers, key personnel and other individuals who have made significant contributions to a unit's or ship's history. These people, if living, may provide the location of the particular person you are seeking.

These historical organizations have station lists, unit directories and order of battle information which can assist in determining the location of a ship or unit on a particular date. They also may provide designation of the units assigned to a particular city on a specific date.

Air Force Museum Foundation          (513) 258-1218
PO Box 1903                      FAX  (513) 258-3816
Wright-Patterson AFB, OH  45433-0624

The Air Force Museum Foundation publishes "The Journal" which lists Army Air Force and Air Force reunion notices.

15th Air Force Historian          Historian, Air Training Cmd
Travis AFB, CA  92535             100 H Street  STE 5
(707) 424-3241                    Randolph AFB, TX  78150
                                  (210) 652-6564
                                  FAX  (210) 652-4319

Historian, Tactical Air Cmd
162 Dodd Blvd  Ste 132
Langley AFB, VA  23665-1994
(804) 764-3186

HQ, US Air Force Historical
Research Agency
USAFHRA/HRS
Maxwell AFB, AL  36112-6424
(334) 953-5723
(334) 953-5733
FAX  (334) 953-4096

Air Force Historical Office
170 Luke Ave  Ste 408
Bolling AFB, DC  20332-5113
(202) 767-5764
FAX  (202) 767-5527

US Air Force Museum
1100 Staatz St  Bldg 489
W. Patterson AFB, OH  45433
(513) 255-4644
FAX  (513) 255-3910

US Army Ctr Military History
1099 14th Street NW
Washington, DC 20005-3402
(202) 504-5420 (unit histories)

USA Military History Institute
Attn:  Historical Ref. Branch
Building 22, Upton Hall
Carlisle Barracks, PA  17013
(717) 245-3611
FAX  (717) 245-3711

The Institute of Land Warfare
Association of the US Army
2425 Wilson Boulevard
Arlington, VA  22201
(703) 841-4300
FAX  (703) 525-9039

US Coast Guard Museum
US Coast Guard Academy
New London, CT  06320
(203) 444-8444

US Coast Guard Museum NW
1519 Alaskan Way South
Seattle, WA  98134

Marine Corps Historical Center
2701 S Capitol St SE
Washington, DC  20374
(202) 433-3483
(202) 433-3386

National Guard Assn Library
1 Massachusetts Avenue NW
Washington, DC  20001
(202) 789-0031

NG Bureau Historical Svcs
Branch NGB-PAH
5109 Leesburg Pike Freeway
Falls Church, VA  22041-3201
(703) 756-5770 (unit histories)

Naval Museum and
  Naval Historical Center
901 M Street SE
Washington, DC  20374-5060
(202) 433-4882
(202) 433-2585 (ship's histories)

The American Legion
Nat'l Headquarters Library
700 N Pennsylvania Street
Indianapolis, IN  46204
(317) 630-1200

Command Historian
HQ US Forces Korea/8th Army
ATTN:  SJS Historian
APO San Francisco  96301

National Archives and
  Records Administration
Washington, DC  20408
(202) 501-5402
FAX  (202) 501-5005

# Base And Post Libraries

Base and Post libraries can, in many cases, provide limited information concerning units that were assigned to their particular installation.  Unit histories, books about units, officers registers, morning reports, muster rolls, units diaries and journals may be available.  It is suggested you write to the individual library to request information and assistance.  If you desire to contact them by telephone, call the appropriate information operator listed in Chapter Two (Base and Post locator service) to obtain the correct telephone number and hours of operation.  You do not have to have a military affiliation to obtain information from these libraries.

Listed below are military libraries that have extensive collections of the military information listed above.  The majority have large collections of Officers Registers of their appropriate branch.  It is suggested you contact the information section of these libraries.

Air Force University Library
600 Chennault Cir Bldg 1405
Maxwell AFB, AL  36112-6424
(334) 953-2888

USAF Academy Library
2354 Fairchild Dr #3A10
USAF Academy, CO 80840-6214
(719) 472-4664
FAX (719) 472-4754

US Military Academy Library
Building 757
West Point, NY  10996-1799
(914) 938-2230
FAX (914) 938-3752

USA War College Library
AWCSL
Carlisle Barracks, PA  17013
(717) 245-3660
FAX (717) 245-3323

Ft. Sam Houston Library
Building 1222
Ft Sam Houston, TX  78234
(210) 221-4702
FAX (210) 227-5921

Marine Corps RC Library
Code C40RCL
2040 Broadway
Quantico, VA  22134-5107
(703) 784-4348
FAX (703) 784-4306

US Naval Academy Library
589 McNair RD
Annapolis, MD  21402-5029
(410) 293-2420
FAX (410) 293-3669

Library of Congress
101 Independence Ave SE
Washington, DC  20540
(202) 707-5000
FAX (202) 707-5844

Pentagon Library
6605 Army Pentagon
Washington, DC  20310-6605
(703) 697-4301
(703) 693-6543

# Military Magazine

*Military* is a monthly magazine that likes to say it "tells it like it was, and is - not like some bureaucrat would like you to think it should have been."

Published monthly, *Military* is oriented toward a readership of former service members from all services. Subscribers write the articles about their personal experiences in war and peace from World War II through Korea, Vietnam and right up to the present.   Also included each month is commentary regarding the current world situation from such military personnel as Lt. Gen. V

H "Brute" Krulak, USMC (Ret), Col. Harry Summers, Jr. USA (Ret) and columnist Reed Irvine. Intelligence reports compiled by the staff from sources in Asia, the Americas and Europe keep readers on the cutting edge of world events even before they happen. A free monthly locator service, along with a list of unit reunions and military book reviews are also regular features.

For the modest price of $14.00 per year (+ $1.09 tax if you live in California), twelve monthly issues will be delivered to your door. To subscribe, write to:

Military                     (916) 457-8990
2122 28th St.
Sacramento, CA 95818

## Army and Air Force Unit Histories

James T. Controvich assists individuals and associations in locating titles and reference materials concerning their units. He also prepares bibliographies concerning Army and Air Force units. He maintains the most comprehensive listing of published and printed histories available. Using his own large library as a base he is also familiar with the holdings of most military and institutional library holdings for those looking for specific titles. For assistance, send a self-addressed envelope or call after 7 p.m. EST. He also asks to be informed when authors or associations prepare new histories so that he can incorporate them into his bibliographic files and library. James Controvich is one of the most outstanding unit historians in the United States. For additional information contact:

James T. Controvich             (413) 734-4856
97 Mayfield St.
Springfield, MA 01108

# Records Of Civil Service Personnel And Military Dependents

The following information may be obtained under the Freedom of Information Act from records of most present and former federal employees:

- name
- present and past position titles and occupational series
- present and past grades
- present and past annual salary rates
- present and past duty stations
- position descriptions

To obtain personnel records of individuals who were employed by the Federal Civil Service, US Postal Service and medical records of dependents of active duty (Army and Air Force) and retired military personnel contact:

National Personnel Records Center     (314) 425-5761
Civilian Personnel Records
111 Winnebago Street
St. Louis, MO  63118

Medical records of Navy, Marine Corps and Coast Guard dependents are located at:

National Personnel Records Center     (314) 538-4141
9700 Page Boulevard
St. Louis, MO  63132-5100

Requests for retirement, insurance information or medical records of Civil Service personnel should be sent to:

Office of Personnel Management
Compensation Group
1900 E Street NW
Washington, DC  20415

# Chapter Seven

# How To Locate Anyone
# (Civilian Or Military)

*This chapter provides numerous ways to locate anyone, whether civilian or military. It explains how federal, state and local government agencies may provide assistance. The same is true of publications and private organizations.*

## Churches

Churches can be of great assistance in many searches. Most priests, ministers and rabbis know the addresses of their current and former members. Most churches and synagogues maintain records of membership, baptisms, confirmations, first communions, bar mitzvahs, weddings and burials. Also, many religious groups have church sponsored clubs and organizations which should be contacted for information. You should also contact other members of the church that the subject attended. If you know the religious affiliation of the person you are seeking, this can be a valuable place to obtain addresses and information (e.g., date of birth, former address, information concerning divorces, names and addresses of friends, relatives and former spouses).

# Colleges, Universities And Alumni Associations

The federal Family and Educational Rights and Privacy Act allows colleges and universities to release "directory information" to the public without the consent of the student. A student may request that all or part of this information be withheld from the public by making a written request to do so (but few do). "Directory Information" includes, but is not limited to, student's name, current address, telephone listing, major, date and place of birth, dates of attendance, degrees and awards received and previous educational agencies or institutions attended. Some colleges may release a student's SSN. Contact college registrars for this information.

College alumni associations try to keep current addresses of former students and most will either provide the address or will forward a letter. They also publish directories of former students (some list graduates only) with current addresses and employment. If the alumni association will not give you an address, then contact the college library, which will have a copy of the directory. They normally will provide you with an address or other identifying information. Alumni associations and college libraries will also have copies of yearbooks. which can sometimes provide the individual's legal name, hometown, degree and other information. See *"Peterson's Guide to Four-year Colleges or Accredited*

*Institutions of Post Secondary Education"* for additional information on this subject in the library section of this chapter.

# Congressional Assistance

If you are not getting results or answers from federal agencies or the military, you can write or call your United States Representative or Senator and ask for their assistance. Federal agencies and the armed forces are very responsive to inquiries from Members of Congress. You can expect a quick reply to your letter, usually within two weeks.

Include all the information you can about the person you are trying to locate, why you need to contact him, what steps you have taken so far and the results of these steps.

The telephone number for the US Capital in Washington, DC is (202) 224-3121. Tell the operator the name of your Senator or Representative and the state he represents. You will be connected to his office.

To write your Representative, the address is:

Honorable John Doe
United States House of Representatives
Washington, DC  20515

To write your Senator the address is:

Honorable John Doe
United States Senate
Washington, DC  20510

See your local telephone book for your Congressman's name and telephone number. It will help if you call the local office first and talk to the administrative assistant about the difficulties you are encountering.

# The Court House And City Hall

Government records such as deeds to property, automobile registration, marriage licenses, business names, voter registration, professional licenses, tax records, record of trials (civil or criminal) can be a source of information that can give you current addresses and possibly a SSN of people you are searching for. Military people often buy real estate near the bases where they are stationed. As they move, they usually rent the property and the tax bill is mailed to them. This information is public record. Check both the courthouse and city hall for tax and deed information. This is best achieved by mail, in person or through computerized search services. In many areas utility users (water, gas, electricity, cable television) addresses are available, if requested.

Most employees in local government offices can be very helpful especially if you tell them the urgency and reason for your search.

A trip to your local library can help you to identify county and civil jurisdictions as well as their addresses. This information is also available in the National ZIP Code Directory published by the US Postal Service.

# Federal Parent Locator Service

The Federal government will make a computer search of IRS, VA, and Social Security files of anyone who has a child support order against them. It will provide the current address of the individual, if it is listed, if you provide the name and Social Security number.

To obtain a search, you must first contact the State Parent Locator Service in the Child Support Enforcement Bureau of the state in which you reside. Check your local telephone directory for address and telephone number.

# Genealogical Libraries

The Church of Jesus Christ of Latter-day Saints (Mormons) has the largest family history (genealogical) library in the world. They also operate numerous local family history libraries in major cities throughout the United States. Local libraries can obtain endless amounts of genealogical information from the main library in Salt Lake City. Local libraries are extremely helpful to searchers. Many libraries have the Social Security Master Death Index, local birth and death records and excellent collections of local telephone books. For additional information, contact the nearest local family history library or write to:

Church of Jesus Christ of Latter-day Saints
Family History Department
35 North West Temple
Salt Lake City, UT  84150

# Immigration And Naturalization Service

The Immigration and Naturalization Service (INS) has duplicate records of all naturalizations that occurred after September 26, 1906.  Inquiries about citizenship granted after that date should be sent to the INS on a form that can be obtained from any of the INS district offices.  Local postmasters can provide the address of the nearest district office or check your telephone book.

For additional information, write to:

Immigration and Naturalization Service
US Department of Justice          (202) 633-5231
425 I Street, NW                  FAX (202) 633-3296
Washington, DC  20536

# Internal Revenue Service

The Internal Revenue Service (IRS) will forward letters for humane reasons to people in their files that they can identify with a Social Security number.  Such cases are:

• Urgent or compelling nature, such as a serious illness.
• Imminent death or death of a close relative.
• A person seeking a missing relative.

A reunion or tracing a family tree does not qualify as a humane purpose.   The IRS will not forward letters concerning debts.  If a letter is forwarded by the IRS and is undeliverable by the post office and returned to the IRS, it will be destroyed and the sender will not be notified.

If an address can be found, the letter will be placed in an IRS envelope and the addressee will be advised that the letter is being forwarded in accordance with current IRS policy. The IRS will not divulge the recipient's current address, nor any tax information, and the decision to reply is entirely up to the recipient. Check your telephone book for the IRS office closest to you.

### To Obtain An Ex-Spouse's
### Social Security Number

Individuals who are divorced and cannot remember the SSN of their former spouse may request a copy of any joint income tax returns from the IRS for a small fee. These returns will contain the SSN of the former spouse.

# The Library

City and county public libraries have a wealth of information for searchers. The same may be true of college, private and other specialized libraries. They are resources that should be utilized either in person, by written communication, by telephone or FAX. Visit your local library and ask the librarian for assistance. Tell the librarian what you are doing and you will definitely get a lot of valuable assistance. This is especially true for information in libraries located in cities where your subject once resided.

Many libraries take part in the Interlibrary Loan and the On-line Computer Library Center programs. With the Interlibrary Loan program, one library might be able to send the books or materials you need to a library closer to you. With the On-line Computer Library Center program, you can find out which libraries have what reference materials so you can go to that particular library. Ask your librarian for details and procedures.

Most military installations have base libraries and museums. Many have some information about the units that were stationed there. Call the information operator of the base concerned to obtain the telephone number of the base library and museum. Remember to ask for help from the library staff. They can be of great assistance to you in your search. See Chapter Six for addresses of military base libraries.

The following books and resources have proven to be of immense value to searchers. We have divided them into the categories of General Reference, Search Related and Databases and Microfilm Information.

## General Reference

*All in One Directory by Gebby Press* - contains addresses, telephone numbers and FAX numbers of daily and weekly newspapers, radio and television stations, business, trade, black and hispanic press and general and consumer magazines. This unique publication is used by professional public relations practitioners and professional searchers.

*Directories in Print* - lists the names and addresses of where to acquire membership directories of hundreds of trade organizations and professional associations.

*Directory of American Libraries With Genealogical and Local History* - provides a comprehensive listing of private and public libraries in the US which have genealogical and local history sections. Published by Ancestry.

*Directory of Associations* - contains the addresses and telephone numbers of thousands of associations in the United States. The associations vary from business orientated, veterans groups, professional and trade and numerous other types. This book is a great source to obtain addresses of missing people.

*Directory of Special Libraries and Information Centers* - lists over 15,000 public libraries and over 19,000 special libraries, archives, research libraries and information centers in the United States.

*Directory of United States Libraries* - lists all of the libraries in the country. Published by the American Library Association.

*Knowing Where to Look: The Ultimate Guide to Research* - contains numerous ideas on using libraries. Written by Lois Horowitz. Available from Writer's Digest Books.

*The National Yellow Book of Funeral Directors* - lists names, addresses and telephone numbers of most funeral homes and directors in the United States. Listings are by city within each state. This is a priceless source of information for searchers who are attempting to locate information about a deceased person. Funeral directors keep files which may list names and addresses of relatives and friends of the deceased. This is particularly valuable source if an obituary was not published or a death certificate is not obtainable.

*National ZIP Code Directory* - in addition to ZIP codes for every city and town in the nation, this book also identifies county and civil jurisdictions as well as their addresses. Published by the US Postal Service, this book is also available for use or sale at all post offices.

*Newspapers in Microform: United States* - a helpful reference in locating newspapers stored on microfilm. Published by the Library of Congress.

*Order of Battle (1939-1946 US Army)* - lists all major and subordinate Army units involved in WWII. Written by Shelby L Stanton.

*Peterson's Guide to Four-year Colleges or Accredited Institutions of Post Secondary Education* - useful if you wish to obtain the address of an alumni association or a college library. If either group does not have a record of your subject, you may place a "locator notice" in the alumni publication.

*US Military Museums, Historic Sites and Exhibits*, by Bruce D. Thompson and published by Military Living, is one of the most comprehensive books available on this subject. It includes listings of Air Force, Army, Coast Guard, Marine Corps, Navy and NOAA museums in the United States and overseas. It also lists all American military cemeteries and military sites in the National Park System. This 300 page book is a must for people doing military research, reunion planning or who have an interest in our country's military history.

*US War Ships of WWII* - A complete list of Army, Navy and Coast Guard ships used during WWII. Includes dates of commissioning and de-commissioning, and disposition of each de-commissioned ship. Written by Paul H Silverstone. Published by the Naval Institute Press.

*US War Ships Since 1945* - A complete list of Army, Navy and Coast Guard ships used since 1945. Includes dates of commissioning and de-commissioning, and disposition of each de-commissioned ship. Written by Paul H Silverstone. Published by the Naval Institute Press.

*Vietnam Order of Battle: Army and Allied Ground Forces and Air Force Units (1961-1973)* - lists all major and subordinate Army and Air Force units involved in the Vietnam war. Written by Shelby L Stanton.

**Maps and Atlases** - often a map is a valuable tool in a search to determine the location of a street or even the location of a city. Libraries have abundant maps that may be useful in your search.

### Search Related

*City Directories* and *Crisscross Directories* - public libraries, especially larger systems, maintain collections of city directories and criss-cross directories of their city and surrounding cities. These two directories can be some of your best search tools. Began with the edition for the last year you knew your subject lived in a particular city. Check more current editions to find the last year he is listed and at which address. You can then identify neighbors or former neighbors who might know where the person you are looking for now lives. You can also do a computer address update if the address is not over ten years old. Call or write the library and ask them to search for you. In the event they will not search, ask them for names of local researchers you can contact. Also see "People Searching News" in Chapter Seven for additional information on researchers.

*Telephone Books* - many libraries maintain collections of old telephone books for their city and surrounding area. These telephone books can provide old addresses of your subject and often names and former addresses of spouses, children and other relatives. They are also sources of names of former employers (individual and business names). Use these books in conjunction with your search of city directories.

*Biographic Register* - annual list (register) of civil service employees published by the Department of State. It includes biographic information on State Department employees as well as personnel of the Agency for International Development, the Peace Corps, the Foreign Agricultural Service, and the United States Information Agency. Many registers include date and place of birth, colleges attended, foreign service posts, and spouse's name.

*Birthright: The Guide to Search and Reunion for Adoptees, Birthparents and Adoptive Parents* - excellent resource for anyone trying to find a birth parent, adoptive parent or a child who was adopted. Written by Jean A. S. Strauss. It is published by Penguin Books.

*Dictionary of Surnames* - in the event you are not sure of the spelling of a surname, this book by Patrick Hanks and Flavia Hodges has alternate spellings of thousands of surnames. It also explains the origin and meaning of over 70,000 surnames.

*Find Anyone Fast* - essential resource on locating missing people. Hundreds of current search techniques are explained as well as how to organize and conduct a search. Also includes computer searches that are available to the public. Written by Richard S. Johnson. Available from MIE Publishing.

*Foreign Service Lists* - directories of Foreign Service officers that are published three times a year by the Department of State. They list field staffs of the US Foreign Service, the US Information Agency, AID, the Peace Corps, the Foreign Agricultural Service. A brief job title appears, as well as date arrived in the country they are assigned and their civil service grade.

*Military Officers Registers* - excellent resource for obtaining information on individuals who served as officers and warrant officers in the armed forces. Each branch of the service published a register of regular, reserved and retired officers annually. Earlier editions contain name, rank, service number, DOB, colleges and universities attended and some assignment information. Later editions (1968-80) list name, rank, SSN, DOB and other miscellaneous service data. Registers were discontinued in 1981 due to the Privacy Act. Some copies are available on microfiche.

*US Air Force Register* -- annual list of commissioned retired officers -- active and retired. Includes service number (pre mid-1969) or Social Security number and date of birth.

*US Army Register* -- yearly lists of active, reserve and retired officers. Lists service number (pre mid-1969) or Social Security number and date of birth. Pre-1969 active lists include state of birth and military training.

*Register of Commissioned and Warrant Officers -- Navy and Marine Corps and Reserve Officers on Active Duty -- of the United States Naval Reserve*

*Register of Retired Commissioned and Warrant Officers, Regular and Reserve of the United States Navy and Marine Corps* -- annual lists that include service number (pre 1972) or Social Security number and date of birth.

*Directories of Alumni* of the military academies:

The *Register of Graduates of the United States Air Force Academy* has begun to appear in a "condensed" version. The 1989 register is the most recent "complete" version. It contained date of birth, full biographical sketches listing awards, decorations and special honors. Wife's name and notations indicating most recently known place of employment may appear. Rank, reserve status, year and circumstance of leaving service also may appear. Names of deceased alumni appear in italics. The 1994 Register will contain complete historical biographic information.**

The *Register of Graduates and Former Cadets of the United States Military Academy* includes state and date of birth. Every effort has been made to include awards, separation dates and ranks, prior military service, colleges and degrees earned, current address and current employment. Deceased graduate's names are printed in italics.

The *Register of Alumni: Graduates and Former Naval Cadets and Midshipmen* includes date and place of birth, last known address, decorations and awards, special assignments, retirements and rank attained. Marine Corps officers are designated. A letter "D" denotes deceased alumni. If known, the name and address of the widow is included.

*The MVR Book: Motor Services Guide* - describes in detail where and how to obtain driver and vehicle registration records in all states. This is one of the outstanding and easy to use public records research books published by BRB Publications. Check this book before attempting to locate people through state drivers license and MVR offices.

Register of Doctors - *The Directory of Medical Specialists* by Marquis Who's Who and *The American Medical Directory* published by the American Medical Association.

Medical Associations are excellent resources to locate doctors. Also state and county medical associations often publish registers and directories of their members. In addition to names, these books also provide information on medical specialty, schooling, business address and other useful information to searchers.

*The Sourcebook of Federal Courts: U.S. District and Bankruptcy* - provides complete information on how to obtain criminal and civil court records and bankruptcy files from federal courts. It outlines jurisdictions and boundaries of these courts. Federal court records can provide addresses of your subject as well as other individuals who have knowledge of his former and present locations. Another excellent source book for searchers published by BRB Publications.

*The Sourcebook of State Public Records* - explains how to obtain records at the state level for business records, liens and security interest records (UCC), criminal records, workers compensation and vital records, MVR, occupational licensing, and business names and permits. Another essential reference book for searchers published by the experts in the public records field, BRB Publications.

*Who's Who in America* series - this series of books contains thousands of names and additional information on prominent people in several different career fields.

## Database and Microfilm Information

The following resources and assets have proven to be of immense value to searchers. There are numerous other resources available in libraries that can be of assistance also.

**Computer Files and Searches** - the National Telephone Directory and the Social Security Master Death Index. Some larger libraries have these CD-ROM databases. The National Telephone Directory contains over 80 million listings of people who have listed telephone numbers. The Social Security Master Death Index lists over 60 million people who have died since 1962.

**Draft Registration Records** - some libraries have copies of draft registration records of the county where they are located for World War I, II, Korean and Vietnam wars. These records contain legal names, addresses and DOB.

**Voter Registration Records** - libraries may have access to many years of voter registration lists from the board of elections (voter registration offices) of their local area. Most of these records contain legal names, addresses, DOB and SSN of registered voters.

**Microfilm and microfiche files of Real Estate Owners** - lists (current and old) of real estate owners is often available in local libraries. This data is usually indexed by name and address.

**Newsbank** - most libraries have access to local newspaper indexes that may list the name of the person you are seeking. In addition to news articles, names may be listed under birth, engagements, marriages, divorces funeral and death announcements. Many libraries can search national databases available through vendors. Searches can be made for an individual whose name appears in a major newspaper or who may be an officer of a company (even a sole proprietorship). Check with your librarian concerning capabilities for searches and fees.

**Newspaper Obituary Files** - most libraries maintain an obituary file of local deaths. This information is usually obtained from local newspapers and goes back many years. Most libraries will respond to telephone request for information from these files. Others will only respond to a written request and some require a search fee. Their response time is usually a few days and some libraries will FAX you the requested information. The information section is usually the place where the obituary file is kept, however some libraries keep it in their genealogical section.

**PHONEFICHE** - many main libraries have most of the complete telephone directories of cities in the nation on microfiche. In the event the library does not have the National Telephone Directory on CD-ROM, this is a good alternative source of addresses and telephone numbers. The disadvantage is that you must look through each city for listings and addresses. You cannot do a national search with this system as you can with the CD-ROM version of the telephone files.

# To Locate Military Dependents

Sometimes the best way to contact or locate an individual is by first locating their children. The following organizations may be of help.

## Military Brats of America

Military Brats of America (MBA) is an organization for all current and former armed forces dependents, foreign service dependents, and spouses of either. Members network together, provide detailed background information about duty tours and schools, publish a newsletter, plan events and participate in charitable activities. MBA is also compiling a comprehensive roster of all Military Brats from 1930 through the present. The roster will become accessible by telephone in 1996.

MBA also sponsors the MBA electronic bulletin board on America Online which is accessed by over 112,000 military brats. The MBA bulletin board lists reunion information, a locator service for individuals and dozens of topics of interest. Their EMAIL address is USBRATS@AOL.COM

For additional information, please contact:

Military Brats of America
POB 1165 LD
New York, NY 10159

### Overseas Brats

Overseas Brats was founded in 1986 as a service organization. It acts as an umbrella organization for the over 200 alumni associations of overseas American private, State Department and Department of Defense high schools. The combined membership of former students and faculty members totals more than 60,000.

While the Overseas Brats organization does not maintain a list of individual students, it does maintain a list of active alumni associations. Requests for specific alumni associations can be made to:

Overseas Brats                    (210) 349-1394
PO Box 29805 DJ
San Antonio, TX 78229

## American Overseas Schools Archives

The American Overseas Schools Archives maintains memorabilia pertaining to all aspects of kindergarten through fourteenth grade education of American children abroad.   The Archives has yearbooks, scrapbooks, curricula, newspaper, magazine and journal articles, photographs, official papers and documents, personal histories and memorabelia of all kinds.   For more information, contact:

American Overseas Schools Archives
University of Northern Arizona          (602) 523-2611
Box 5774                                 FAX  (602) 523-1929
Flagstaff, AZ  86011-5774

# Newspapers And Magazines

There are several periodicals which may be of assistance in locating missing people.   When seeking military or former military people, the following weekly newspapers are recommended: *Army Times, Navy Times, Air Force Times and Federal Times.* These are the most popular and most widely read newspapers of the Armed Services and Civil Service personnel.   Federal Times is read primarily by present and former Civil Servants, a large portion of whom are military veterans, retired military or members of the Reserve Components. *Army Times, Navy Times, Air Force Times and Federal Times* have locator columns that may help you.   Readers include current military members, but also many reserve, National Guard, retired and former members.   You will probably get a response to any published assistance you request. Following is the address for all the newspapers:

Army Times Publishing Co.          (800) 424-9335
6883 Commercial Drive
Springfield, VA  22159

The largest veteran oriented newspaper in the United States is *Stars and Stripes: The National Tribune.* When seeking a veteran or publicizing a reunion this publication should be considered.

> *Stars and Stripes:*                     (202) 829-3225
> *The National Tribune*          FAX (202) 829-5657
> PO Box 1803
> Washington, DC  20013

The *Airborne Static Line* is a monthly publication for, by and about paratroopers and men with airborne hearts. This publication is dedicated to the perpetuation of the airborne ideals of brotherhood, fellowship and camaraderie established in warfare, strife and duress of combat.    Published 12 times per year, dues for this publication are $25 per year.

The Airborne Static Line publishes a locator column in every edition.

> *Airborne Static Line*                    (404) 478-5301
> PO Box 87518
> College Park, GA  30337

Also an effective newspaper is the one sold in the last known location where the person you are seeking lived. Place an advertisement in the personal section. Thousands of people read the classified section and you may get a response.   Write an advertisement similar to the following:

> Chief Master Sgt. Joe L. James
> Urgent, anyone who knows his
> whereabouts call collect (513) 555-5555

A letter to the editor of a small town newspaper will usually bring you some help in your search. Your local library can give you names and addresses of newspapers that you will need to contact, from *Gale's Directory of Publications.*

*People Searching News (PSN)* is an excellent magazine with emphasis on adoption and missing person searches ($18.00 - six issues per year; sample copy + registry forms - $6.95). *PSN* sells a variety of search books and can offer the services of more than 1,000 researchers world-wide. *PSN* also has a large "in-search-of" classified ad section; subscribers are likely to offer you help and information. Their no-fee search hot-line is (407) 768-2222.

*People Searching News*
PO Box 100444
Palm Bay, FL  32910-0444

## To Locate People In Prison

All states operate prison locators. These locators are usually operated by the State Department of Corrections. Telephone the information operator in the appropriate state capital. If the individual you are looking for may be in a federal prison, telephone the US prison federal locator at (202) 307-3126 (aliases may be available). To determine if a former military member is or has been imprisoned in the US Disciplinary Barracks (military prison) at Ft. Levenworth, Kansas, call (913) 684-4629. Most prison locators keep records of former inmates for up to ten years. Surname searches may be completed without date of birth or Social Security number.

# To Locate People
# Traveling Overseas

To locate US citizens traveling abroad call the State Department's Citizens Emergency Center: (202) 647-5225.

# To Locate People Who Are Due
# Unclaimed Assets

There are numerous companies that search for people who are heirs or who are eligible to receive unclaimed assets held by probate courts and state unclaimed property offices. These companies receive a percentage of all moneys recovered by the persons they locate. You may wish to contact the author if unclaimed assets are involved. The author searches for people due unclaimed assets and has located individuals who have received millions of dollars of inheritances and other unclaimed moneys. See Chapter Twelve for information and address.

# To Locate Pilots Who Are
# Licensed By The FAA

The Federal Aviation Administration (FAA) will provide a pilot's current address if you provide the name and date of birth or a SSN or a certificate number. If the name is unique, they can provide the information without these identifying items. The pilot's records are annotated with the name and address of the person who requested the information.

FAA Airmen Certification Branch, AVN-460
PO Box 25082                                    (405) 954-3261
Oklahoma City, OK  73125

# The US Postal Service

For many years you could obtain an individual's new address from the US Post Office under the FOIA if the individual had submitted a change of address card.  This practice was discontinued as of April 1994.  However, the US Postal Change of Address file is still available to credit bureaus, other information providers and in many computer databases (see Chapter Nine for details).

You may still be able to obtain an individual's new address by doing the following:  mail a letter to the person you are seeking to the last known address and write "ADDRESS CORRECTION REQUESTED" on the lower edge of the envelope or below the return address.  The post office will place a label showing the new address and return your letter to you.  You may also put "DO NOT FORWARD" and the letter will be returned to you with the individual's new address.  Change of address information is retained by the post office for eighteen months, but they will forward mail for only 12 months.  There is a fee of thirty five cents for this service.  You might want to use this method when you forward letters through the armed forces world-wide locators, base locators, alumni associations and the Social Security Administration.  You may find the person's current address in this manner.

You may also write the postmaster (especially smaller towns) of the town where the person once lived.  You might obtain some useful information and assistance.  Many small town postmasters have held their job for 30 to

40 years and know the location or relatives of numerous people who once lived there.

## The National ZIP Code Directory

The US Postal Service publishes the National ZIP Code Directory which lists all cities in the US with a post office, their ZIP codes, and the county where the city is located. Streets are listed for larger cities. This book is available for purchase or use in all US Post Offices. It is also available in most libraries. It provides a great deal of valuable information for searchers.

# Locating Missing People
# Through Professional Searchers

Some difficult cases may need the help of a professional searcher. These can include private investigators, specialized searchers and attorneys. Listed below are professional searchers recommended by the author.

### Private Investigators

The National Association of Investigative Specialists (NAIS) is a world-wide network of private investigative professionals and/or agencies. With over 1,500 members, it is one of the largest associations in the world for private investigators. NAIS also publishes and sells training manuals and books for the private investigative and security industry. For a catalog of products, contact:

National Association of               (512) 928-8190
   Investigative Specialists
PO Box 33244
Austin, TX  78764

Darrin Fansler is a private investigator who resides and practices in Germany. He is a former US Army Military Police investigator. He specializes in locating US active and retired military who are stationed or reside in Germany. He is also available for debt collection, background investigation, etc.

For information and fees, contact:

Detective Darrin Fansler        011-49-6181-5280
Central Texas College
20233
APO AE 09165

## Attorney

Charles Eric Gordon is an attorney concentrating on locating persons who have been missing for a substantial period of time or about whom little information is known. He is a consultant to law firms, corporations, government agencies and foreign governments in tracing missing witnesses, heirs, beneficiaries, relatives, debtors and others. He will also counsel individuals with regard to difficult or unusual cases.

With his world-wide contacts and many years of experience as both an attorney and an investigator, he can also assist in obtaining information and public records which are difficult to access: e.g., vital records, voter registration and court records.

Charles Eric Gordon, Esq.        (516) 433-5065
5 Joyce Road
PO Box 514
Plainview, NY  11803-0514

## To Locate American Fathers of Amerasians

Asian American Initiatives (AAI) conducts searches for US military fathers of Amerasian children.   AAI has extensive information on military personnel (all branches) who served in Southeast Asia.   AAI also maintains a registry of thousands of children born in Vietnam who are searching fo their American fathers.

For information and fees, contact:

Samatha Wright                FAX (502) 955-8047
Asian American Initiatives
343 Marvin Ave
Brooks, KY  40109-5229

## To Locate American Fathers of European Children

Lt. Col. Philip C. Grinton (Ret) assists the children of British mothers to find their American GI fathers.   His main area of expertise is finding men who served in the European Theater of Operation during World War II.

For information and fees, contact:

Lt. Col. Philip C. Grinton          (707) 545-1520
828 Beaver St
Santa Rosa, CA  95404-3731

## To Locate People in German Speaking Countries

The following team of searchers specialize in locating people (birth parents, children and others) who live or have lived in Germany, Austria and Switzerland.   Both were born in Germany and have extensive experience and numerous contacts in Europe.

For information and fees, contact:

Leonie Boehmer                    (505) 268-1310
805 Alvarado NE
Albuquerque, NM  87108

Margit S Benton                   (803) 747-6156
38 Bailey Dr
Charleston, SC  29405

# Regional Government Depository Libraries

Many libraries are members of the Regional Government Depository Library Program.  Although public libraries and university libraries usually participate in this program, not all have the facilities for maintaining extensive collections of federal publications.  Regional depositories are charged with receiving all new and revised government publications authorized for distribution to depository libraries.

Many documents and books published by the federal government and the armed forces may not be available in many libraries.  These publications can be obtained on a loan basis by libraries who participate in this program from Regional Government Depository Libraries.  These depository libraries are located in every state.  Example of publications that may be available for loan from these Regional Government Depository Libraries are armed forces officers registers, Department of State employee registers and lists, federal government telephone books, US Government pamphlets on such diverse matters as census data, commercial laws, bankruptcies courts, federal tax matters, etc.  Consider using this valuable resource if you are involved with a difficult search.  Ask your librarian how you can use this service to obtain publication you may need in your search.

You can use the services of these Regional Government Depositories direct. Call the Federal Information Office for the telephone number of the library closest to you. See your telephone book for your local number.

# The Salvation Army

The Salvation Army conducts searches of missing people for immediate family members only through their national missing person network. Contact your local Salvation Army Social Service Center for information and a registration form. There is a $10.00 fee for this service.

There are also four territorial headquarters for the Salvation Army that can assist you in a search.

Regional addresses for the Salvation Army Missing Persons Services are:

Southern US Salvation Army
Missing Persons Services
1424 NE Expressway
Atlanta, GA  30329

Western US Salvation Army
Missing Persons Service
30840 Hawthorne Boulevard
Rancho Palos Verdes, CA  90274

Eastern US Missing Persons Services
120 W 14th Street
New York, NY  10011

Central US Salvation Army
Missing Persons Services
860 N Dearborn Street
Chicago, IL 60610

# Social Security Administration

The Social Security Administration (SSA) will forward some unsealed letters to people whose names are listed in their files. This will be done for certain humanitarian reasons that will be beneficial to the receiver e.g., locating missing relatives, medical needs, locating heirs to estates, assisting people with claims, etc. Letters that are accepted will be forwarded to their employers or directly to the individual if he is drawing Social Security benefits.

Before offering assistance, the SSA must determine that it is reasonable to assume the person to be contacted would want to receive the letter and want to reply.

The SSA will not offer to forward any correspondence unless the following conditions are met:

1. Strong compelling reasons exist, e.g.,

    a. a strong humanitarian purpose will be served (e.g., a close relative is seriously ill, is dying, or has died).
    b. a minor child is left without parental guidance.
    c. a defendant in a felony case is seeking a defense witness.
    d. a parent wishes to locate a son or daughter.
    e. consent of the missing person is needed in connection with an adoption proceeding for his/her child.

2. The missing person would want to know the contents of the letter.

3. The missing person's disappearance occurred recently enough that SSA could reasonably expect to have a usable mailing address.

4. All other possibilities for contacting the missing person have been exhausted.

### Forwarding Procedures

You must submit your request in writing to the SSA, giving the following information:

1. Missing person's name and Social Security number (SSN).

2. If SSN is unknown, give date and place of birth, name of parents, name and address of last known employer and period of employment.

3. Reason for wanting to contact the person.

4. Last time seen.

5. Other contacts that have been exhausted.

Enclose your letter to be forwarded in an unsealed stamped envelope.

SSA will try to find an address in their records for the missing person. If an address is found they will forward your letter.

They will tell you if they cannot forward a letter because they cannot locate a Social Security number for the missing person.

They cannot tell you whether:

• they found an address for the missing person, or
• they were able to forward a letter to the missing person.

## If Monetary Consideration Exists

A strong compelling reason may be deemed to exist if a monetary or other consideration is involved and it is reasonable to assume that the missing person does not know it.  For example:

- missing person is a beneficiary of an estate.
- insurance proceeds are due the missing person.
- an important document is being held.  (ssa will not forward the document.)

The procedures are the same as above except include a personal check, cashier's check, or money order payable to the Social Security Administration in the amount of $3.00 per letter.

Always ask for a receipt if you make a payment as sometimes the clerks will write the individual's SSN on the receipt.  Also, if you are seeking someone who has changed their name, the new name may be listed on the receipt.   If you do obtain a receipt with some new information on it, you can then attempt some of the computer searches in Chapter Nine.

In the event they cannot help you and you have prepaid a fee, the Treasury Department will send you a refund. They will state that you overpaid them or that they do not charge a fee in your case.

Mail all correspondence to:

Social Security Administration          (800) 772-1213
Office of Central Records Operations
300 N Greene Street
Baltimore, MD  21201

## Telephone Company

Contact your local telephone company and ask if they have telephone books for other cities, especially if the local library does not have the one you need.

The directory assistance (long distance information) operator can give you valuable information in addition to telephone numbers. You can request the information operator check the entire area code for the person you are seeking. Most area code operators will do this search for you. Dial 1-XXX-555-1212. (XXX = the area code you are seeking).

MCI also has a directory assistance service to locate both domestic and international telephone numbers with a single call. For 75¢, you can receive two telephone numbers if you provide the name and city, domestic or international, of the person you want to call. Use of the traditional directory assistance as described above requires dialing directory assistance in any of the 144 area codes in the US. The MCI directory service is available to anyone by calling 1-800-CALL-INFO (1-800-225-5463).

You can get addresses or you can find out if a certain person has a telephone even if it is unlisted in some areas. There are different rules in each state and area code concerning unlisted telephone numbers. If you find out the person you are looking for does have an unlisted number, call the operator and have them call the person and ask them to contact you. This service is done only in some areas for emergencies or important matters, so inform the operator of its importance. Many people can be located easily through the telephone company or through telephone books.

# Find Anyone Fast

It is highly recommend that you obtain a copy of *Find Anyone Fast.* This book discusses numerous methods of locating missing people in great detail. For additional information, see the order form at the back of this book.

# Chapter Eight

# How To Locate Veterans For A Military Reunion

*This chapter provides recommended steps to locate former members of a military unit for a reunion.*

## How To Locate Veterans With Service Numbers

The following steps are the best method to locate veterans who served when service numbers were used, between 1918 and the early 1970s.

1. Obtain a unit roster or ship muster roll from the National Archives or appropriate military service (see Chapter Six). These contain the name, rank and service number of all members. (If they were prepared before the services converted from service number to Social Security number). There are no Army rosters for 1944, 1945 or 1946 as they were

destroyed. For these years, you must create a roster from morning reports, unit and individual orders and payrolls. By using all of these, you will have a "master" list of the correct spelling and legal names of all of the people you will want to contact.

2.  Appoint a "reunion organizer". Have him or her create a database of names, service numbers and eventually addresses and phone numbers using either index cards or a computer.

3.  Register your reunion with The American Legion and VFW "VETS", the National Reunion Registry, and the Office of Secretary of the Army (Army units only). See below.

4.  Prepare a good news release or reunion notice. Make it as brief as possible, but be sure to include your organization, branch of service, the war or period of time, name,address and telephone number of the reunion organizer, date and place of the reunion. For example: "The 111 Mess Kit Repair Battalion (US Army) (WWII) will hold its first reunion on September 5, 1995 at the Waldorf Astoria Hotel in New York City. Former members or widows are asked to contact Joe Jones, Reunion Organizer, 123 Maple St, Anytown, USA 78125, (999) 123-4567".

Send reunion notices or news releases to all appropriate veterans organizations and request that they be published in their magazines, bulletins and newsletters. Use the CO-OP mail program provided by the National Reunion Registry and Press Service which sends notice of your reunion to over 2,300 newspapers, public library and veterans organizations. The fee for this unique service is only $53.00. Send them to the National Reunion Registry and Press Service,. PO Box 355 Bulverde, Texas 78163-0355 (210) 438-4177

5. Send a copy of your roster with names and service numbers to the VA Records Processing Center (VARPC). They will in turn give you the VA claim number of the individual, tell you if the individual is deceased or tell you they do not have a record of the individual. The fee for this service is $2.00 per name. See Chapter Five.

6. Prepare a letter informing each individual about your planned reunion. Have the VARPC forward these letters to each of the individuals for whom there is a VA claim number.

7. Have individuals you have been in contact with search their own personnel files, footlockers, scrapbooks, letters, etc. for any orders. Orders (unit orders, reassignment orders, orders for promotions, awards, etc.) are very valuable because they contain the correct spelling of the name and service numbers. Have them send copies of all these orders to the reunion organizer.

0. Check appropriate *Officers Registers* for information on unit or ship officers such as date of birth, service number, state where they entered service. See chapters Five and Six.

9. Have the retired locator of the appropriate branch forward letters to individuals who have retired from the service. See Chapter Four.

10. If you know the city and state where the veteran entered the service, contact the postmaster, mayor, historical organizations, veterans organizations, churches, schools and reunion groups of that city or

town and ask if they the current location of the veteran or his family.

11. Attempt to locate individuals who may belong to veterans organizations e.g. VFW, DAV, The American Legion, AMVETS, The Retired Officers Association, NCO Association, Fleet Reserve Association, Marine Corps League, etc.

12. Obtain addresses from the National Telephone Directory listings of all remaining veterans. Mail letters or postcards to these addresses advising them of the reunion. Address listings may be obtained from many main public libraries or the Nationwide Locator, PO Box 39903, San Antonio, Texas 78218.

13. Contact college and university alumni associations for the addresses of veterans who attended their schools. If the alumni association will not supply you with an address, contact the college library and ask if they have a copy of the directory of former students. Ask the librarian to give you the individual's address.

14. Check with each individual that you have located to see if he knows address or location of other missing members.

15. Continue to advertise your reunion. Have individuals send news releases to their local newspapers. Put notices of your reunion on computer bulletin board services. Use specialty advertising such as bumper stickers, T-shirts, baseball caps, badges, etc. which show your reunion organization, telephone number and date of reunion.

# How To Locate Veterans
# With Social Security Numbers

The following steps are the best method to locate veterans who served when Social Security numbers (SSNs) were used.  The Army and Air Force switched to SSNs in July 1969, the Navy and Marine Corps in July 1972 and the Coast Guard in October 1974.

The best and most economical way to locate a veteran is by running a computer trace using their SSN.  A Social Security trace can obtain the most current reported address from the header information of 160 million credit files.  87 to 92% of the time, the most current reported address will be returned.  Also, if the individual is deceased, the date of death will usually be reported.

1.  Obtain a unit roster or ship muster roll from the National Archives or appropriate military service.  (see Chapter Six)  These contain the name, rank and SSN of all members assigned to that unit or ship the date the document was prepared, however the SSNs will be marked out.  Nonetheless, this will give you a "master" list of the correct spelling and legal names of all of the people you will want to contact.

2.  Appoint a "reunion organizer".  Have him or her create a database of names, SSNs and eventually addresses and phone numbers using either index cards or a computer.

3.  Request a brochure and a group price list from the Nationwide Locator, PO Box 39903, San Antonio, Texas 78218 to obtain more information and rates for Social Security traces.  The prices vary from $30.00 for one computer trace to as low as $3.00 for three hundred.

4. Register your reunion with The American Legion and VFW "VETS", the National Reunion Registry, and the Office of Secretary of the Army (Army units only). See below.

5. Prepare a good news release or reunion notice. Make it as brief as possible, but be sure to include your organization, branch of service, war or period of time, name, address and telephone number of the reunion organizer, date and place of the reunion. For example: the USS Fireball (US Navy) (Vietnam) will hold its first reunion on December 25, 1995 at the Las Vegas Hilton, Las Vegas, NV. Former members or widows are asked to contact Fred Applemeyer, Reunion Organizer, 4779 Penelope Dr., Anytown, USA 63645, (999) 965-4123.

Send reunion notices or news releases to all appropriate veterans organizations and request that they be published in their magazines, bulletins and newsletters. Use the CO-OP mail program provided by the National Reunion Registry and Press Service which sends notice of your reunion to over 2,300 newspapers, public library and veterans organizations. The fee for this unique service is only $53.00. Send them to the National Reunion Registry and Press Service,. PO Box 355 Bulverde, Texas 78163-0355 (210) 438-4177

6. Have individuals you have been in contact with search their own personnel files, footlockers, scrapbooks, letters, etc. for any orders. Orders (unit orders, reassignment orders, orders for promotions, awards, etc.) are very valuable because they contain names and SSNs. Have them send copies of all these orders to the reunion organizer.

7.  Check appropriate *Officer's Registers* to obtain Social Security numbers of officers assigned to the unit or ship who do not appear on the rosters or muster rolls. See chapters Five and Six.

8.  Make a list of SSNs and matching names. Mail it, with the appropriate payment, to The Nationwide Locator, PO Box 39903, San Antonio, Texas 78218.

9.  Have the retired locator of the appropriate branch forward letters to individuals who have retired from the service. See Chapter Four.

10. If you know the city and state where the veteran entered the service, contact the postmaster, mayor, historical organizations, veterans organizations, churches, schools and reunion groups of that city or town and ask if they the current location of the veteran or his family.

11. Attempt to locate individuals who may belong to veterans organizations e.g. VFW, DAV, The American Legion, AMVETS, The Retired Officers Association, NCO Association, Fleet Reserve Association, Marine Corps League, etc.

12. Obtain addresses from the National Telephone Directory listings of all remaining veterans. Mail letters or postcards to these addresses advising them of the reunion. Address listings may be obtained from many main public libraries or the Nationwide Locator, PO Box 39903, San Antonio, Texas 78218.

13. Contact college and university alumni associations for the addresses of veterans who attended their schools. If the alumni association will not supply you with an address, contact the college library and ask if they

have a copy of the directory of former students.  Ask the librarian to give you the individual's address.

14. Use the newly acquired addresses to contact missing members.  Ask them to join your reunion association and pay a small membership fee to cover the costs of locating other former members.

15. Ask newly found members to search for orders and send them to the reunion organizer to start the search process over again.

16. Continue to advertise your reunion.  Have individuals send news releases to their local newspapers.  Put notices of your reunion on computer bulletin board services.  Use specialty advertising such as bumper stickers, T-shirts, baseball caps, badges, etc. which show your reunion organization, telephone number and date of reunion.

The 11th Armed Cavalry's Veterans of Vietnam and Cambodia used this method and, with the help of the author, located over 14,000 of their former members in two years.  This is the fastest growing reunion association in the country.  With the increase in dues from new members, they have paid for all locating costs and have also increased the amount in their treasury substantially.

If you cannot locate an address for the veteran through a Social Security trace, you may need to contact the Social Security Administration or have the Nationwide Locator search the Social Security Death Index to see if the veteran has died.

If you cannot find a service number or a Social Security number for a veteran, search the National Telephone Directory using the services of the local library or the Nationwide Locator.

# Army Unit Reunions

The Public Affairs Office of the Secretary of the Army maintains a free computer roster of associations of Army organizations. It contains addresses, telephone numbers and contact persons for approximately 1,600 associations and organizations. To obtain a copy of the roster, send a blank 3.5 HD computer diskette with your return address to the address below. If you are a member of an Army association, be sure it is listed with this office.

Bob King                          (703) 695-4660
SAPA-ZDA (Room 2E645)
Chief of Public Affairs
1500 Army, Pentagon
Washington, DC 20310-1500

# The American Legion Magazine's Veterans Electronic Telecommunication Service (VETS)

The American Legion Magazine subscribes to a 24 hour a day telephone and computer service to provide information about military reunions. Dial 1-900-773-VETS for dates of reunions and how to contact the reunion organizers. The call cost $1.95 per minute. The American Legion Magazine is attempting to enroll 10,000 reunion organizations into VETS. For free registration write:

VETS                          (900) 773-VETS
PO Box 1055
Indianapolis, IN 46206

## Veterans Of Foreign War's (VFW) Veterans Electronic Telecommunication Service (VETS)

The VFW Magazine also subscribes to a 24 hour a day telephone and computer service to provide information about military reunions. Dial 1-900-933-VETS for dates of reunions and how to contact the reunion organizers. The call costs $1.95 per minute. This is the same service as The American Legion uses, however, different codes are assigned to unit reunion organizations. For free registration write:

VETS                                    (900) 993-VETS
c/o VFW
PO Box 901
Columbia, MO  65205-0901

## Reunions Magazine

*Reunions Magazine* is the only national publication that concentrates on reunions of all kinds. In addition to articles on searching, genealogical research and military reunions, it also provides tips, leads and hints to help you search for missing people. Other articles focus on adoptees and birth parents searches. To subscribe ($24.00 per year) or for a sample copy, send $2.00 to:

Reunions Magazine                       (414) 263-4567
PO Box 11727                            FAX (414) 263-6331
Milwaukee, WI  53211                    Reunions1@aol.com

# Reunions For Desert Storm, Grenada And Panama

If you were involved in any of these military activities or have friends or relatives who were, preparation for a future military reunion should be done now. The following recommendations should be accomplished:

1. Appoint one or more people who were in the units involved to be reunion organizers.

2. Collect rosters of the unit that include names, ranks and Social Security numbers of the members.

3. Obtain home addresses of all unit members through the Nationwide Locator (see Appendix B).

4. Place all information in a computer database.

5. Keep in touch with all original unit members by letter or a newsletter at least once a year.

6. Prepare for your reunion now. Select a sight and date. Inform all members.

7. Seek donations from unit members to defray mailing and organizational costs.

8. Register your reunion organization as soon as possible with:

    a. National Reunion Registry
    b. Secretary of the Army
    c. The American Legion's and VFW VETS

9. Subscribe to Reunions magazine.

If the above recommendations are completed now it will be easier to locate all former members of a unit. All future reunions will be easier to conduct and will have greater participation.

# The National Reunion Registry And Press Service

The National Reunion Registry is a database of over 6,000 military reunion organizations and their planners. Reunion organizers may list their reunions free of charge (copy the form on next page).

Persons seeking reunions can request a records search at no charge. Send a self-addressed stamped envelope along with the reunion being sought.

Military reunion organizers may use the National Reunion Press Service to publicize their reunion. For a one-time charge of $53.00 (less than 3 cents per release) notice of your reunion is sent to over 2,300 demographically selected outlets. These include veterans associations, civilian and military newspapers, VA facilities and Veterans Service Officers, and public libraries. Millions of people may see your announcement. User testimonials report this is both a successful and cost-effective way to reach long-lost shipmates and buddies.

National Reunion Registry
　　and Press Service
PO Box 355
Bulverde, TX  78163-0355

(210) 438-4177
FAX (210) 438-4114

# Registration Form

Service _____

Unit (be very specific)_____

Period: WWII____ Korea____ Vietnam____ Beirut _____

Grenada_____ Panama____ Desert Storm____ Other ___

Reunion Dates: _____
                 Month       Days       Year

Where: _____
           City     State        Hotel

Contact: _____
            First Name     Last Name

Address: _____
       House #    Street Name     Apartment #

Address: _____
          City        State     ZIP plus 4

Phone: (_____) _____

Estimated Attendance at last/next reunion: _____

National/Regional Reunion: _____

Frequency:   Annual_____   Biennial_____

National Reunion Registry        (210) 438-4177
    and Press Service        FAX (210) 438-4114
PO Box 355
Bulverde, TX  78163-0355

# Professional Reunion Organizers

Ted Day, of Armed Forces Reunions, is a professional reunion organizer who conducts military reunions throughout the United States. You can have his organization plan and conduct every aspect of your reunion and your group's fee will be as low as $3.00 per person attending. The bulk of the compensation is in the form of a commission from the hotels where the reunions are held. For additional information, contact:

Ted Dey                            (800) 562-7226
Armed Forces Reunions
PO Box 11327
Norfolk, VA 23517

Larry Eckard has been an outstanding professional military reunion organizer for several years. He and his staff will plan, coordinate and conduct every aspect of your reunion. He also locates missing unit members for your reunion. For additional information and fees, contact:

Larry Eckard                        (704) 256-6274
PO Box 5145
Hickory, NC 28063

# Chapter Nine

# How To Locate People Through State Governments

*This chapter provides information on how to obtain identifying information and addresses of individuals through birth, marriage and divorce records, motor vehicle registration, driver license records and professional regulating agencies of the various states.*

### State Parent Locator Service

The federal government will make a computer search of IRS, VA and the Social Security Administration files for anyone who has a child support court order against them. If the name is listed, the address and SSN of the individual will be provided.

To obtain this service, all requests must be made to the appropriate state parent locator service in the child support enforcement bureau. Check the local telephone book for address and telephone number or call the state information number listed later in this chapter.

## To Obtain Identifying Information Through Birth, Marriage And Divorce Records

Vital records consists of birth and death certificates, marriage licenses, divorce and annulment decrees. (See Chapter Eight concerning alternate way to determine if an individual is deceased). Each Vital Records office has different fee and information requirements according to the laws of their state/area. Some states will release these records to family members only.

Provide as much of the following information as possible in order to obtain birth or death records:

- Full name of person whose record is being requested
- Sex and race
- Parents' names, including maiden name of mother
- Place of birth or death (city or town, county and state; and name of hospital, if any)
- Purpose for which copy is needed
- Relationship to person whose record is being requested

Provide as much of the following information as possible in order to obtain marriage records:

- Full names of bride and groom (including nicknames)
- Residence addresses at time of marriage
- Ages at time of marriage (or dates of birth)
- Month, day and year of marriage
- Place of marriage (city or town, county and state)
- Purpose for which copy is needed
- Relationship to person whose record is being requested

Provide as much of the following information as possible in order to obtain divorce and annulment records:

- Full names of husband and wife (including nicknames)
- Present residence address
- Former addresses (as in court records)
- Ages at time of divorce (or dates of birth)
- Date of divorce or annulment
- Place of divorce or annulment
- Type of final decree
- Purpose for which copy is needed
- Relationship to person whose record is being requested

Below are the addresses of the offices where copies of birth, death, marriage, divorce and annulment records can be obtained. Also listed are the charges required by each state.

ALABAMA
Center for Health Statistics
PO Box 5625
Montgomery, AL 36103-5625
(334) 242-5033
$12.00

ALASKA
Dept of Health & Social Srvcs
Bureau of Vital Statistics
PO Box H-02G
Juneau, AK 99811-0675
(907) 465-3391
$7.00

AMERICAN SAMOA
Registrar of Vital Statistics
Govern't of American Samoa
Pago Pago, AS 96799
(684) 633-1222, ext. 214
$2.00

ARIZONA
Vital Records Section
Arizona Dept of Health Srvcs
PO Box 3887
Phoenix, AZ 85030
(602) 255-3260
$8.00

ARIZONA
Vital Records Section
Arizona Dept of Health Srvcs
PO Box 3887
Phoenix, AZ 85030
(602) 255-3260
$8.00

ARKANSAS
Division of Vital Records
Arkansas Dept of Health
Little Rock, AR 72201
(501) 661-2336
$5.00

ARKANSAS
Division of Vital Records
Arkansas Dept of Health
Little Rock, AR  72201
(501) 661-2336
$5.00

CALIFORNIA
Vital Statistics Section
Dept of Health Services
PO Box 73041
Sacramento, CA  94244-0241
(916) 445-2684
$12.00

CANAL ZONE
Panama Canal Commission
Vital Statistics Clerk
APO AA  34011
$2.00

COLORADO
Vital Records Section
Colorado Dept of Health
4300 Cherry Creek Drive S
Denver, CO  80222-1530
(303) 756-4464
$12.00

CONNECTICUT
Vital Records
Dept of Health Services
150 Washington Street
Hartford, CT  06106
(203) 566-2334
$5.00

DELAWARE
Office of Vital Statistics
Division of Public Health
PO Box 637
Dover, DE  19903
(302) 739-4721
$5.00

DISTRICT OF COLUMBIA
Vital Records Branch
Room 3009
425 I Street, NW
Washington, DC  20001
(202) 727-9281
$12.00

FLORIDA
Dept of Health & Rehab Svcs
Office of Vital Statistics
PO Box 210
1217 Pearl Street
Jacksonville, FL  32231
(904) 359-6900
$9.00

GEORGIA
Georgia Dept of Hmn Rscs
Vital Records Unit
Room 217-H
47 Trinity Avenue, SW
Atlanta, GA 30334
(404) 656-4900
$10.00

GUAM
Office of Vital Statistics
Dept of Pub Hlth/Social Svcs
Government of Guam
PO Box 2816
Agana, GU, M.I. 96910
(617) 734-4589
$5.00

HAWAII
Office of Health Status Monit
State Dept of Health
PO Box 3378
Honolulu, HI 96801
(808) 586-4533
$2.00

IDAHO
Vital Statistics Unit
Idaho Dept of Health/Welfare
450 West State Street
State House Mail
Boise, ID 83720-9990
(208) 334-5988
$8.00

ILLINOIS
Division of Vital Records
Illinois Dept of Public Health
605 West Jefferson Street
Springfield, IL 62702-5097
(217) 782-6553
$15.00

INDIANA
Vital Records Section
State Dept of Health
1330 West Michigan Street
PO Box 1964
Indianapolis, IN 46206-1964
(317) 633 0274
$6.00

IOWA
Iowa Dept of Public Health
Vital Records Section
Lucas Office Building
321 East 12th Street
Des Moines, IA 50319-0075
(515) 281-4944
$6.00

KANSAS
Office of Vital Statistics
Kansas State Dept of Health
and Environment
900 Jackson Street
Topeka, KS 66612-1290
(913) 296-1400
$10.00

KENTUCKY
Office of Vital Statistics
Dept for Health Services
275 East Main Street
Frankfort, KY 40621
(502) 564-4212
$7.00

MAINE
Office of Vital Statistics
Maine Dept of Human Srvcs
State House Station 11
Augusta, ME 04333-0011
(207) 289-3184
$10.00

MASSACHUSETTS
Registry Vital Records/Stats
150 Tremont St, Room B-3
Boston, MA 02111
(617) 727-7388
$11.00

MINNESOTA
Minnesota Dept of Health
Section of Vital Statistics
717 Delaware Street, SE
PO Box 9441
Minneapolis, MN 55440
(612) 623-5121
$11.00

LOUISIANA
Vital Records Registry
Office of Public Health
325 Loyola Avenue
New Orleans, LA 70112
(504) 568-5152
$10.00

MARYLAND
Division of Vital Records
Dept of Hlth&Mental Hygiene
Metro Executive Building
4201 Patterson Avenue
PO Box 68760
Baltimore, MD 21215-0020
(301) 225-5988
$4.00

MICHIGAN
Office of the State Registrar
& Center for Health Statistics
Michigan Dept of Pub Health
3423 North Logan Street
Lansing, MI 48909
(517) 335-8655
$13.00

MISSISSIPPI
Vital Records
State Dept of Health
2423 North State Street
Jackson, MS 39216
(601) 960-7450
$12.00

MISSOURI
Missouri Dept of Health
Bureau of Vital Records
1730 East Elm
PO Box 570
Jefferson City, MO 65102
(314) 751-6400
$10.00

MONTANA
Montana Dept of Health
Vital Records
1400 Broadway
Cogswell Bldg Rm C118
Helena, MT 56920
(406) 444-4228
$10.00

NEBRASKA
Bureau of Vital Statistics
State Dept of Health
301 Centennial Mall South
PO Box 95007
Lincoln, NE 68509-5007
(402) 471-2871
$8.00

NEVADA
Divsn of Health-Vital Statistics
Capitol Complex
505 East King Street #102
Carson City, NV 89710
(702) 687-4480
$11.00

NEW HAMPSHIRE
Bureau of Vital Records
Health and Welfare Building
6 Hazen Drive
Concord, NH 03301
(603) 271-4654
$10.00

NEW JERSEY
State Dept of Health
Bureau of Vital Statistics
South Warren & Market Strts
CN 370
Trenton, NJ 08625
(609) 292-4087
$4.00

NEW MEXICO
Vital Statistics
New Mexico Hlth Srvcs Div
PO Box 26110
Santa Fe, NM 87502
(505) 827-2338
$10.00

NEW YORK
Vital Records Section
State Dept of Health
Empire State Plaza
Tower Building
Albany, NY 12237-0023
(518) 474-3075
$15.00

NEW YORK CITY
Division of Vital Records
New York City Dept of Hlth
PO Box 3776
New York, NY 10007
(212) 693-4637
$15.00

NORTH CAROLINA
Dept of Environment, Health,
  and Natural Resources
Division of Epidemiology
Vital Records Section
225 North McDowell Street
PO Box 29537
Raleigh, NC 27626-0537
(919) 733-3526
$10.00

NORTH DAKOTA
Division of Vital Records
State Capitol
600 East Boulevard Avenue
Bismarck, ND 58505
(701) 224-2360
$7.00

NORTHERN MARIANA ISLS
Superior Court
Vital Records Section
PO Box 307
Saipan, MP 96950
(670) 234-6401, ext. 15
$3.00

OHIO
Bureau of Vital Statistics
Ohio Dept of Health
PO Box 15098
Columbus, OH 43215-0098
(614) 466-2531
$7.00

OKLAHOMA
Vital Records Section
State Dept of Health
1000 Northeast 10th Street
PO Box 53551
Oklahoma City, OK 73152
(405) 271-4040
$5.00

OREGON
Oregon Health Division
Vital Statistics Section
PO Box 14050
Portland, OR 97214-0050
(503) 731-4095
$13.00

PENNSYLVANIA
Division of Vital Records
State Dept of Health
Central Building
101 South Mercer Street
PO Box 1528
New Castle, PA 16103
(412) 656-3100
$4.00

PUERTO RICO
Dept of Health
Demographic Registry
PO Box 11854
Fernandez Juncos Station
San Juan, PR  00910
(809) 728-7980
$2.00

RHODE ISLAND
Division of Vital Records
Rhode Island Dept of Health
Room 101, Cannon Building
3 Capitol Hill
Providence, RI  02908-5097
(401) 277-2811
$10.00

SOUTH CAROLINA
Office of Vital Records
  and Public Health Stats
South Carolina Dept of Hlth
  and Environmental Ctrl
2600 Bull Street
Columbia, SC  29201
(803) 734-4830
$8.00

SOUTH DAKOTA
State Dept of Health
Center for Health Policy Stats
Vital Records
523 E. Capitol
Pierre, SD  57501
(605) 773-3355

TENNESSEE
Tennessee Vital Records
Dept of Health
Cordell Hull Building
Nashville, TN  37247-0350
(015) 741 1763
₵10.00

TEXAS
Bureau of Vital Statistics
Texas Dept of Health
1100 West 49th Street
Austin, TX  78756-3191
(512) 458-7111
$11.00

UTAH
Bureau of Vital Records
Utah Dept of Health
288 North 1460 West
PO Box 16700
Salt Lake City, UT  84116
(801) 538-6105
$12.00

VERMONT
Vermont Dept of Health
Vital Records Section
Box 70
60 Main Street
Burlington, VT  05402
(802) 863-7275
$5.00

VIRGINIA
Division of Vital Records
State Health Dept
PO Box 1000
Richmond, VA 23208-1000
(804) 786-6228
$5.00

VIRGIN ISLANDS
Registrar of Vital Statistics
Knud Hansen Complex
Hospital Ground
Charlotte Amalie
St. Thomas, VI 00802
(809) 774-9000, ext. 4621
$10.00

WASHINGTON
Dept of Health
Center for Health Statistics
PO Box 9709
Olympia, WA 98507-9709
(206) 753-5936
$11.00

WEST VIRGINIA
Vital Registration Office
Division of Health
State Capitol Complex Bldg 3
Charleston, WV 25305
(304) 558-2931
$5.00

WISCONSIN
Vital Records
1 West Wilson Street
PO Box 309
Madison, WI 53701
(608) 266-1371
$10.00

WYOMING
Vital Records Services
Hathaway Building
Cheyenne, WY 82002
(307) 777-7591
$8.00

OVERSEAS BIRTHS
Authentication Office
21st St & Virginia Ave NW
Washington, DC 20025
($3.00)

OVERSEAS BIRTHS
Passport Services
State Department
Washington, DC 20524
($4.00)

## To Obtain Information Through
## State Driver License Offices

At present, sixteen states usually use the Social Security number (SSN) as the driver's license number:  AZ, AR, DC, GA, HI, IA, KS, KY, MA, MO, MS, MT, ND, OK, SD,

VA.  Some other states, including FL and OH, make the SSN part of the driver's record.  Obtaining a copy of the driving record in most of these states will provide you the individual's SSN.

Nevada derives driver license (DL) numbers from the driver's SSN using a mathematical formula.  If you know that formula, you can reverse the process and obtain the SSN from the DL number.

Forty-six states and the District of Columbia will provide the current reported address of individuals who have a driver license or identification card in their respective states.  Four states (California, Georgia, Massachusetts and Virginia) will not provide an address, but will forward letters to the individual.  There are computer searches available that will provide the current, reported address from state driver license files.

Contact each state office for information and fee requirements.

ALABAMA
DPS, Driver License Division
PO Box 1471
Montgomery, AL  36102
(334) 242-4400

ALASKA
DMV, Driver's Records
PO Box 20020
Juneau, AK  99802
(907) 465-4335

ARIZONA
Motor Vehicle Division
Record Services Section
POB 2100 Mail Drop 504M
Phoenix, AZ  85001
(602) 255-7865

ARKANSAS
Dept of Driver Services
Driver Records Division
PO Box 1272, Rm 127
Little Rock, AR  72203
(501) 682-7207

CALIFORNIA
Dept. of Motor Vehicles
Info Request Counter
POB 944231 Mail Sta C198
Sacramento, CA 94244
(916) 657-8098

COLORADO
Motor Vehicle Division
Traffic Records
104 W 6th Ave, Rm 103
Denver, CO 80204
(303) 623-9463

CONNECTICUT
Dept of Motor Vehicles
Copy Records Section
60 State St Room 305
Wethersfield, CT 06109
(203) 566-3197

DELAWARE
Division of Motor Vehicles
Driver Services
PO Box 698
Dover, DE 19903
(302) 739-4343

DISTRICT OF COLUMBIA
Dept of Motor Vehicles
Driver Records Division
301 "C" St NW, Rm 1157
Washington, DC 20001
(202) 727-6761

FLORIDA
Dept of Public Safety
Division of Drivers Licenses
2900 Apalachee Pky Rm B239
Tallahassee, FL 32399
(904) 487-2369

GEORGIA
Dept of Motor Vehicles
Driver's License Section
MVR Unit, PO Box 1456
Atlanta, GA 30371
(404) 624-7487

HAWAII
Driver Violations Bureau
Abstract Section
1111 Alakea St
Honolulu, HI 96813
(808) 548-5735

IDAHO
Idaho Transportation Dept
Driver's Services
PO Box 34
Boise, ID 83701
(208) 334-8736

ILLINOIS
Driver Analysis Section
Drivers Services Dept
2701 S Dirksen Prky
Springfield, IL 62723
(217) 782-2720

INDIANA
Bureau of Motor Vehicles
Driver Records
Rm N405, IN Gov Cen, N
Indianapolis, IN  46204
(317) 232-2894

IOWA
Dept. of Transportation
Driver Service Records Sec
PO Box 9204
Des Moines, IA  50306
(515) 237-3070

KANSAS
Department of Revenue
Driver Control Bureau
PO Box 12021
Topeka, KS  66612
(913) 296-3671

KENTUCKY
Division of Driver's Licensing
MVRS-State Office Building
501 High Street, 2nd Fl
Frankfort, KY  40622
(502) 564-4711

LOUISIANA
Dept of Public Safety
  and Corrections
Office of Motor Vehicles
PO Box 64886
Baton Rouge, LA  70896
(504) 925-6009

MAINE
Bureau of Motor Vehicles
Driver License & Control
State House Station 29
Augusta, ME  04333
(207) 287-2576

MARYLAND
Motor of Motor Vehicles
Motor Vehicle Admin
6601 Richie Hwy, NE
  Counter 212
Glen Burnie, MD  21062
(410) 787-7705

MASSACHUSETTS
Registrar of Motor Vehicles
1135 Tremont St
Boston, MA  02120
(617) 351-9834

MICHIGAN
Dept of State Police
Commercial Look-up Unit
7064 Crowner Dr
Lansing, MI  48918
(517) 322-1624

MINNESOTA
Driver and Vehicle Services-
  Investigation Unit
Record Request
395 John Ireland Blvd Rm 108
St. Paul, MN  55155
(612) 296-2023

MISSISSIPPI
Dept of Public Safety
Driver Records
PO Box 958
Jackson, MS  39205
(601) 987-1274

MONTANA
Motor Vehicle Division
Drivers' Services
PO Box 201419
Helena, MT  59620
(406) 444-4590

NEVADA
Dept. of Motor Vehicles
  and Public Safety
555 Wright Way
Carson City, NV  89711
(702) 687-5505

NEW JERSEY
Motor Vehicle Services
Driver's Abstract Section
CN 142
Trenton, NJ  08666
(609) 603-8255

NEW YORK
Dept. of Motor Vehicles
Div of Data Prep & Control
Rm 430, Empire St Plaza
Albany, NY  12228
(518) 474-2381

MISSOURI
Dept of Revenue
Driver License Bureau
PO Box 200
Jefferson City, MO  65105
(314) 751-4600

NEBRASKA
Dept of Motor Vehicles
Driver Records
PO Box 94789
Lincoln, NE  68509
(402) 471-4343

NEW HAMPSHIRE
Dept of Motor Vehicles
Driving Records
10 Hazen Dr
Concord, NH  03305
(603) 271-2322

NEW MEXICO
Dept of Motor Vehicles
Driver Services Bureau
PO Box 1028
Santa Fe, NM  87504
(505) 827 2241

NORTH CAROLINA
Dept of Motor Vehicles
Driver's License Section
1100 New Bern Ave
Raleigh, NC  27697
(919) 733-4241

NORTH DAKOTA
Dept of Transportation
Driver License & Traffic
  Safety Division
608 E Boulevard Ave
Bismarck, ND 58505
(701) 224-2603

OKLAHOMA
Dept of Public Safety
Driver's Record Services
PO Box 11415
Oklahoma City, OK 73136
(405) 425-2026

PENNSYLVANIA
Dept of Transportation
Information Sales Unit
PO Box 68691
Harrisburg, PA 17106
(717) 787-3130

SOUTH CAROLINA
Dept of Public Safety
Driver Records Section
PO Box 1498
Columbis, SC 29216
(803) 251-2940

TENNESSEE
Dept of Safety, Financial
  Responsibility Section
Driving License & Driving
  Records
1150 Foster Ave
Nashville, TN 37249
(615) 741-3954

OHIO
Dept of Motor Vehicles
Bureau of Motor Vehicles
4300 Kimberly Pkwy
Columbus, OH 43232
(614) 752-7600

OREGON
Dept of Motor Vehicles
1905 Lana Ave NE
Salem, OR 97314
(503) 945-5000

RHODE ISLAND
Driving Records Clerk
Operator Control
345 Harris Ave
Providence, RI 02909
(401) 277-2994

SOUTH DAKOTA
Div of Commerce & Reg
Driver's License Program
118 W Capitol
Pierre, SD 57501
(605) 773-3191

TEXAS
License Issuance &
  Driver Records
Driver Records Section
PO Box 15999
Austin, TX 78761
(512) 465-2032

UTAH
Dept of Public Safety
Driver's License &
 Driving Records Section
PO Box 30560
Salt Lake City, UT  84119
(801) 965-4430

VIRGINIA
Dept of Motor Vehicles
Motorist Info Administration
PO Box 27412
Richmond, VA  23269
(804) 367-0538

WEST VIRGINIA
Division of Motor Vehicles
Safety & Enforcement
1900 Kanawha Blvd
Charlston, WV  25317
(304) 558-0238

WYOMING
Wyoming Dept of Trans
Driver Services
PO Box 1708
Cheyenne, WY  82003
(307) 777-4802

VERMONT
Dept of Motor Vehicles
Driver Improvement Info
120 State St
Montpelier, VT  05603
(802) 828-2050

WASHINGTON
Dept of Licensing
Driver's Responsibility Div
PO Box 9030
Olympia, WA  98507
(206) 753-6976

WISCONSIN
Dept of Motor Vehicles
License Record Section
PO Box 7918
Madison, WI  53707
(608) 264-7060

## To Obtain Addresses Through State
## Motor Vehicle Registration Offices

To obtain someone's address from an automobile license, vehicle plate number, registration or title, you can contact the appropriate state office below.  This service usually requires a fee.  Check with the office for further information.

ALABAMA
Motor Vehicle Division
Title & Registration Section
PO Box 327640
Montgomery, AL 36132
(334) 242-9000

ALASKA
Dept. of Motor Vehicles
 ATTN: Research
2150 E Dowling Rd
Anchorage, AK 99507
(907) 563-5589

ARIZONA
Motor Vehicle Division
Records Services Section
PO Box 2100 Mail Drp 504M
Phoenix, AZ 85001
(602) 255-7865

ARKANSAS
Office of Motor Vehicles
IRP Unit
PO Box 1272, Rm 106
Little Rock, AR 72203
(501) 682-3333

CALIFORNIA
Dept. of Motor Vehicles
Consulting Room
POB 944247, Mail Sta C198
Sacramento, CA 94244
(916) 657-8098

COLORADO
Dept of Motor Vehicles
Vehicle Records Section
140 W 6th Ave
Denver, CO 80204
(303) 623-9463

CONNECTICUT
Dept. of Motor Vehicles
Copy Record Unit
60 State St, Branch Ops
Wethersfield, CT 06109
(203) 566-3090

DELAWARE
Division of Motor Vehicles
ATTN. Correspondence Sec
PO Box 698
Dover, DE 19903
(302) 739-3147

DISTRICT OF COLUMBIA
Dept of Motor Vehicles
Vehicle Control Division
301 "C" St NW, Rm 1063
Washington, DC 20001
(202) 727-4768

FLORIDA
Division of Motor Vehicles
Information Research Section
Neil Kirkman Bldg Room A126
Tallahassee, FL 32399
(904) 488-5665

GEORGIA
Dept of Revenue
ATTN: Research
270 Washington St SW
  Room 105
Atlanta, GA 30334
(404) 656-4145

HAWAII
Restricted Access
Not available to the public

IDAHO
Idaho Transportation Dept
Titles/Dealers Ops Section
PO Box 7129
Boise, ID 83707
(208) 334-8663

ILLINOIS
Vehicles Services Dept.
Record Inquiry
408 Howlett Building
Springfield, IL 62756
(217) 782-6992

INDIANA
Bureau of Motor Vehicles
Vehicle Records
100 N Senate Ave Rm N405
Indianapolis, IN 46204
(317) 232-2795

IOWA
Dept of Transportation
Office of Vehicle Reg
PO Box 9204
Des Moines, IA 50306
(515) 237-3077

KANSAS
Division of Vehicles
Title and Registration Bureau
915 Harrison
Topeka, KS 66616
(913) 296-3621

KENTUCKY
Dept of Motor Vehicles
Div of Motor Vehicle Licensing
State Office Bldg, 3rd Floor
Frankfort, KY 40622
(502) 564-2737/4076

LOUISIANA
Dept. of Public Safety
  and Corrections
Office of Motor Vehicles
PO Box 64884
Baton Rouge, LA 70896
(504) 925-6146

MAINE
Dept of Motor Vehicles
Registration Section
State House Station 29
Augusta, ME 04333
(207) 287-3556

MARYLAND
Dept of Motor Vehicles
Vehicle Reg Division
6601 Richie Hwy, NE
  Room 206
Glen Burnie, MD 21062
(410) 768-7250

MASSACHUSETTS
Registry of Motor Vehicles
Customer Assistance-
  Mail Listing Dept.
1135 Tremont St
Boston, MA 02120
(617) 351-4400

MICHIGAN
Dept of State Police
Commercial Look-Up Unit
7064 Crowner Dr
Lansing, MI 48919
(517) 322-1624

MINNESOTA
Driver and Vehicle Services
Records Dept
395 John Ireland Blvd Rm 214
St Paul, MN 55155
(612) 296-6911

MISSISSIPPI
State State Tax Comm
Registration Dept.
PO Box 1140
Jackson, MI 39215
(601) 359-1248

MISSOURI
Dept of Motor Vehicles
Motor Vehicle Bureau
PO Box 100
Jefferson City MO 65105
(314) 751-4509

MONTANA
Dept of Justice
Title & Registration Bureau
925 Main St
Deer Lodge, MT 59722
(406) 846-1423

NEBRASKA
Dept of Motor Vehicles
Titles & Registration Sec
PO Box 94789
Lincoln, NE 68509
(402) 471-3910

NEVADA
Dept. of Motor Vehicles and
  Public Safety
Motor Vehicle Record Sec
555 Wright Way
Carson City, NV 89711
(702) 687-5505

NEW HAMPSHIRE
Dept of Public Safety
Bureau of Title Registration
10 Hazen Dr
Concord, NH 03305
(603) 271-3111

NEW JERSEY
Motor Vehicle Services
Certified Info Unit
CN 146
Trenton, NJ 08666
(609) 588-2424

NEW MEXICO
Dept of Motor Vehicles
Vehicle Services Bureau
PO Box 1028
Santa Fe, NM 87504
(505) 827-2220

NEW YORK
Div of Data Prep & Control
Empire State Plaza
Swan St Bldg, Room 430
Albany, NY 12228
(518) 474-0642

NORTH CAROLINA
Dept of Motor Vehicles
Vehicle Registration Sec
1100 New Bern Ave
Raleigh, NC 27697
(919) 733-3025

NORTH DAKOTA
Dept of Transportation
Records Sec/Motor Veh Div
608 E Boulevard Ave
Bismarck, ND 58505
(701) 224-2725

OHIO
Bureau of Motor Vehicles
Motor Vehicle Records
4300 Kimberly Parkway
Columbus, OH 43232
(614) 752-7634

OKLAHOMA
Oklahoma Tax Comm
Motor Vehicle Division
 ATTN: Research
2501 Lincoln Blvd.
Oklahoma City, OK 73194
(405) 521-3221

OREGON
Driver & Motor Vehicle Ser
Customer Assistance
1905 Lana Ave NE
Salem, OR 97314
(503) 945-5000

PENNSYLVANIA
Dept of Transportation
Information Sales Unit
PO Box 68691
Harrisburg, PA 17106
(717) 787-3130

RHODE ISLAND
Registry of Motor Vehicles
 c/o Registration Files
Two Capital Hill
Providence, RI 02903
(401) 277-2064

SOUTH CAROLINA
Dept of Motor Vehicles
Titles and Reg Records Sec
PO Box 1498
Columbia, SC 29216
(803) 251-2960

SOUTH DAKOTA
Div of Motor Vehicles
Information Section
118 W Capital Ave
Pierre, SD 57501
(605) 773-3541

TENNESSEE
Dept of Motor Vehicles
Titling & Registration Div
1283 Murfreesboro Rd,
 Ste 100
Nashville, TN 37243
(615) 741-3101

TEXAS
Dept of Transportation
Production Data Control
40th St and Jackson
Austin, TX 78779
(512) 465-7611

UTAH
State Tax Commission
Motor Vehicle Records Sec
1095 Motor Ave
Salt Lake City, UT 84116
(801) 538-8300

VERMONT
Dept of Motor Vehicles
Registr'tn & License Info/Rec
120 State St
Montpelier, VT 05603
(802) 828-2000

VIRGINIA
Management Info Admin
Vehicle Research Section
PO Box 27412
Richmond, VA 23269
(804) 367-6729

WASHINGTON
Dept of Licensing
Vehicle Services
PO Box 0030
Olympia, WA 98507
(206) 753-6990

WEST VIRGINIA
Division of Motor Vehicles
Titles and Registration Div
1608 Washington St E
Charleston, WV 25317
(304) 558-0282

WISCONSIN
Dept of Transportation
Vehicle Records Section
PO Box 7911
Madison, WI 53707
(608) 266-3666

WYOMING
Dept of Transportation
Motor Vehicle Licensing
 and Titles
PO Box 1708
Cheyenne, WY  82003
(307) 777-4717

## To Locate People In
## State Prisons

Most states operate prison locators.  These locators are usually operated by the State Department of Corrections or Prisons.  If the individual you are looking for may be in a federal prison, telephone the US prison federal locator at (202) 307-3126.  To determine if a former military member is or has been imprisoned in the US Military Prison at Ft. Leavenworth, Kansas, call (913) 684-4629.

Most prison locators keep records of former inmates for up to ten years.  Surname searches may be completed without date of birth or Social Security number.  Aliases may be available.  The telephone numbers for the State Prison Locators are as follows:

Alabama
 (334) 242-9400

Alaska
 (907) 465-3376

Arizona
 (602) 542-5586

Arkansas
 (501) 247-1800

California
 (916) 445-6713

Colorado
 (719) 579-9580

Connecticut
 (203) 566-5710

Delaware
 New Castle County
 (302) 739-5601

Delaware
  Sussex County
  (302) 653-9261

Florida
  (904) 488-2533

Georgia
  (404) 651-6800

Hawaii
  (808) 847-4491

Idaho
  (208) 334-2318

Illinois
  (217) 522-2666 ext. 2008

Indiana
  (317) 232-5715

Iowa
  (515) 281-4816

Kansas
  (913) 296-7220

Kentucky
  (502) 564-2433

Louisiana
  (504) 342-6641

Maine
  (207) 287-2711

Maryland
  NONE

Massachusetts
  (617) 727-3300

Michigan
  (517) 335-1426

Minnesota
  (612) 642-0200

Mississippi
  (601) 745-6611

Missouri
  (314) 751-8488

Montana
  (406) 444-3930

Nebraska
  (402) 471-2654

Nevada
  (702) 887-3285

New Hampshire
  (603) 271-5600

New Jersey
  (609) 292-0328

New Mexico
  (505) 827-8200

New York
  (518) 457-0034

North Carolina
  (919) 733-3965

North Dakota
(701) 221-6100

Ohio
(614) 752-1159

Oklahoma
(405) 425-2500

Oregon
NONE

Pennsylvania
(717) 737-6538

Rhode Island
(401) 464-3000

South Carolina
(803) 896-8500

South Dakota
(605) 773-3478

Tennessee
(615) 741-2071

Texas
(409) 295-6371

Utah
(801) 265-5571

Vermont
(802) 241-2305

Virginia
(804) 674-3000

Washington
(206) 753-1573

West Virginia
(304) 558-2036

Wisconsin
(608) 266-4548

Wyoming
(307) 777-7405

## To Locate People Through
## State Licensing Agencies

All states license or register trades and professions. Those that are regulated vary by state. Many cities and counties also have some licensing requirements. The following are examples of some trades and professions that are regulated. If the person you are looking for is a member of any of these occupations, contact the appropriate state, city or county licensing or regulating agency. Most agencies consider the address of these individuals to be public information, so you may be able to obtain a former or current address in this manner. A list of state information offices is at the end of this chapter. Call them for telephone numbers of the appropriate agency.

Accountants
Acupuncture
Aircraft Mechanics
Airports
Alarm Installers
Alcohol Sales
Appraisers
Architects
Athletic Announcers
Attorneys
Auctioneers
Audiologist
Auto Adjuster
Auto Appraiser
Auto Inspectors
Auto Wreckers
Bankers
Barbers
Beauticians
Builders/Carpenters
Building Contractors
Building Wreckers
Butchers
Carpet Cleaners
Certified Public
  Accountants
Check Cashing Service

Child Care/Daycare
  Centers
Chiropractors
Consumer Collection
  Agencies
Cosmetologist
Cosmetology Instructor
Counselors
Credit Unions
Debt Adjusters
Dentists/Hygienists
Detectives
Dietitians
Driving Instructors
Electricians
Embalmer
Engineers
Explosives
Food Processing
Fuel Storage
Fuel Transportation
Funeral Director
Furniture Manufacturing
Gambling
Garment Cleaners
Geologists
Hairdresser
Health Care Professionals

Hearing Aid Dealer
Heating/Air Conditioning
  Technicians
Homeopath
Hypertrichologist
Hypnotherapist
Insurance Agents
Insurance Brokers
Insurance Companies
Insurance Consultants
Insurance Investigators
Interior Designers
Investment Advisers
Laboratories
Landscape Architecture
Licensed Nurse Midwife
Licensed Practical Nurse
Liquor Licensees
Locksmiths
Lottery Control Board
Manicurist
Marriage and Family
  Therapist
Massage Therapist
Mattress Rebuilders
Meat Packers
Meat Storage
Mechanics
Medical Technicians
Mining
Money Orders/Travelers
  Checks Services
Naturopath
Notary Publics

Nursing Home
  Administrators
Nursing Homes
Occupational Therapists
Occupational Therapists
  Assistants
Ocularists
Oil Drilling
Opticians
Optometrists
Osteopathic Physician/
  Surgeon
Painters
Pawnbrokers
Pest Controllers/
  Exterminators
Pesticide Applicators
Pet Groomers
Pharmacists
Physical Therapists
Physicians
Physician Assistants
Pilots
Plumbers
Podiatrists
Private Investigators
Private schools
Process Servers
Psychiatrists
Psychologists
Public Transportation
  (Taxis, etc.)
Public Utilities
Radiological Technologists

Real Estate Agents and
  Brokers
Registered Nurses
Respiratory Care
  Practitioners
Restaurants
Savings and Loan
  Companies
Schools
Scrap Dealers
Security Guards
Service Stations
Social Workers
Stock Brokers

Surveyors
Taxi Owners/Operators
Teachers
Therapists
Timbering
Trade Schools
Veterinarians
Waste Disposal
Waste Removal
Waste Storage
Water Taxis
Water Well Drillers
Weights and Measures
X-Ray Technicians

## State Assistance Numbers

Call the appropriate number below to find out addresses
and telephone numbers for state agencies, offices and
activities not listed in this book which might be additional
sources of assistance or information. Examples of these
are state libraries, state archives, state National Guard
headquarters (Adjutants General offices) state military
archives and museums, state historical offices, state
genealogical societies, state hunting and fishing license
offices, state regulating offices, state parent locators,
state child support offices, state professional regulatory
boards, state tax offices, state civil service personnel
offices (locators) and state government officials, etc.

Alabama
  (334) 242-8000

Alaska
  (907) 465-2111

Arizona
  (602) 542-4900

Arkansas
  (501) 682-3000

California
North  (916) 322-9900

California
South  (213) 620-3030

Colorado
(303) 866-5000

Connecticut
(203) 566-2211
CT only  (800) 842-2220

Delaware
Sussex  (302) 856-5011

Delaware
NewCastle (302) 577-2011

Florida
(904) 488-1234

Georgia
(404) 656-2000

Hawaii
(808) 586-0222

Hawaii - Outer Islands
Only  (800) 468-4644

Idaho
(208) 334-2411

Illinois
(217) 782-2000

Indiana
(317) 232-1000

Iowa
(515) 281-5011

Kansas
(913) 296-0111

Kentucky
(502) 564-3130

Louisiana
(504) 342-6600

Maine
(207) 582-9500

Maryland
Not In Service

Massachusetts
(617) 727-7030

Michigan
(517) 373-1837

Minnesota
(612) 296-6013

Mississippi
(601) 359-1000

Missouri
(314) 751-2000

Montana
(406) 444-2511

Nebraska
(402) 471-2311

Nevada
(702) 687-5000

New Hampshire
(603) 271-1110

New Jersey
(609) 292-2121

New Mexico
(505) 827-4011

New York
(518) 474-2121

North Carolina
(919) 733-1110

North Dakota
(701) 224-2000

Ohio
(614) 466-2000

Oklahoma
(405) 521-2011

Oregon
None

Pennsylvania
(717) 787-2121

Rhode Island
(401) 277-2000

South Carolina
(803) 734-1000

South Dakota
(605) 773-3011

Tennessee
(615) 741-3011

Texas
(512) 463-4630

Utah
(801) 538-3000

Vermont
(802) 828-1110

Virginia
(804) 786-0000

Washington
(206) 753-5000

West Virginia
(304) 558-3456

Wisconsin
(608) 266-2211

Wyoming
(307) 777-5910

# Chapter Ten

# If The Person You Are Trying To Locate Is Deceased

*This chapter provides addresses of government and private organizations that may be able to tell you if the person you are looking is deceased. It also explains how to obtain official military casualty reports and find out where a military veteran is buried.*

## To Determine If An Individual Is Deceased Through The Social Security Administration

The Social Security Administration will tell you if they have a report that an individual is deceased, if you provide them with a SSN or a name and date of birth. It is also helpful if you have the names of the parents of the individual. Call the SSA at (800) 772-1213.

# To Determine If A Veteran
# Is Deceased Through
# The Department Of Veterans Affairs

The VA will tell you if a veteran is deceased if they can identify him in their files.  They will also give you his date of death and place of burial, if known.   The VA is informed  of veterans death by funeral homes, family members and other government agencies and have excellent records in this regard.  Call any VA regional office for assistance (see Chapter Five for additional details and telephone numbers).

# To Locate Next Of Kin
# Of Military Casualties

You may write to the appropriate armed service for assistance if you wish to contact the next of kin of military members who were casualties during recent wars. Names and addresses of next of kin are contained on all casualty reports.  Casualty information normally is only made through written request.  Casualty reports are for release primarily to the next-of-kin.  Any reports that are released to other parties under the Freedom Of Information Act are normally sanitized; i.e., next of kin information is deleted.

Casualty records covering 1942 to present (Marine Corps) and World War II to present (Navy), containing names and service numbers of personnel who are deceased or missing and those injured in a battle zone.

Headquarters, US Marine Corps      (703) 696-2069
Casualty Branch MHP-10            FAX (703) 696-2072
Washington, DC  20380-0001

HQ AFMPC/DPMCB                          (210) 652-5513
550 C Street West, Room A315
Randolph AFB, TX  78150-6001

Bureau of Naval Personnel, BNP-633
Casualty Assistance Branch              (703) 614-2934
Washington, DC  20370-5663              (800) 443-9297
                                   FAX (703) 325-5300

The US Army Mortuary Affairs and Casualty Support
Division has access to individual deceased personnel
records for Americans who died overseas during World
War II and the Korean War.  They have access to
individual deceased personnel files for Army members,
only who died in Southeast Asia during the Vietnam War.

The files contain information pertaining to the disposal of
remains to include place of death and place of burial.
The files do not contain information pertaining to awards
and decorations.

Director, Army Casualty and Memorial
Affairs Operation Center                (703) 325-5300
Total Army Personnel Agency, DAPC-PED
2461 Eisenhower Avenue
Alexandria, VA  22331

# To Locate Grave Sites Of
# US Servicemen Buried Overseas

The American Battle Monuments Commission (ABMC)
can provide names of 124,912 US war dead of World
War I and II who are interned in American burial grounds
in foreign countries.  The ABMC also can provide the
names of any of 94,093 US servicemen  and women who

were missing in action or lost or buried at sea during the World Wars, the Korean and Vietnam Wars. For further information contact:

American Battle Monuments Commission
Casemir Pulaski Building
20 Massachusetts Ave., NW          (202) 272-0532
Washington, DC  20314-0300         (202) 272-0533
                          FAX  (202) 272 1375

# To Locate Grave Sites Of Veterans And Their Dependents Buried In VA Cemeteries

The National Cemetery System (NCS), Department of Veterans Affairs, provides limited genealogy services and burial location assistance to the next-of-kin or close friends of decedents.

NCS personnel can research records to determine if a specific decedent is interred in one of the VA National Cemeteries. However, all requests must relate to an individual since research cannot be conducted on groups on the basis of surname, military unit, war period or place of residence.

To request a burial search on a specific individual, it is requested that the following information be provided:

• full name (first, middle, and last)
• date and place of birth
• date and place of death
• state from which entered military service
• rank and military unit in which served on active duty

No form is required and no fee is charged for this service. Simply provide the above information in a letter addressed to:

Director for Technical Support (401B)
National Cemetery System      (202) 273-5400
Department of Veterans Affairs
810 Vermont Avenue, NW
Washington, DC  20420

# To Obtain Copies Of
# Military Casualty Reports

## Casualties Of All Military Services

**Korean Conflict Casualty File** contains data of all US Military personnel who died by hostile means as a result of combat duty in the Korean conflict.  There are 32,642 records with dates of death from 1950-57.

**Southeast Asia Combat Area Casualties Database** contains 58,152 records of all US Military personnel who died as a result of hostilities or other causes in Cambodia, China, Laos, North Vietnam, South Vietnam or Thailand from 1957-89.

## Army Casualties

**Korean War Casualty File-US Army** contains 109,975 records of both fatal and non-fatal Army casualties.

**The Casualty Information System** for the periods 1961-1981 contains records of casualties suffered by all US Army personnel and their dependents.  Extracts of records for all US Army active duty personnel who have died are available.

For fee and information requirements on any of the above, contact:

Center for Electronic Records (NSX)
National Archives and Records Administration
8601 Adelphi Road                    (301) 713-6630
College Park, MD 20740-6001

### World War II Army Air Force
### Accident Reports

World War II Army Air Force and other USAF Accident Reports are in the custody of:

HQ USAF Safety Agency
AFSA/IMR
9700 Ave G SE
Kirkland AFB, NM 87117-5670

# To Locate Children Of
# World War II Casualties

The American World War II Orphans Network is a network of sons and daughters of World War II casualties and an orphan registry. At present, they have over 600 orphans in their database. They provide a locator service to help orphans, war buddies and family members find each other. They also provide information on locating deceased veterans government records and other public records, publish a newsletter with information about finding records and discuss issues pertinent to their members. They share information and help one another in any way they can. They have a goal of locating all World War II orphans and to locate all US memorials which list the names of World War II casualties. This is a non-profit organization. Entry into the database is free.

Self-addressed stamped envelopes are appreciated when making inquiries.

American World War II Orphans Network
PO Box 4369                               (206) 733-1678
Bellingham, WA  98227                FAX (206) 733-5259

# To Locate Families And Friends Of Deceased Vietnam Veterans

"In Touch" is a locator service whose main goal is to connect Vietnam veterans and the families of those who died in Vietnam.  Many Vietnam veterans need to locate the families of their fallen comrades to share memories, anecdotes, pictures, tapes, etc. or just to keep a 20 year old promise to their lost buddy or to themselves.

At the same time, families are trying to find fellow veterans of their loved ones who were lost in Vietnam. The children of those who were lost in Vietnam want to talk to their fathers, comrades. They want to learn what their fathers were like when they were their age.

Also, under the "In Touch" program, support networks for Sons and Daughters In Touch and Siblings In Touch connect family members who benefit from communicating with each other.  The sharing of common experiences brings the comforting knowledge that they are not alone.

In cooperation with other locator services, "In Touch" also helps Vietnam veterans find each other.  There is no charge for any of the "In Touch" services which are sponsored by Friends of the Vietnam Veterans Memorial, a non-profit, largely volunteer organization whose purpose is to continue the healing effects begun by the building of the Vietnam Veterans Memorial.

"In Touch" has an account on CompuServe. Their address for electronic mail is 71035,3126.

"In Touch"                  (703) 525-1107
Friends of VN Vet Memorial
2030 Clarendon Boulevard, Suite 412
Arlington, VA 22201

# To Determine If Someone Is Deceased Through The Social Security Death Index Rapidly

If you provide the name and date of birth, name and Social Security number or name only, the Nationwide Locator will provide a list of people who are deceased, their SSN, date of birth, and the date and place of death as reported by the Social Security Administration. The information will be returned by mail or fax within 24 hours of receipt. The fee for this service is $30.00 per name. For additional information, see Appendix B.

The Nationwide Locator         FAX (210) 828-4667
PO Box 39903
San Antonio, TX 78218

# Chapter Eleven

# Locating Family History Information For Veterans

To do thorough genealogical research for a family history of a person who was in the armed forces, the following steps are recommended. These are in addition to the normal genealogical research conducted for a family history. The assistance of a genealogist who specializes in military records may save you a great deal of time.

Determine if individual is listed in the separate military schedule of the national census of 1890 (Union veterans), 1900, 1910 and 1920, if appropriate.

Obtain copies of the individual's induction (draft) records, military personnel and medical records. If the individual served in more than one branch of the service, separate requests must be made as the records are not combined. For additional information, see Chapter Six.

Obtain copies of pension records in the federal and state archives and all records held by the Department of Veterans Affairs. See Chapter Six.

If the individual ever served as an officer, obtain copies of entries in *Officers Registers* for each year that he or she served as an officer.  The entries usually give information on promotion date, civilian and military schools attended and awards and decorations received.  See the library section in Chapter Seven.

Obtain copies of unit histories of all units in which the individual served.  See Chapter Six.

Obtain appropriate copies of unit rosters, muster rolls, after action reports, daily staff journals, deck logs, morning reports, and daily journals for all units and ships the individual was assigned.  See Chapter Six.

If the individual was wounded or killed while in the service, attempt to obtain copies of casualty reports if those reports were not in their official military personnel records.  See Chapter Ten.

If the individual was a prisoner-of-war, obtain copies or excerpts of database and records retained by the National Archives.  See Chapter Six.

Obtain records of membership in veteran, military and patriotic organizations as well as military unit reunion organizations.  See Chapter Five.

Apply for medals and awards that the individual earned but may not have received.   Write to the National Personnel Records Center for additional information.

Obtain copies of membership records, yearbooks, cruise books, newspapers, etc., in military fraternal organization, military colleges and high school alumni associations. Also, obtain records of churches on or near military bases to which he may have belonged.

Obtain a copy of the individual's obituary. Research military newspaper files for articles about the individual. See Chapter Seven.

Determine location of burial site in military cemeteries, national (VA) cemeteries, or overseas American burial grounds. See Chapter Ten.

# Chapter Twelve

## Conclusion

Now that you have read this book, you should realize there are many methods available to locate people who are or have been in the military. It may take more than one attempt to be successful, but if you are persistent, you will ultimately find the person you are trying to locate.

If you have any questions or problems concerning this book, write to the author, Lt. Col. Richard S. Johnson at the address below. We would also appreciate hearing about any successful searches. Since the information contained in this book changes at times, revised editions will be published annually. If you have any comments that may improve future copies of this book they will certainly be appreciated. Please write us at the following address:

Lt. Col. Richard S. Johnson      FAX (210) 828-4667
MIE Publishing
PO Box 340081
San Antonio, Texas 78234

# Individual Data Worksheet

Complete legal name, nick names, maiden name, previous married names, and aliases - _____

_____

Social Security number - _____

Date of birth - _____

Place of birth - _____

Parents' names- _____

Spouse and former spouse's name - _____

Names of brothers and sisters - _____

_____

Names of other relatives - _____

Children's names and addresses - _____

_____

Previous addresses - _____

Previous telephone number - _____

Military service number - _____

VA claim number/VA insurance number - _____

Branch of military service - _____

Dates of military service - _____

Unit or ship assigned - _____

Installation or base assigned - _____

Assignments in Vietnam, Korea, etc. - _____

Rank or rating (if not known, officer or enlisted) - _____

# Individual Data Worksheet (cont.)

Membership in Veterans and military reunion organizations -

_____

Membership in the reserve or National Guard units/dates of assignment - _____

Real estate owned - _____

Automobiles, motorcycles and boats owned/state in which registered - _____

Elementary, high schools, colleges and universities attended, locations and dates - _____

Previous employment/dates and locations - _____

_____

Church or synagogue affiliation - _____

Union membership - _____

Professional membership/licenses - _____

Lodges, fraternal and service organization membership - ____

Physical description: height, weight, color of hair and eyes, tattoos, scars, etc. (obtain photos) - _____

_____

Hunting, boating or fishing licenses - _____

Pilot, amateur radio, driver and motorcycle licenses - _____

Names, addresses and telephone numbers of friends and fellow employees - _____

Hobbies, talents and avocations - _____

Political party affiliation and voter's registration - _____

Foreign and national travel history - _____

Dates and places of bankruptcy - _____

Miscellaneous information - _____

# The Nationwide Locator

The Nationwide Locator will provide addresses and other important information to people seeking friends and relatives, to attorneys, private investigators, collection agencies, reunion planners and others.  Our data is obtained from various databases that contain information on over 160 million individuals.  Our data is highly accurate and reasonably priced.

## Social Security search

Provide us the nine digit Social Security number (SSN) and we will provide you the person's name, most current reported address, date reported and all previous reported addresses, if this number is contained in a national credit file.  If a report of death has been submitted, it will be listed.  **$30.00** per SSN for a nationwide search.

## Address update

Provide us the name and last known address (not over ten years old) and we will provide you the most current reported address and the names and telephone numbers of five neighbors. **$30.00** per name submitted.

## National Surname search

Provide us the first name, middle initial and last name and we will use the National Telephone Directory to provide you the names, addresses and listed telephone numbers of everyone in the nation with a matching name. **$30.00** per name submitted.

## Date of Birth search

Provide us first and last name, approximate date or year of birth and Social Security number (if known) and we will provide all matching names, city and state of residence.  May be able to provide street address and phone number.  **$75.00** per name and date of birth submitted.

## Social Security Death Index search

Provide us either the name and date of birth, name and Social Security number or name only and we will provide you a list of people who are deceased, their SSN, date of birth, and the date and place of death as reported by the Social Security Administration. **$30.00** per name.

Information will be provided to you within 24 hours of receipt. Information will be returned by mail or by FAX if requested. Volume discounts are available. Prices are subject to change without notice. Other specialized searches are available. Texas residents add 7.75% tax.

Client agrees that all information obtained through the Nationwide Locator will be used for lawful purposes and agrees to hold the Nationwide Locator harmless for any use of this service. Client states that the client understands and agrees the the Nationwide Locator does not warrant and does not guarantee information obtained from database searches. Client agrees to pay for all searches made by the Nationwide Locator regardless of results (to include "no record"). The Nationwide Locator is owned by Military Information Enterprises, Inc., is a member of the San Antonio Retail Merchants Association and is listed by Dun and Bradstreet.

If you would like to have the Nationwide Locator perform any of these searches, please write or FAX the information required to perform the search along with the following:

1. Payment in full: check, money order or credit card. If using Visa, MasterCard or American Express, please include your card number, the expiration date, the amount charged, and your signature.
2. Your name
3. Phone number
4. Address
5. City, State and ZIP
6. A self addressed stamped business size envelope.
7. FAX number if you wish to have information sent by FAX.

The Nationwide Locator
PO Box 39903
San Antonio, Texas 78218
FAX (210) 828-4667

# Computer Access Programs

The Nationwide Locator also markets two computer access programs to locate missing people. These programs are for use by private investigators, collection agencies, attorneys, heir searchers, reunion planners, and others who are searching for a large number of people.

*The Nationwide Locator Direct Access Package* is a low cost program that lets you enter the finest database in the country. This program enables you to obtain addresses of people you are searching for at the lowest possible price. There are no restrictions on who can use the Nationwide Locator Direct Access Package. The database does not provide any credit information or reports. None of the provided information is regulated by the Fair Credit Reporting Act. This access package includes five major categories of searches:

- Social Security trace
- Surname search
- Subject verification
- Address verification
- Telephone number ownership

All your searches are on-line and you receive instant responses. Most searches are $6.00 each. Social Security traces are less with volume usage.

- No minimum usage requirements
- No monthly user fee
- No large up-front fee
- No line charge
- No sales tax
- Instant reports
- 24 hour a day access
- User friendly access program

All that is required is an IBM compatible computer, a modem, a telephone line and a major credit card (VISA, Master Card or American Express).

*The NIS Online Information Services* is the nation's most versatile computer access package. This package provides access to the files of all major information databases. This package is used by hundreds of private investigators, researchers and other professionals. Some of the available searches are:

- Social Security searches
- National criss-cross
- Surname searches
- Address updates
- Postal forwarding
- Commercial credit
- Asset searches
- Motor vehicle registration traces
- Driver license traces
- Criminal history
- Worker's compensation

and numerous other online searches. The cost of each search varies. Most searches give you instant online results, while some searches will be returned within 3-5 days. You do not need a computer to use this program. It can be accessed by phone, FAX or mail.

*The NIS Online Information Services* is user friendly, menu driven, available 24 hours a day and accessible by phone, mail, FAX and E-mail.

The cost of the the **Nationwide Locator Direct Access Package** is $290.00. The cost of the **NIS Online Information Services** is $395.00. You can be online within 3-5 days. For a brochure of either of these access programs, write or FAX:

The Nationwide Locator
PO Box 39903
San Antonio, Texas 78218
FAX (210) 828-4667

# Standard Form 180

| REQUEST PERTAINING TO MILITARY RECORDS | Please read instructions on the reverse. If more space is needed, use plain paper. |
|---|---|

**PRIVACY ACT OF 1974 COMPLIANCE INFORMATION.** The following information is provided in accordance with 5 U.S.C. 552a(e)(3) and applies to this form. Authority for collection of the information is 44 U.S.C. 2907, 3101, and 3103, and E.O. 9397 of November 22, 1943. Disclosure of the information is voluntary. The principal purpose of the information is to assist the facility servicing the records in locating and verifying the correctness of the requested records or information to answer your inquiry. Routine uses of the information as established and published in accordance with 5 U.S.C. a(e)(4)(D) include the transfer of relevant information to appropriate Federal, State, local or foreign agencies for use in civil, criminal, or regulatory investigations or prosecution. In addition this form will be filed with the appropriate military records and may be transferred along with the record to another agency in accordance with the routine uses established by the agency which maintains the record. If the requested information is not provided, it may not be possible to service your inquiry.

## SECTION I — INFORMATION NEEDED TO LOCATE RECORDS (Furnish as much as possible)

| 1 NAME USED DURING SERVICE (Last, first, and middle) | 2 SOCIAL SECURITY NO | 3 DATE OF BIRTH | 4 PLACE OF BIRTH |
|---|---|---|---|
| | | | |

5 ACTIVE SERVICE, PAST AND PRESENT    (For an effective records search, it is important that ALL service be shown below)

| BRANCH OF SERVICE (Also, show last organization, if known) | DATES OF ACTIVE SERVICE | | Check one OFFI- EN- CER LISTED | SERVICE NUMBER DURING THIS PERIOD |
|---|---|---|---|---|
| | DATE ENTERED | DATE RELEASED | | |
| | | | | |
| | | | | |
| | | | | |

6 RESERVE SERVICE, PAST OR PRESENT    If "none," check here ▶ ☐

| a. BRANCH OF SERVICE | b DATES OF MEMBERSHIP | | c Check one OFF- EN CER LISTED | d SERVICE NUMBER DURING THIS PERIOD |
|---|---|---|---|---|
| | FROM | TO | | |

| 7 NATIONAL GUARD MEMBERSHIP    (Check one) | a ARMY ☐ | b AIR FORCE ☐ | c NONE ☐ |
|---|---|---|---|

| d STATE | e ORGANIZATION | f DATES OF MEMBERSHIP | | g Check one OFF- EN CER LISTED | h SERVICE NUMBER DURING THIS PERIOD |
|---|---|---|---|---|---|
| | | FROM | TO | | |

| 8 IS SERVICE PERSON DECEASED  ☐ YES  ☐ NO    If "yes," enter date of death | 9 IS (WAS) INDIVIDUAL A MILITARY RETIREE OR FLEET RESERVIST  ☐ YES  ☐ NO |
|---|---|

## SECTION II — REQUEST

| 1 EXPLAIN WHAT INFORMATION OR DOCUMENTS YOU NEED. OR. CHECK ITEM 2. OR. COMPLETE ITEM 3 | | | | 2 IF YOU ONLY NEED A STATEMENT OF SERVICE check ☐ |
|---|---|---|---|---|

| 3 LOST DOCUMENT REPLACEMENT REQUEST (Complete a or b, and c.) | a. REPORT OF SEPARATION (DD 214 or equivalent) ☐ | YEAR ISSUED | This contains information normally needed to determine eligibility for benefits. It may be furnished only to the veteran, the surviving next of kin, or to a representative with veteran's signed release (item 5 of this form). |
|---|---|---|---|
| | b. DISCHARGE CERTIFICATE ☐ | YEAR ISSUED | This shows only the date and character of discharge. It is of little value in determining eligibility for benefits; may be issued only to veterans discharged honorably or under honorable conditions, or, if deceased, to the surviving spouse. |
| | c. EXPLAIN HOW SEPARATION DOCUMENT WAS LOST | | |

| 4 EXPLAIN PURPOSE FOR WHICH INFORMATION OR DOCUMENTS ARE NEEDED | 6 REQUESTER |
|---|---|
| | a. IDENTIFICATION (check appropriate box) ☐ Same person identified in Section I    ☐ Surviving spouse  ☐ Next of kin (relationship)  ☐ Other (specify) |
| | b. SIGNATURE (see instruction 3 on reverse side)    DATE OF REQUEST |

| 5 RELEASE AUTHORIZATION, IF REQUIRED (Read instruction 3 on reverse side)  I hereby authorize release of the requested information/documents to the person indicated at right (item 7)    VETERAN SIGN HERE ▶  (If signed by other than veteran show relationship to veteran) | 7 Please type or print clearly —    COMPLETE RETURN ADDRESS  Name number and street, city, State and ZIP code    TELEPHONE NO (include area code) ▶ |
|---|---|

180-108                NSN 7540-00-142-9360                STANDARD FORM 180 (Rev. 4-82)
Presc. and by NARA .36 CFR .228  62 A0

# INSTRUCTIONS

1. **Information needed to locate records.** Certain identifying information is necessary to determine the location of an individual's record of military service. Please give careful consideration to and answer each item on this form. If you do not have and cannot obtain the information for an item, show "NA," meaning the information is "not available." Include as much of the requested information as you can. This will help us to give you the best possible service.

2. **Charges for service.** A nominal fee is charged for certain types of service. In most instances service fees cannot be determined in advance. If your request involves a service fee you will be notified as soon as that determination is made.

3. **Restrictions on release of information.** Information from records of military personnel is released subject to restrictions imposed by the military departments consistent with the provisions of the Freedom of Information Act of 1967 (as amended in 1974) and the Privacy Act of 1974. A service person has access to almost any information contained in his own record. The next of kin, if the veteran is deceased, and Federal officers for official purposes, are authorized to receive information from a military service or medical record only as specified in the above cited Acts. Other requesters must have the release authorization, in item 5 of the form, signed by the veteran or, if deceased, by the next of kin. Employers

and others needing proof of military service are expected to accept the information shown on documents issued by the Armed Forces at the time a service person is separated

4. **Location of military personnel records.** The various categories of military personnel records are described in the chart below. For each category there is a code number which indicates the address at the bottom of the page to which this request should be sent. For each military service there is a note explaining approximately how long the records are held by the military service before they are transferred to the National Personnel Records Center, St. Louis. Please read these notes carefully and make sure you send your inquiry to the right address. Please note especially that the record is not sent to the National Personnel Records Center as long as the person retains any sort of reserve obligation, whether drilling or non-drilling.

*(If the person has two or more periods of service within the same branch send your request to the office having the record for the last period of service.)*

5. **Definitions for abbreviations used below:**
NPRC — National Personnel Records Center     PERS — Personnel Records
TDRL — Temporary Disability Retirement List     MED — Medical Records

| SERVICE | NOTE (See paragraph 4 above.) | CATEGORY OF RECORDS — WHERE TO WRITE ADDRESS CODE | | ▼ |
|---|---|---|---|---|
| **AIR FORCE (USAF)** | Except for TDRL and general officers retired with pay. Air Force records are transferred to NPRC from Code 1, 90 days after separation and from Code 2, 150 days after separation | Active members (includes National Guard on active duty in the Air Force), TDRL, and general officers retired with pay | | 1 |
| | | Reserve, retired reservist in nonpay status, current National Guard officers not on active duty in Air Force, and National Guard released from active duty in Air Force | | 2 |
| | | Current National Guard enlisted not on active duty in Air Force | | 13 |
| | | Discharged, deceased, and retired with pay | | 14 |
| **COAST GUARD (USCG)** | Coast Guard officer and enlisted records are transferred to NPRC 7 months after separation | Active, reserve, and TDRL members | | 3 |
| | | Discharged, deceased, and retired members (see next item) | | 14 |
| | | Officers separated before 1/1/29 and enlisted personnel separated before 1/1/15 | | 6 |
| **MARINE CORPS (USMC)** | Marine Corps records are transferred to NPRC between 6 and 9 months after separation. | Active, TDRL, and Selected Marine Corps Reserve members | | 4 |
| | | Individual Ready Reserve and Fleet Marine Corps Reserve members | | 5 |
| | | Discharged, deceased, and retired members (see next item) | | 14 |
| | | Members separated before 1/1/1905 | | 6 |
| **ARMY (USA)** | Army records are transferred to NPRC as follows: Active Army and Individual Ready Reserve Control Groups About 90 days after separation. U.S. Army Reserve Troop Unit personnel About 120 to 180 days after separation | Reserve, living retired members, retired general officers, and active duty records of current National Guard members who performed service in the U.S. Army before 7/1/72 * | | 7 |
| | | Active officers (including National Guard on active duty in the U.S. Army) | | 8 |
| | | Active enlisted (including National Guard on active duty in the U.S. Army) and enlisted TDRL | | 9 |
| | | Current National Guard officers not on active duty in the U.S. Army | | 12 |
| | | Current National Guard enlisted not on active duty in the U.S. Army | | 13 |
| | | Discharged and deceased members (see next item) | | 14 |
| | | Officers separated before 7/1/17 and enlisted separated before 11/1/12 | | 6 |
| | | Officers and warrant officers TDRL | | 8 |
| **NAVY (USN)** | Navy records are transferred to NPRC 6 months after retirement or complete separation | Active members (including reservists on duty) — PERS and MED | | 10 |
| | | Discharged, deceased, retired (with and without pay) less than six months. TDRL, drilling and nondrilling reservists | PERS ONLY | 10 |
| | | | MED ONLY | 11 |
| | | Discharged, deceased, retired (with and without pay) more than six months (see next item) — PERS & MED | | 14 |
| | | Officers separated before 1/1/03 and enlisted separated before 1/1/1885 — PERS and MED | | 6 |

*Code 12 applies to active duty records of current National Guard officers who performed service in the U.S. Army after 6/30/72
Code 13 applies to active duty records of current National Guard enlisted members who performed service in the U.S. Army after 6/30/72

| ADDRESS LIST OF CUSTODIANS (BY CODE NUMBERS SHOWN ABOVE) — Where to write / send this form for each category of records | | | | | | | |
|---|---|---|---|---|---|---|---|
| 1 | Air Force Manpower and Personnel Center Military Personnel Records Division Randolph AFB, TX 78150-6001 | 5 | Marine Corps Reserve Support Center 10950 El Monte Overland Park, KS 66211-1408 | 8 | USA MILPERCEN ATTN: DAPC-MSR 200 Stovall Street Alexandria, VA 22332-0400 | 12 | Army National Guard Personnel Center Columbia Pike Office Building 5600 Columbia Pike Falls Church, VA 22041 |
| 2 | Air Reserve Personnel Center Denver, CO 80280-5000 | 6 | Military Archives Division National Archives and Records Administration Washington, DC 20408 | 9 | Commander U.S. Army Enlisted Records and Evaluation Center Ft. Benjamin Harrison, IN 46249-5301 | 13 | The Adjutant General (of the appropriate State, DC, or Puerto Rico) |
| 3 | Commandant U.S. Coast Guard Washington, DC 20593-0001 | 7 | Commander U.S. Army Reserve Personnel Center ATTN: DARP-PAS 9700 Page Boulevard St. Louis, MO 63132-5200 | 10 | Commander Naval Military Personnel Command ATTN: NMPC-036 Washington, DC 20370-5036 | 14 | National Personnel Records Center (Military Personnel Records) 9700 Page Boulevard St. Louis, MO 63132 |
| 4 | Commandant of the Marine Corps (Code MMRB-10) Headquarters, U.S. Marine Corps Washington, DC 20380-0001 | | | 11 | Naval Reserve Personnel Center New Orleans, LA 70146-5000 | | |

# Military Records Authorization

Military Information Enterprises, Inc. can acquire records rapidly from the National Personnel Records Center and the Army Reserve Personnel Center in St. Louis, MO. All requests are properly prepared and hand carried to the appropriate Center, thus assuring that you will receive the records you need in the most rapid manner possible. The following records may be obtained:

1. Certified copies of **Report of Separation (DD-214)** for anyone discharged or retired from any of the armed forces and army reservists who have been separated from active duty. Fee is $50.00. Allow four to six weeks for delivery.

2. A copy of the **complete military personnel and medical records** (every item in the file is copied) of an individual may be provided to the veteran or his next of kin if the veteran is deceased. Fee is $100.00. This includes records of individuals who are retired from any armed forces, most individuals who are discharged and have no reserve obligation for all branches and current members of the Army reserve. Copies of military records of individuals on active duty, current members of the Army National Guard and Air National Guard, current members of the Navy, Marine and Air Force reserves cannot be obtained. These records are not at St. Louis. MO.*

   **NOTE**: Requests for DD-214 and military records are made with the authorization form shown on the next page. It must be completed and signed by the veteran or his next of kin, if deceased.

3. Certified copies of **complete military personnel and medical records** may also be obtained for attorneys and private investigators in four to six weeks **for court**

**cases**. A court order signed by a federal or state judge is required. A sample of how the court order should be worded will be mailed or faxed upon request. The fee for this service is $200.00. *

4. **Organizational records** can also be obtained. Write for details.

* In July 1973, a fire at the NPRC destroyed 75-80% of the records for the Army (discharged from 1912 to 1960) and Air Force (H through Z discharged 1947 through 1964). Some of these records have been partially reconstructed and others were only partially destroyed. An exact determination of their condition can only be made by reviewing the records.

All fees are for research and in the event the records requested are not available or have been destroyed, the fee is not refundable. All requests must be prepaid and all information concerning the request should be included. All orders are shipped by first class mail but may be shipped by Federal Express for an additional fee of $10.00. Checks should be made payable to Military Information Enterprises, Inc. (not affiliated with the federal government) or you may make payment by VISA, MasterCard or AMEX. For additional information or to order records, mail or FAX authorization to:

**Military Information Enterprises, Inc.**
**PO Box 340081**  **FAX (210) 828-4667**
**Ft Sam Houston, TX 78234**

# Military Records Authorization

I request and authorize that representatives of Military Information Enterprises, Inc. be allowed to review my Military Service Personnel and Medical Records in the same manner as if I presented myself for this purpose. I specifically authorize the National Personnel Records Center, St. Louis, MO, or other custodians of my military records, to release to Military Information Enterprises, Inc. a complete copy of my military personnel and related medical records.

I am willing that a photocopy and or FAX of this authorization be considered as effective and valid as the original.

Signature _____ date _____

If veteran is deceased, date of death_____
and relationship _____

## Instructions: Type or print this authorization.

Name _____
         Last                    First                    Middle initial

_____
         Street address              Apt. #

_____
         City                    State       ZIP

Social Security number _____

Date of birth_____ Place of birth _____

Telephone number _____

Service number _____ Branch of service _____

Dates of service _____

Current military status ( )reserve,  ( ) retired,
( ) separated with Army reserve obligation,  ( ) none

Please obtain  ( ) DD-214, ( ) complete military records,
( ) other _____

Enclosed is ( ) check, ( ) money order, charge my ( ) Visa
( ) MasterCard  ( ) AMEX  for $ _____

Card number _____ Expir. date _____

Signature _____

Address of where records are to be sent, if different from
above _____

# Glossary

**Armed Forces**
The armed forces are composed of the Air Force, Army, Coast Guard, Marine Corps and the Navy.

**Base or Post Locator**
An office or organization that has names and units of assignment of all military personnel assigned to a particular installation.

**Department Of Veterans Affairs**
The Department of Veterans Affairs is the new name for the Veterans Administration. The abbreviation VA is used in this book.

**Freedom Of Information Act Of 1974**
Federal law requiring US government agencies and the armed forces to release records to the public on request unless information is exempted by the Privacy Act or for national security reasons.

**Identifying Information**
Information used to identify and locate someone such as name, SSN, service number, date of birth, ship, unit or former unit of assignment.

**National Archives**
The depositories of historical documents of the federal government. The National Personnel Records Center is part of the Archives.

**Merchant Marines**
The civilian maritime fleet.

**Privacy Act Of 1974**
Federal law designed to protect an individual's constitutional right to privacy. The law also provides disclosure to an individual of information that the federal government maintains on that individual.

**Rank**
The grade or rating an individual holds in his military organization.

## Reserve Components
The Reserve Components include the Air Force, Army, Coast Guard, Marine Corps and the Navy reserve and the Army National Guard and Air National Guard.

## Retired Military Member
A person who has completed twenty or more years of duty in any of the military components is receiving retired pay. He may be retired from an active or reserve component of a service (a member of the Reserve Components is not eligible for retired pay until age 60). A military member may be retired from active duty for disability due to injury or illness with less than 20 years of active service.

## Service Number
A number formerly used by the armed forces to identify individual members. The Army and Air Force discontinued using service numbers on July 1, 1969, the Navy and Marine Corps on July 1, 1972 and the Coast Guard on October 1, 1974. The SSN is now used in place of the service number.

## Social Security Number
The nine digit number used by the uniformed services to identify individual members.

## The Uniformed Services
The Uniformed Services are composed of the armed forces, the Public Health Service, and the National Oceanic and Atmospheric Administration.

## VA
The abbreviation for the Department of Veterans Affairs.

## Veteran
A person who has served on active duty in one or more of the armed forces.

## World-Wide Locator
An office or organization operated by each of the Uniformed Services which maintains the name, rank, SSN, date of birth, unit assignment and world-wide location of members of their respective service.

# Index

# Index (Cont.)

# Index (Cont.)

# Index (Cont.)

# Other Publications Available

**Find Anyone *FAST*** by Richard S. Johnson the nationally renowned expert on locating missing people, has brought together state of art methods necessary to find anyone quickly. This informative book describes hundreds of proven search techniques. It list resources and assistance available form federal, state and local government agencies as well as private organizations and business sources. Numerous computer searches that are available to the general public are described in detail. **$14.95**

**How To Investigate By Computer** by Ralph D. Thomas. A manual of the new investigative technology that gives you the sources and teaches you to investigate by computer. Learn about hard-to-find sources of information and how to access them. 102 pages **$39.95**

*The following books by BRB Publicationsare available:*

**The Sourcebook Of Federal Courts, US District And Bankruptcy** The definitive guide to searching for case information at the local level within the federal court system. 672 pages **$33.95**

**The Sourcebook Of County/Asset/Lien Records** national guide to all county/city government agencies where real estate transactions UCC financing statement and federal/state tax liens are recorded. 1995 edition 448 pages **$29.95**

**The MVR Book Motor Service Guide** A national reference detailing and summarizing in practical terms the description, access procedures, regulations and privacy restrictions of driver and vehicle records in all states. 1995 edition 256 pages **$19.95**

**The Sourcebook Of State Public Records** The definitive guide to searching for public record information at the state level. 304 pages **$29.95**

Order Form
# MIE Publishing
PO Box 5143
Burlington, NC  27216
1-800-937-2133

We Accept Government Purchase Orders.

| Publication | Price | Num | Amt |
|---|---|---|---|
| How To Locate Anyone Who Is Or Has Been In The Military | $19.95 | | |
| Other books desired | | | |
| | | | |
| | | | |
| | | | |

TOTAL: $ _____

North Carolina orders please add 6% Sales Tax.　$ _____

Postage and Handling　$  4.05

Please add $1.00 for each additional book.　$ _____

Consult Publisher for International Mail Prices.

Total Amount Enclosed: $ _____

Visa, MasterCard, American Express Card Number:
_____ Expiration Date __/__/__

Signature _____

Name: _____

Street/Apt no: _____

City/State/Zip: _____

Telephone: (____) _____

Please remit entire order form.